Online Communities for Doctoral Researchers and their Supervisors

Bringing together accounts of online community engagement from a range of perspectives, this book considers how the changing landscape of doctoral communities might be used to inform institutional level decisions about doctoral provision and support.

Despite the increasing availability of online communities dedicated to doctoral supervisors, there has been little consideration of how they form and operate. This book surveys the landscape of these online communities and examines their impact on the production of the doctorate, and on the experience of doctoral researchers and supervisors. Bringing together accounts of online community engagement from a range of perspectives – doctoral students, supervisors, content curators, and research support practitioners, one of the overarching aims of this volume is to explore these communities in action.

With the supporting doctoral research through online media catalysed as the 'new normal', this book allows stakeholders in doctoral education to better understand how students are using social media in their PhD studies, how online communities of practice impact upon researcher/supervisor relationships and support, and ways in which student experiences of various platforms might converge to create an augmented experience.

Julie Sheldon is Dean of the Doctoral Academy at Liverpool John Moores University, UK.

Victoria Sheppard is Researcher Development Manager at Liverpool John Moores University, UK.

Online Communities for Doctoral Researchers and their Supervisors
Building Engagement with Social Media

Edited by
Julie Sheldon and Victoria Sheppard

LONDON AND NEW YORK

First published 2022
by Routledge
2 Park Square, Milton Park, Abingdon, Oxon OX14 4RN

and by Routledge
605 Third Avenue, New York, NY 10158

Routledge is an imprint of the Taylor & Francis Group, an informa business

© 2022 selection and editorial matter, Julie Sheldon and Victoria Sheppard; individual chapters, the contributors

The right of Julie Sheldon and Victoria Sheppard to be identified as the authors of the editorial material, and of the authors for their individual chapters, has been asserted in accordance with sections 77 and 78 of the Copyright, Designs and Patents Act 1988.

All rights reserved. No part of this book may be reprinted or reproduced or utilised in any form or by any electronic, mechanical, or other means, now known or hereafter invented, including photocopying and recording, or in any information storage or retrieval system, without permission in writing from the publishers.

Trademark notice: Product or corporate names may be trademarks or registered trademarks, and are used only for identification and explanation without intent to infringe.

British Library Cataloguing-in-Publication Data
A catalogue record for this book is available from the British Library

Library of Congress Cataloging-in-Publication Data
Names: Sheldon, Julie, 1963- editor. | Sheppard, Victoria, 1980- editor.
Title: Online communities for doctoral researchers and their supervisors : building engagement with social media / edited by Julie Sheldon and Victoria Sheppard.
Description: First Edition. | New York : Routledge, 2022. | Includes bibliographical references and index.
Identifiers: LCCN 2021019325 (print) | LCCN 2021019326 (ebook) | ISBN 9780367224004 (Hardback) | ISBN 9780367224097 (Paperback) | ISBN 9780429274749 (eBook)
Subjects: LCSH: Social media in education. | Doctoral students--Case studies. | Doctoral students--Supervision of. | Mentoring in education--Case studies. | Dissertations, Academic--United States--Authorship.
Classification: LCC LB1044.87 .O433 2022 (print) | LCC LB1044.87 (ebook) | DDC 378.2--dc23
LC record available at https://lccn.loc.gov/2021019325
LC ebook record available at https://lccn.loc.gov/2021019326

ISBN: 978-0-367-22400-4 (hbk)
ISBN: 978-0-367-22409-7 (pbk)
ISBN: 978-0-429-27474-9 (ebk)

DOI: 10.4324/9780429274749

Typeset in Times New Roman
by Taylor & Francis Books

Contents

List of illustrations vii
List of contributors viii
Acknowledgements xi

Introduction 1
JULIE SHELDON AND VICTORIA SHEPPARD

1 The open dissertation: how social media shaped – and scaled – my PhD process 8
BONNIE STEWART

2 Doctoral candidates' experiences of social media: I don't think I could do the PhD without it 23
LIZ BENNETT AND SUE FOLLEY

3 It started with a tweet: how doctoral researchers become social media savvy 38
JULIE SHELDON AND VICTORIA SHEPPARD

4 Intersubjective reflections of @PhDForum: a doctoral community on Twitter 50
DONNA PEACH

5 Online communities that support postgraduate well-being 66
KAY GUCCIONE AND CHRIS BLACKMORE

6 Online communities of practice for academic practice and a sense of belonging 83
JANET DE WILDE, GABRIEL CAVALLI AND STEPHANIE FULLER

7 Blending online and offline in a community of practice model for research degree supervisor development 95
SIAN VAUGHAN AND GEOF HILL

8	*The Supervision Whisperers*: why a virtual community of practice for research supervisors did (not) work EVONNE MILLER AND INGER MEWBURN	110
9	Academic identity, the supervisor and online communities of practice JANET DE WILDE AND GABRIEL CAVALLI	124
10	Interview with Mel Haines: Julie Sheldon and Victoria Sheppard interviewing Mel Haines	133
11	Interview with Katy Peplin: Julie Sheldon and Victoria Sheppard interviewing Katy Peplin	140
12	Interview with Amy Bonsall: Julie Sheldon and Victoria Sheppard interviewing Amy Bonsall	146
13	Interview with Pat Thomson and Anuja Cabraal: Victoria Sheppard interviewing Pat Thomson and Anuja Cabraal	151
	Afterword JULIE SHELDON	160
	Index	162

Illustrations

Figures

5.1	The STEP Padlet board	77
8.1	Heat map of *The Thesis Whisperer* readership, by location from 2011 to 2019	115
8.2	*The Supervision Whisperers* homepage	115

Tables

3.1	Online communities' questions added into PRES	40
3.2	Motivations for engaging with online content and social media as a postgraduate researcher	41

Contributors

Liz Bennett is Director of Teaching and Learning within the School of Education and Professional Development at the University of Huddersfield, UK. Liz completed her doctorate as a part time student in 2012 and since then has had plenty of experience of supervising and examining doctorates from UK and internationally.

Chris Blackmore is a Senior University Teacher and Researcher in Mental Health at the University of Sheffield, UK. He has special interests in student mental health, the role of narratives in our lives and the impact of technology on well-being. Chris is developing expertise in the use of immersive technologies for mental health through the LifePathVR project.

Gabriel Cavalli is Reader in Science and Engineering Education, Director of Teaching Development and Scholarship and Director of the International Centre for Teaching and Learning at the School of Engineering and Materials Science, Queen Mary University of London, UK. He is interested in language and disciplinary discourse and inclusive pedagogies in STEM Education.

Janet De Wilde is Director of Queen Mary Academy and a Professor of Engineering and Education at Queen Mary University of London, UK. She is interested in communities of practice, academic identities, and collective leadership in education.

Sue Folley is an Academic Developer at the University of Huddersfield, UK, with a remit to support academic staff with the use of digital technologies. Sue has a doctorate in Education and is a Senior Fellow of the Higher Education Academy. Her research interests include online teaching and student dashboards.

Stephanie Fuller is Academic Practice Taught Programmes Manager at the Queen Mary Academy, Queen Mary University of London, UK, leading and delivering taught programmes in academic practice for university staff. She has research interests in communities of practice, online and blended learning design and interdisciplinarity in HE.

List of contributors ix

Kay Guccione is Head of Researcher Development at the University of Glasgow, UK. She specialises in mentoring for academic development, publishing on mentoring, thesis writing, hidden curriculum, and the value of the doctorate. Kay edits two blogs – *Supervising PhDs* and *Hidden Curriculum in Doctoral Education* – and founded the annual Researcher Education and Development Scholarship conference.

Geof Hill is a Management Consultant. His training in the 1980s as a Work Study analyst, provided the foundation for later consultancies supporting and advocating professional practice change in Business, Health, Education and Mining. Geof is the instigator and principal author of *The (Research) Supervisor's Friend* – a Wordpress blog.

Inger Mewburn is currently the Director of Researcher Development at The Australian National University where she oversees professional development workshops and programs for all ANU researchers. Aside from creating new posts on *The Thesis Whisperer* blog, she writes scholarly papers, books and book chapters about research education, with a special interest in post PhD employability.

Evonne Miller is Professor of Design Psychology in the School of Design, Faculty of Creative Industries, Education and Social Justice at Queensland University of Technology, in Brisbane, Australia. She has supervised and graduated over 34 PhD, Masters and Doctorate of Creative Industries students, and advised on many student-supervisor dialogues.

Donna Peach is a Lecturer in Social Work and Integrated Practice (Learning Disabilities) at the University of Salford, UK. Donna is the founder and curator of the online Twitter community @PhDforum and its study room www.thephdforum.com/study-room

Julie Sheldon is Dean of the Doctoral Academy at Liverpool John Moores University, UK. She is also a Professor of Art History and has published widely on nineteenth and twentieth century art. She is a board member and Honorary Secretary for the UK Council for Graduate Education (UKCGE).

Victoria Sheppard is the Researcher Development Manager at Liverpool John Moores University, UK. She has a doctorate in English Literature, and her current interests are in doctoral peer communities, transnational skills development and employability.

Bonnie Stewart is an educator and social media researcher interested in what digital networks mean for institutions and society. Assistant Professor of Online Pedagogy and Workplace Learning in the University of Windsor's Faculty of Education, Canada, Bonnie was an early MOOC researcher and ethnographer of Twitter. Bonnie's current research interests include the data literacies of educators, and what it means to know, to learn, and to be a citizen in our current information ecosystem.

Sian Vaughan is Reader in Research Practice at Birmingham School of Art, Birmingham City University, UK, and a Site Director for Midlands4Cities, an Arts & Humanities Research Council funded Doctoral Training Partnership. She has published widely on doctoral education, supervision, artistic research practices, archives and public art.

Acknowledgements

The authors would like to thank the UK Council for Graduate Education for supporting the workshop that led to this production. Our thanks also go to Janet De Wilde for co-convening the session.

Introduction

Julie Sheldon and Victoria Sheppard

This edition has its origins in a UK Council for Graduate Education (UKCGE) workshop held in Liverpool in the UK in April 2018. At the workshop attendees shared experiences of supporting doctoral research through online media. It was an upbeat day of facilitated discussion, show and tell demonstrations, breakout groups, and filling out flip charts to arrive at shared summaries. Participants were in the main fellow travellers, and their take-home message was optimistic and uncomplicated – online communities of research would play a greater role in all our futures. To be sure, we talked about digital-sceptics and recalcitrant researchers but we reasoned that, in time, they would be nudged into an acceptance of interactions underpinned by digital technologies.

No one could have foreseen that push would come to shove so abruptly.

The great online pivot occasioned by Covid-19 shifted most doctoral supervision to Skype, Zoom or Teams meetings, researcher development programmes went online, and postgraduate students formed support networks through departmental Facebook or WhatsApp groups.[1] This slide into the cloud campus was eased by the pre-existence of considerable online researcher support. Over the last decade there has been a substantial growth in blogs, Twitter accounts, online networks, special interest groups, and coaching programmes offering doctoral candidates support and advice on their PhD. There is also an emerging landscape of online communities dedicated to doctoral supervisors. But despite the increasing availability of these modes of researcher support, there has been little consideration of how they form and operate. One of the overarching aims of this volume is to explore these communities in action, bringing together accounts of online community engagement from a range of perspectives – doctoral students, supervisors, content curators, and research support practitioners.

What is clear is that digital scholarship has dramatically changed academic working practices (Weller, 2011; Veletsianos, 2016; Carrigan, 2016; Lupton et al., 2018). Online education was one of the fastest growing areas of Higher Education, even before social distancing measures hastened the shift to online or blended learning for the majority of students in 2020. Open courses, including MOOCs, offer huge potential to widen access (although not without problems, as charted by Toven-Lindsey et al., 2015 and Freund et al., 2018), while the use of technology

DOI: 10.4324/9780429274749-1

has enabled a 'flipped classroom' model, and online access to digitised scholarly materials, open educational resources, and open access publishing has changed the day-to-day teaching and learning experience. Meanwhile the use of digital technologies is widely embedded in many commonplace research activities, from managing and storing content, to collecting, managing and analysing data, engaging in informal peer learning and participating in researcher networks (Gouseti, 2017; Veletsianos, 2016).

Social media is now integrated into the scholarly communications system, and as Sugimoto et al summarise, many studies show high usage of social media for dissemination and promotion (Sugimoto et al., 2017; Van Noorden, 2014), with the use of Altmetrics set to encourage this further. Social media is also being used by academics in a more generative way, to construct research, through participatory 'networked scholarship' (Veletsianos, 2016), though this is somewhat less commonplace than its use for dissemination (JISC, 2012; Procter et al., 2010). Studies that have focused specifically on doctoral researchers' use of social media, however, are rare. Some research has suggested that virtual networks, forums and Twitter are helpful in combatting the loneliness of the doctoral researcher (Janata et al., 2014; Rainford, 2016), while others conversely suggest that these communities are not truly interactive and that most doctoral researchers would rather follow networks than actively contribute their own content (Gouseti, 2017). Investigations of doctoral researchers who blog suggest it is a means of community building and professional development (Frost, 2018), and a valuable way of creating an academic self (Mewburn and Thomson, 2018). Less discussed are the doctoral researchers who might be lurking, or quietly engaging with blogs, advice sites, Twitter conversations, or are participants in closed social media groups and are harder to track. And supervisors are largely absent from much of the literature – what is their relationship with doctoral online networks, and what networks and communities are available to support them in their practice as supervisors?

This book surveys the landscape of these online communities and examines their impact on the production of the doctorate, and on the experience of doctoral researchers and supervisors. In a networked world in which researchers are 'less defined by the institution to which they belong and more by the network and online identity they establish' (Weller, 2011, p. 7), contributors also consider the role of institutions, and how online communities might inform institutional level decisions about doctoral provision and support.

The first three chapters bring together empirical and authoethnographic research focusing on the doctoral researcher perspective, and how they engage with social media as both consumers and producers to develop a researcher identity. Bonnie Stewart's concept of 'The Open Dissertation', a doctoral research project conducted under the scrutiny of a social media network, argues a role for social media in shaping and scaling the PhD. Stewart 'thought out loud', blogging and tweeting as the study took shape and testing work in progress amongst members. Inviting what she calls 'choral commentary' from the network, Stewart argues, not only allowed her to rehearse her ideas in the community, but made the research accountable to wider and varied interests. Blogging can also be a tool of professional profile building. Stewart shows how, through blogging, individuals develop their professional identity, aligning their outcomes to the field.

Stewart demonstrates the extent to which scholarly identities are developed and recognised in and through social media. Liz Bennett and Sue Folley, Julie Sheldon and Victoria Sheppard look at Twitter as a means of informal professional development. Bennett and Folley explore doctoral students' experiences of Twitter and blogs as a means of building relationships within the 'tribe' and learning how to 'try on' or 'try out' the disciplinary norms and conventions. They see the student 'oscillates between the persona of the novice as the identity of a 'doctor'. Sheldon and Sheppard uncover some of these self-regulating norms of behaviour, in their chapter, charting how researchers become social media savvy. They examine the factors that influence the move from more passive consumption to active participation, and the development of an online voice that is professional but still feels authentic.

All of the contributions in this edition acknowledge the mental health challenges of the online pivot. It has long been understood that postgraduate research can be a solitary experience, but that being deprived of peer support can lead to mounting feelings of isolation. Donna Peach, Kay Guccione and Chris Blackmore all examine the crucial role of curators and facilitators in establishing and maintaining networks to support the well-being of doctoral researchers. Peach's Twitter site @PhDForum attracts a transient population of PhD students hopping on and off according to their needs. In her chapter she conceptualises @PhDForum as a 'cyberstreet' within the larger cyberdistrict of Twitter. Peach, like others, describes her role as one of 'content curation', but also as 'guardianship' (Massa, 2017). She reflects on her own learning journey within these roles, and the need to be responsive to the evolving needs of the community.

Blackmore and Guccione analyse two case studies of initiated online communities for doctoral researchers – special interest networks and a project using photography for well-being. Unlike the public, global 'cyberdistrict' of Twitter, these are examples of smaller, closed communities within an institution, in which the facilitator has an important role in establishing ground rules and creating an atmosphere where participants are willing to engage and share often sensitive information. With appropriate care and facilitation, they argue, online environments can be used to build new networks and provide a meaningful source of peer support for research students.

Janet De Wilde, Gabriel Cavalli, and Stephanie Fuller also consider affiliation within institutional online communities. They draw upon two educational case studies to examine the ways in which online communities of practice foster a sense of belonging for doctoral students and staff entering the unfamiliar environment of academic practice. Their chapter looks at the creation of a 'shared repertoire' in which experiences, problem solving tools and guidance are traded between participants (and rated through 'likes') as users strive to be competent academic practitioners. Like Sheldon and Sheppard, De Wilde et al show that users adopt different identities for different social networking platforms, ostensibly separating their sociable from their professional. However, both show that research can be another form of socialization in which doctoral researchers and academic staff not only learn the competencies with which to enact their profession but develop and sustain friendships.

Supervisors of doctoral research remain indivisible from the postgraduate researcher experience. But as suggested in some of the final chapters of this edition, and the interviews that follow them, they have yet to fully understand the part they play in promoting self-agency, resilience and independence amongst researchers. De Wilde and Cavalli are eager to counter the narrative that supervisor indifference or negligence is driving students to online proxies. Vaughan and Hill show that supervisors are not opposed to or threatened by their students' use of online resources: the word 'Useful' is the most common verdict rendered by supervisors in their control group. However, the motivational affordances that drive students to online platforms are not the same for supervisors and, as Evonne Miller and Inger Mewburn show, supervisors are reluctant to share 'a story of failure'. *Thesis Whisperer* founder Mewburn joined with Miller in 2017 to launch an ancillary service, the *Supervision Whisperers*. In their chapter, Miller and Mewburn discuss their attempts to create a supervision community. *The Supervision Whisperers* site is significantly less used than *The Thesis Whisperer*, which Miller and Mewburn attribute in part to the identity of the supervisor as an 'authorised knower', which 'seems to work against full disclosure of the discomfort and "unknowingness" of practice'.

The place of supervision in academic identity formation is discussed by De Wilde and Cavelli in 'Academic identity, the supervisor and online communities of practice'. The challenges and gains and losses of non-face-to-face supervision (such as the diminution of spontaneous 'coffee machine small talk', the threat of 'torn pedagogy' and the dangers of online disinhibition) are well posed by De Wilde and Cavalli. They argue that in order to be a meaningful proxy online supervision should not be reduced to reporting meetings but should include finding other online spaces to work together. Blending online and offline in a Community of Practice model for research degree supervisor development is discussed by Sian Vaughan and Geof Hill. They explore blended supervisor-student interactions as a process that is 'brought full circle', with online leading to face-to-face experiences and vice versa.

The final section of this volume gives voice to facilitators of online communities for researchers, content creators and content curators, through a series of interviews. Mel Haines runs the *Write that PhD* Twitter and Facebook site, with almost 200,000 followers. Katy Peplin has been running Thrive PhD, a 12-week online coaching programme, since 2017. Both attest that their services are often sought by students whose needs are not met in traditional student–supervisor interactions. Peplin divides her clients into three groups: the first have lost their way, the second are disconnected from campus-based research, and the third 'are truly under supervised'. Compensating for the deficiencies of the dyadic relationship (commonly called the 'master apprentice model') of supervision, Haines' writing advice site helps users who are 'too scared to ask their supervisor ... because they don't want to look like an idiot'.

The immediacy, impartiality and constancy of support are widely reported benefits. As Haines puts it: 'I think largely I provide a just-in-time service and people feel like they can dip into the resources that I share at any time'. That 24/7 global service is also an advantage for a diverse PhD population that is geographically dispersed, time-poor, and over-committed to other things. Similarly, Amy Bonsall describes the formation of *Women in Academia Support Network* #WIASN Facebook group and attributes its global membership to 'the immediacy of suggestions and advice'.

> I think it's also the levels of expertise you're able to access. If you need the advice of the vice dean, and somebody's there, you can tag them, and if they're available, they can give you that advice. I don't know where else that would be possible.

The final interview in the book provides a fitting conclusion to the issues considered in the chapters. Pat Thomson and Anuja Cabraal established *VirtualnotViral* as a series of resources for doctoral students facing severe disruption to their research in 2020. It began as a Twitter feed sourcing and retweeting topical feeds, and invigorated by weekly tweet chats. Each chat includes expert guest speakers and is focused on a single theme such as 'staying well', 'networking online', 'working with the new normal' and 'making online supervision work for you'. It also has a website of curated resources for doctoral researchers with content organised into sections on working from home, well-being, research and writing advice.

The speed with which Thomson and Cabraal established the resources and weekly tweet chats is indicative of the responsiveness and agility of social media. It is a story of Twitter as a force for good, a platform that can 'make positive things possible'. It connected collaborators on opposite sides of the world who had never met or even spoken in person, and enabled them to share supportive, practical advice with doctoral students trying to manage the impact of the pandemic on their research. Of course this response did not appear from a vacuum but was built on a decade of online researcher support and communities, many of which are represented and discussed in this volume. The website component of *VirtualnotViral* curates already-existing resources from a wealth of researcher-related blogs, online courses, open access articles, podcasts and interactive content. The guest speakers for the tweet chats are well established academics researching digital scholarship, methods or researcher development and are all highly active on social media.

Even the tweet chat format itself was a resurrection of an established form that had died down somewhat in recent years, but successfully rejuvenated for a new context. Perhaps most significant is *VirtualnotViral*'s foundations in a decade of blogging. Thomson's *Patter* blog, established in 2011, along with Mewburn's *The Thesis Whisperer* (2010) were the prototype blogs for postgraduate researchers, and in the last decade they have published hundreds of posts with pragmatic, accessible advice for doctoral researchers in a vernacular and reassuring tone. While not itself a blog in form, *VirtualnotViral* is a clear example of the blogging ethos Mewburn and Thomson identified in a study of 100 academic blogs in 2013. They argued that blogs functioned in 'a kind of scholarly "gift economy" in which online mentoring, peer support and information sharing is the norm' (Mewburn and Thomson, 201, p. 1115). *VirtualnotViral*, like the other networks and communities discussed in this volume, are examples of 'scholars keen to act more collectively with others rather than in competition' (Mewburn and Thomson, 2018, p. 33).

To sum up, it was never the intention of this volume to proselytise on behalf of digital academia, although its contributions harmonise in the positive. In any case, the pandemic has catalysed all forms of online experience and our intuitions have become the *new normal*. What can we learn from this volume? There is a wealth of material for online support on numerous digital platforms, but postgraduate students benefit from orientation services at the outset of the doctoral journey. The creation and maintenance of effective online communities requires ongoing investment in time and resource to foster effective spaces of interaction. And we have to leverage the online environment to integrate well-being content.

Note

1 With the caveat that the internet and digital platforms and tools have been insufficient proxies for much lab-based research in universities.

References

Brit Toven-Lindsey, B., Rhoads, R.A. and Berdan Lozano, J. (2015). Virtually unlimited classrooms: Pedagogical practices in massive open online courses. *The Internet and Higher Education*, 24, 1–12. doi:10.1016/j.iheduc.2014.07.001

Carrigan, M. (2016). *Social Media for Academics*. London: Sage.

Freund, K., Kizimchuk, S., Zapasnik, J., Esteves, K. and Mewburn, I. (2018). A labour of love: a critical examination of the "labour icebergs" of massive open online courses, in Lupton, D., Thomson, P. and Mewburn, I. (eds). *The Digital Academic: Critical Perspectives on Digital Technologies in Higher Education*. London: Routledge, 122–139. doi:10.4324/9781315473611

Frost, C. (2018). Going from PhD to platform, in Lupton, D., Thomson, P. and Mewburn, I. (eds). *The Digital Academic: Critical Perspectives on Digital Technologies in Higher Education*. London: Routledge, 122–139. doi:10.4324/9781315473611

Gouseti, A. (2017). Exploring doctoral students' use of digital technologies: What do they use them for and why? *Educational Review*, 69(5), 638–654. doi:10.1080/00131911.2017.1291492

Janata, H., Lugosi, P., and Brown, L. (2014). Coping with loneliness: A netnographic study of doctoral students. *Journal of Further and Higher Education*, 38(4), 553–571. doi:10.1080/0309877X.2012.726972

JISC (2012). Researchers of tomorrow. The research behaviour of Generation Y doctoral students. Available at: www.jisc.ac.uk/reports/researchers-of-tomorrow

Lupton, D., Thomson, P. and Mewburn, I. (eds) (2018). *The Digital Academic: Critical Perspectives on Digital Technologies in Higher Education*. London: Routledge. doi:10.4324/9781315473611

Massa, F.G. (2017). Guardians of the Internet: Building and sustaining the anonymous online community. *Organization Studies*, 38(7), 959–988. https://doi.org/10.1177/0170840616670436

Mewburn, I. and Thomson, P. (2013). Why do academics blog? An analysis of audiences, purposes and challenges. *Studies in Higher Education*, 38(8), 1105–1119. doi:10.1080/03075079.2013.835624

Mewburn, I. and Thomson, P. (2018). Towards an academic self? Blogging during the doctorate, in Lupton, D., Thomson, P. and Mewburn, I. (eds) *The Digital Academic: Critical Perspectives on Digital Technologies in Higher Education*. London: Routledge, 122–139. doi:10.4324/9781315473611

Procter, R., Williams, R. and Stewart, J. (2010). If you build it, will they come? How researchers perceive and use web 2.0. London: Research Network Information. Available at: http://wrap.warwick.ac.uk/56246/

Rainford, J. (2016). Becoming a doctoral researcher in a digital world: Reflections on the role of Twitter for reflexivity and the internal conversation. *E-Learning and Digital Media*, 13 (1–2),99–105. doi:10.1177/2042753016672380

Sugimoto, C.R., Work, S., Larivière, V. and Haustein, S. (2017). Scholarly use of social media and altmetrics: A review of the literature. *Journal of the Association for Information Science and Technology*, 68, 2037–2062. https://doi.org/10.1002/asi.23833

Van Noorden, R. (2014). Online collaboration: Scientists and the social network. *Nature*, 512, 126–129. http://doi.org/10.1038/512126a

Veletsianos, G. (2016). *Social Media in Academia: Networked Scholars*. London: Routledge. doi:10.4324/9781315742298

Weller, M. (2011). *The Digital Scholar: How Technology Is Transforming Scholarly Practice*. Basingstoke: Bloomsbury Academic.

1 The open dissertation
How social media shaped – and scaled – my PhD process

Bonnie Stewart

Introduction

It was Twitter that got me through my dissertation.

When I set out to study digital networked practices among academics, in the heady first decade of Twitter and Facebook, I wasn't sure that social media platforms would survive my dissertation timeline. 'I should make sure I include blogging in the mix of my study', I thought, sagely. 'Twitter could disappear tomorrow'. By the time I narrowed my research focus to academic Twitter itself, I wasn't entirely sure that *I* would survive my dissertation, whatever its timeline. Apparently, this is normal. But it was Twitter – or rather the people and the participatory practices that were the hallmark of that space as I knew it in that window of time, and the very presence of those people and practices within an otherwise cloistered reality – that made it possible for me to see my journey through to completion.

Five years after my (successful) 2015 dissertation defense, I often look at the tire fire that is social media and think we'd all be better off without the data surveillance and democracy disruption that it's normalized in our society. There is no arc of personal triumph that can offset the urgency of these very real and pervasive concerns. But the societal problems posed by social media are corporate and governmental and regulation failures, more than structural inevitabilities of the web. They are the problems of a time of knowledge abundance.

This chapter explores social media participation as a game-changing factor in my PhD experience as a mid-career educator. Using an autoethnographic approach, I contrast my experiences as a member of a small, inaugural cohort in a geographically-isolated PhD program with my open, online journey towards an in-depth doctoral study that investigated Twitter as a scholarly space.

I examine structural differences in how the two environments – a local, formal program and the ephemeral open space of networked participatory scholarship (Veletsianos & Kimmons, 2012) – fostered my development and confidence as a scholar, as well as the outputs of my scholarship.

Ultimately, the chapter makes a case for rethinking the practices and norms surrounding PhD program structures in a time of knowledge abundance, and

DOI: 10.4324/9780429274749-2

for opening the dissertation process to the supports, scrutiny, and scholarly exemplars that social media communities can offer. It is the story of what open digital practice did – unexpectedly – for my PhD, but also a tale about academia in a time of social media, and the digital literacies scholarship needs to cultivate to survive and thrive today.

Backdrop: scholarship for knowledge abundance

Traditionally, scholarship has been organized around the premises that knowledge is scarce and the artifacts through which it is disseminated, perishable. Ancient libraries like that of Alexandria could be lost, and medieval scrolls consumed by fire or decay. As Eye (1974) notes in one of the early appearances in the literature of the concept of knowledge abundance, 'materials are exhaustible' (p. 445). Even with multiple copies of a given manuscript readily available, as has been the case with print for many generations, individual copies of a book or journal can become dog-eared or destroyed. Also, distribution of print incurs material costs and risks. As a result, print publishing has traditionally been a gatekeeping process, particularly in academia where peer-review processes and funding structures have established and guarded specific status hierarchies (Husu, 2004).

On the other hand, the properties of digital knowledge artifacts are persistence, replicability, scalability, and searchability (boyd, 2011, p. 46). Whether I forward an email to one person or to 500, the costs, effort, and effects on the message itself are nominal. If a piece of paper passes through a thousand hands, there are likely to be traces of dirt and damage on the message, while a tweet or viral meme can pass in front of a thousand eyes in short order without any material impact.

Yet practices of scarcity do not simply disappear in the face of abundance. I have been in classrooms as a teacher and a student much of my life. In spite of widespread and mobile – if inequitably distributed – access to knowledge, much of the techno-cultural system of contemporary scholarship remains 'rooted in the premise of scarcity, or the hierarchies scarcity has fostered' (Stewart, 2015a, para. 5).

My own PhD research made many of academia's status hierarchies visible, especially in relation to the prestige economies of higher education. The reputational economy of traditional scholarship is familiar to most academics. As Willinsky (2010) describes it:

> Those within the academy become very skilled at judging the stuff of reputations. Where has the person's work been published, what claims in priority of discovery have they established, how often have they been cited, how and where reviewed, what institutional ties earned, what organizations led?
>
> (p. 297)

I was interested in what happens when one reputational economy – the academy – collides with that of social media. I had already been on Twitter for more than five years by the time I started my dissertation proposal (Stewart, 2018), and I was curious: what about the academics who not only toil on peer-reviewed articles or conference papers, but who blog their ideas or engage with others in their field on Twitter? Can those be considered forms or extensions of scholarship? How do the scholars themselves understand it? What might networked or digital scholarship have to teach conventional academia?

My study was designed around the premise that networked scholarship operates on equally tacit – if different – 'stuff of reputations', as Willinsky put it. I wanted to identify the terms on which networked scholars understood their social media engagement and influence. I didn't initially plan for the study to be a comparison of reputational economies, but in a sense, it turned out to be. The 2013–2014 research interviews and ethnographic observations within my study focused on participants' perception of influence in digital networks, but since all participants were situated both in academia and in digitally-networked spaces, comparative conversations were part of how the study unfolded. Fourteen participants, all of whom had active academic affiliations, blogs, and academic Twitter accounts, were selected for the ethnography: thirteen remained part of the study throughout. They were located in Canada, the U.S, Mexico, Australia, Singapore, Ireland, Italy, and South Africa. Daily online participant observation was conducted from November 2013 through February 2014, via Twitter, blog sites, Facebook, and Instagram accounts. Participants kept 24-hour reflective logs of particular windows of engagement that they felt were representative of their networked participation and completed profile assessments of other (volunteer) academic Twitter profiles. Ten participants engaged in emergent semi-structured interviews via Skype, following the completion of their reflective logs and profile assessments of others' network profiles. Interview questions focused on participants' practices, experiences, and perceptions of networked scholarship as juxtaposed with their institutional identities and interactions.

In terms of hierarchies, the research process made clear that institutional interactions were often experienced as marginalizing or silencing, particularly among junior and early-career scholars with high network engagement. This collateral conclusion emerged along with my core findings on how scholars in the open read each others' influence and resonated with other research reflections emerging at the time on intersections of academic marginality and digital microcelebrity (McMillan Cottom, 2015). It also resonated with my own experience of being highly visible online while a graduate student, which created status tensions between the two prestige economies I inhabited.

Seven of my study's thirteen participants were PhD students or very early career scholars. Most who shared this junior status in the traditional academic hierarchy – as well as a number with senior or tenured positions – overtly noted negative experiences of hierarchy, scarcity, and zero-sum social behaviours within their PhD programs or institutions more broadly, even though these were not a direct focus of the study. Some participants reported having their input rejected or dismissed due to their lack of status, particularly in faculty meetings or group settings. Others noted confusion or hostility from senior colleagues as responses to media visibility generated through social media channels, since media attention has traditionally been a signal of senior status in the academic prestige economy. One study participant, who had a sizeable and well-known academic Twitter account and an administrative role within her institution, noted, 'I've grown this global network sitting on my ass and it offends people.... It has success. But when you're the one getting keynotes, people who've bought into older notions of success, they feel cheated' (Stewart, 2015b, p. 301). The study served to confirm that many scholars experience academia in hierarchical terms, wherein the success of individuals is perceived competitively by peers and colleagues.

At the same time, the study also indicated that social media networks, even in 2013–2014, were not the hierarchy-flattening spaces acclaimed by Thomas Friedman in *The World is Flat* (2005). While participants shared that by creating relational networks and new sites for conversation, 'the norms of open online participation helped minimize academia's hierarchies' (Stewart, 2015b, p. 305), the platform tended to amplify offline power inequities around race and gender (Stewart, 2016). What social media was shown to shift was not hierarchy at the societal level, but the specific scarcity-based, peer-review-focused reputational economy of academia. My study showed that the reputational economy of academic Twitter is not based in the gatekeeping that marks traditional scholarship, but rather in the participatory yet metrics-conscious terms of an attention economy (Stewart, 2015b). As I noted in a blog post reflecting on my dissertation process: 'participation enrols us in a media machine that is always and already out of our control' (Stewart, 2014, para 10).

That said, the study also indicated that scholars' open networked practices represent and enable a scholarship that is of – and for – a time of knowledge abundance. One participant proposed an alternate form of attention economy that she experienced from her scholarly Twitter network when she was diagnosed with cancer:

> The attention economy ... isn't just about clicks and eyeballs, but also about the ways in which we selectively tend towards each other and tend each others' thoughts – it's an economy of care, not just a map to markets.
> (Stewart, 2014, para 18)

And it was the care I experienced in academic Twitter that really made the difference to my dissertation experience, in the end.

Reputational economies: an autoethnography

While knowledge abundance and Twitter were both familiar to me before I began my PhD, the formal structures of institutional research and the dissertation process were more alien, though I'd worked in higher education for over a decade. I'd worked as a grant writer, project manager, and researcher in the decade since my MA, but my staff and contract status positions meant that I existed largely outside the prestige economy of the tenure track. As a result, I had not fully anticipated the ways in which it keeps the arc of the dissertation process bent towards scarcity.

My study was designed as an ethnography of a broader community to which I belonged, in the tradition of Boas (Boellstorff, 2008). It was not, however, an *auto*ethnography according to the circulation of the term within my faculty and discipline at the time I undertook my research. While Hayano (1979) applied the term autoethnography to 'how anthropologists conduct and write ethnographies of their "own people"' (p. 99), by the time I began my work in a Faculty of Education in 2010, autoethnography had become understood as more distinctly personal. The idea of autoethnography as an 'autobiographical genre of writing and research that displays multiple layers of consciousness, connecting the personal to the cultural' (Ellis and Bochner, 2000, p. 39) was more in keeping with my understanding of the method. I did see academic Twitter as 'my own people' and wrote my dissertation primarily in the first person. However, I was not a subject of my own research, nor was my own experience foregrounded in the data analysis or narration.

I came to my dissertation process from specific places and subjectivities, both online and off. The boundaries between these places and subjectivities are in many ways blurred, but the three that I'll trace most prominently are my personal identity(ies), my institutional identity(ies), and my networked – or digital – identity(ies).

The first two are difficult to untangle, because personal factors determined my institutional identity during my PhD years. I am a first-in-family university graduate, the only child of a single mother from a small Atlantic Canadian city. I went to university on scholarship, lived and taught around the world, then returned home after 15 years to start my own family. Five years on from my return, I began my PhD as one of four inaugural students in a brand-new doctoral program; the first PhD in Educational Studies available in the province.

The university I enrolled at had been my erstwhile employer over that five years, in a variety of casual contracts punctuated by maternity leaves. With two very young children and extended family responsibilities, I was not in a position to consider moving in order to pursue doctoral work, so I was excited when the program opened. There were no other doctoral opportunities in my field within the province, nor online programs without significant residency requirements. But although I chose the institution based almost entirely on proximity, my prior experiences within the university and the faculty had generated a sense of professional belonging within those spaces, for me. I brought a sense of being a relational insider, embedded in trust relationships, to the program.

I also had developed trust relationships within my field more broadly, via social networks and blogging. When I began the PhD program in September

2010, I'd had a blog for nearly five years, and a Twitter account for three. I'd been on the perimeter of early Canadian research in Massive Open Online Courses (MOOCs), though my online presence was predominantly personal rather than academic. Still, my work had intersected with educational technology for over a decade, and I was interested in the educational implications of participatory blogging and social media networks. My networked identity had been my primary site of continuity over the previous few years of parental/professional upheaval, and I had a fine-tuned understanding of networks and of trends in digital education. Due to my partner's long-time presence in online edtech networks, and the fact that my own digital presence referenced our family life, our Twitter networks in particular had become quite entwined (Stewart, 2018) by the time I entered the PhD. I was, therefore, regularly engaged in online conversations with relatively influential people in edtech and media education, particularly in Canada, as well as with significant influencers in the blogging space.

At the time, I didn't fully realize how separate the two spaces – the networked conversation about digital education and the formalized institutional study of education – were. During my MA studies a decade prior, I'd experienced deep connection and intellectual community, and had found this again in some of the online spaces that blogging and social media had unfolded for me. I understood – and had written speculatively about – the ways in which social networks constituted a reputational economy of their own and was curious about the ways this differed from the reputational economy that I understood academia to be. But to an extent, I expected both communities to be curious about the implications of the digital, and to be mutually enhancing environments for intellectual community and inquiry. Instead, although one space ended up being the subject of my studies in the other, that mutuality proved elusive.

Scarcity and abundance: a contrast

The first years of my PhD were marked by three very particular forms of scarcity: time, money, and belonging.

The first is usual: even in a time of knowledge abundance, there are only twenty-four hours to any day, and a PhD is a major undertaking. My own time constraints were amplified by the fact that my children were four and nearly two when I began the PhD program in 2010. My dissertation bears, in part, a dedication of thanks to them 'for sharing their childhoods with the gestation of this rather demanding sibling'.

I'd anticipated an intense workload, but not one that precluded time or clearance for any paid work. PhD students were ineligible to teach or TA when I began, and institutional funding was less than promised. I had two children in daycare, and while I eventually secured external scholarship funding, teaching contracts, and a part-time staff role on campus, my family spent a long time recovering financially from the unexpected scale of expense during that first year.

By December of my first year, my cohort of four had also slipped to three. My cohort colleagues – all mid-career adults – were being mentored from different traditions and corners of the faculty and expressed discomfort with digital communications. After the first year, our faculty's PhD culture was so new that few events or channels existed to keep us in contact. The region we were located in is geographically isolated, with few academic conferences, and travel is expensive. I was limited in terms of local access to an intellectual community in my field of inquiry and felt the lack of a sense of belonging deeply.

I filled this gap by developing a virtual cohort, via blogging and Twitter, among the networked community of academics whom I came to study. But my digital presence, and my capacity to contribute and engage in the collaborative work of understanding digital practice, were not particularly valued within my program. As I began to develop status and recognition in the digital space, doing public talks and radio interviews about digital education and engagement, the consistent message I received from my faculty was 'get your PhD done first'.

I had felt a sense of belonging, even as contract staff, to the institution and to higher ed as a field and a profession. But as a PhD student, that feeling of belonging dissipated, and was replaced by a vague sense that I was – regularly and repeatedly – contravening the tacit order of things by behaving and relating to institutional colleagues in ways that were not legible within their prestige economy. I had not fully understood the extent to which being a graduate student would mean giving up the professional status attached to my institutional identity. Nor had I realized that public visibility in my academic field might be seen as illegitimate, due to my limited institutional status. I learned that where reputational economies collide, a person with low status in one space and relatively high status in another is at risk if they do not perform their dual subjectivity with great care and astuteness. I was not astute.

When I went through a proposal defense process without exemplars or 'what to expect' guidance in advance, in spite of my formal and informal requests, I foundered. I passed, but was left feeling misunderstood, shamed, and powerless. I wondered if I'd wasted two years in the pursuit of an idea that simply wouldn't fit the box that the academy demanded.

From this low point, I eventually got up the courage to request some changes in my co-supervisor situation, and to begin a second draft of my dissertation proposal. I also withdrew much of my invested identity in the PhD program. Had I had a solid job opportunity to go to at that point, I'd likely have simply quit. But professional jobs are scarce in Atlantic Canada, and I still had time left on the external, national PhD scholarship I'd won. So, from a place that felt a lot like abjection, I reached out to try to begin to pull my doctoral journey back together.

I did not reach out institutionally. I reached out to my network.

Networked participatory scholarship: social media shaping

This was the step that led to me opening up my own dissertation. It was an effort to create space for myself as a scholar, on terms that were recognizable to me.

I'd started a new academic blog more than a year before, shortly after I'd begun my PhD. I'd hoped it might be a place to draft ideas and draw my institutional supervisors into a choral, networked conversation about my work. I'd felt it would be one thing to sit at a table and try to recap the emergent perspectives on digital engagement and practices that I encountered on academic Twitter, and another to have my committee present in that emergence along with some of senior scholars in educational technology and digital scholarship whom I cited regularly. I'd used the blog to keep track of my reading and notes while also creating an open record of responses to those notes and ideas, one that my institutional committee could see and be a part of. I had not factored in the extent to which it is difficult for people to shift their practices, or find time for networked engagement, and thus my committee were minimally engaged with the blog as a space for shaping my work. But my network – which was slowly morphing from personal to academic and educator-centric – *was* engaged. And thus, the network effectively become my cohort in the process. It included the senior scholars mentioned, but also a broad range of early career scholars, education practitioners, instructional designers, and fellow PhD students, situated primarily throughout North America and Anglo Europe and Australia. I had the privilege of scale and connections: I had approximately 4,700 Twitter followers at the point in 2013 when I put out my Call for Research Participants.

I never blogged overtly about my program or the experience of the barely-passed proposal defense, but I did eventually write a post acknowledging that I needed to rewrite my proposal. I drafted out the possibility of shifting my focus from networked practice generally to networked scholars and got significant – and generous – response. Fellow PhD students left enthusiastic comments. Tenured faculty from different parts of the world offered affirmation as well as notes of guidance and reading recommendations.

My network reflected my work back to me as worthy, and not just of empty praise or likes, but of time and feedback and commitment to improvement. The commenters helped me see avenues and existing conversations in which my work could be situated. They also helped me begin to regain confidence in the idea that the study of contemporary social media practice had a place in the academy. They made me feel that they *understood* what I was attempting to explore ... and that I could contribute to the broader conversation in my field of inquiry through the work I proposed.

My institutional committee had put genuine effort into trying to help my original proposal fit what they understood as the conversation I was entering, but we had not managed to establish shared premises about what that conversation *was*. My networked audience made me feel that they understood networked practice and what I was stumbling toward in my drafts. Moreover, the networked audience, no matter their academic status, engaged with me as a peer on a learning curve *with* them.

The work I was doing followed an emerging tradition that Veletsianos & Kimmons (2012) frame under the term Networked Participatory Scholarship, or 'scholars' participation in online social networks to share, reflect upon, critique, improve, validate, and otherwise develop their scholarship' (para. 1). This techno-cultural perspective on digital scholarly practice recognizes that networked participation can be used not just to disseminate scholarship and amplify one's readership or citation count (Mewburn & Thompson, 2013), but to build ideas in a participatory fashion. Veletsianos himself – a Canada Research Chair on the opposite coast of Canada – responded to my blog post about my proposal with a detailed appraisal of strengths and weaknesses in my idea. The idea that an established senior colleague would take the time to comment in this validating and caring way was a model of networked participatory scholarship in action for me. The responses to my post motivated me to consider modeling the entire process of my dissertation as an open exploration, accountable to the community it was meant to represent and engage.

I began to redesign my proposal, and to blog core pieces of it as I went. I continued blogging through my research study – releasing my Call for Participants and my Ethics clearance through my blog, amplified by Twitter – and sharing preliminary findings in the open. That meant I got to hear from the networked scholarly community at large, including non-participants, about whether my conclusions regarding networked academic practice resonated for them. The open practice of blogging served to situate my study within the broader conversation on digital scholarship and digital practice and helped make colleagues aware of my work.

I decided not only to blog about formal aspects of my study, but to tweet about digital practice openly and regularly. I polled Twitter for perspectives, informally, and engaged in ongoing meta-talk with the academic Twitter community, particularly around changes in the platform and how users interpreted them. I tweeted back and forth with journalists reporting on Twitter and attempted to gauge the pace of emerging practices and adoption, especially among educators.

Situating my dissertation process in the open, as an ongoing presence on social media and on my blog, had the core effect of making me accountable not just to my committee but to a far wider and more varied collection of interests. I did recognize that I needed to instantiate particular forms and targets in order for my study to qualify as a dissertation, and I set about overtly studying and incorporating those. But from the time I began the second proposal, my dissertation was always turned towards the open, networked community that it documented. That community was not only its subject, but its audience.

This shaped my dissertation by embedding it within a network of relationships, long before publication. People began to be aware of my topic and to contribute where they could. Members of the network regularly shared articles that I might be interested in, just as my formal committee did, thus enhancing my literature review and keeping me up-to-date on emerging ideas. But the most important relational impact of social media and blogging on my dissertation was that open engagement enlarged my cohort from three to an effectively uncountable number, bringing me in contact with other scholars engaged in inquiries similar to my own, including graduate students across a variety of locales and systems. This meant that in addition to sharing of ideas and work, I also had a far broader collection of people with whom to share struggles and build my own sense of belonging to the identity of graduate student, even and especially when I did not feel belonging to my institutional program.

This was the factor that kept me going through my dissertation: Twitter offered me a site where I could be a scholar on networked terms, while still trying to learn and master the terms of the academic reputational economy. Twitter connected me to people who understood my work, but also my networked and institutional social locations – and the tensions between them. Twitter taught me the digital literacies I needed to deal with abundance and with the quick-moving world of ideas in an age of social media. And Twitter gave me friends, and a sense that both my work and I had value. It gave me a place where I could contribute, intellectually and socially. Overall, opening my dissertation to the abundance of social media and open academic communities offered me a way to remain invested in the process of my own work, even when factors of scarcity at the institutional level felt limiting or discouraging.

The open dissertation: social media scaling

Moreover, the process of opening my dissertation scaled my study's impact, bringing it to the attention of a far wider audience than it would likely have had otherwise. To open my dissertation, I effectively brought its development out into the light of networked platforms: I blogged and tweeted about my ideas for the study, shared updates about my proposal being approved, thought out loud. The process served to reap me input, choral commentary, a pile of useful articles, and an informal but ongoing public play-testing of my assumptions, premises, and fledgling conclusions amongst the subculture I was studying.

The circulation of my ideas wasn't extreme: dissertation proposals or updates are not the kind of thing that goes viral. But when my ethics clearance went through, I blogged a Call for Participants, tweeted it out, and eventually saw it retweeted over 150 times. I got a generous response to that call, which is a huge boon for any PhD student. Later, when the first paper from my PhD came out and I tweeted the link, the paper got a significant number of clicks and downloads, and ultimately circulated enough that it's now been cited a respectable 70 times in four years. These are the measurable impacts, if also perhaps the least important.

Having my work circulate in the open also served as a buffer against the power of academic structures. The dissertation tradition is monographic and almost monastic, generally: a closed process that cloisters work away until it is approved by the supervisors and committee and readied for defense. This can amplify the power differentials that already exist within the academic hierarchy, particularly in the intensely individual supervisory relationship. I trusted my committee, but also wanted my work in the open as a buffer between the academic and networked prestige economies, since the project needed to be legible within both. That changed the power relationship between my committee and me. I still had a great deal to learn from them, but they were no longer the sole audience for the work I was doing. Circulating in the open extended my proposal's reach beyond my supervisors, or committee, or institution, and extended my audience from scarcity to abundance.

Once I got past the proposal stage, I continued to pursue the path of an open dissertation. Here again, the abundance in – and of – digital networked spaces served to scale up my efforts and expose me to a much wider array of input than I could have had in any single institution. I found a collection of practices and experiences being shared on hashtags such as #phdchat and #highereducation, as well as within my existing network. And I drew on and developed relationships with other PhD candidates, enabling me to reflect aloud and work with others towards broadening my idea of what a dissertation could be.

My version of the open dissertation ended up consisting primarily of missals from inside the process, in addition to ongoing Twitter commentary. I blogged about working from an alternate research-based Twitter account, shared tentative findings and observations throughout the experience, and tweeted about the shifts that I saw occurring on Twitter's platform during the 2013–2014 window in which my ethnography took place. I also traced the rise of call-out culture and the weaponization of Twitter within academia, particularly for marginalized scholars, in public writing about my dissertation process (Stewart, 2015c). These writing invitations – and the keynote invitations that materialized during my PhD process – all stemmed from my open practice, wherein people discovered my topic online and extended an opportunity to bring my ideas to new audiences.

Thanks to my committee's willingness to support me in experimenting with form, I also opened up the process through a three-paper thesis format. This meant that by the time I cobbled the final version of my dissertation together, core chapters had been through the peer review process, published, and even paraphrased for professional publications like *Inside Higher Ed* (Stewart, 2015d). As a result, I'd had the benefit of peer review, plus additional scholarly and public feedback on how I presented my ideas and tied the overarching threads together. The three-paper format also increased the scale of audience for my work and for my findings, meaning that I could communicate openly with a broader public. I chose a Creative Commons CC-BY license for my published dissertation, which still established me as the originator of the work and the ideas therein but placed it in the tradition of abundance rather than scarcity. I keep a full copy of the thesis openly available and discoverable on the web.

Finally, I made my defense as open as I could. My committee and my institution were game to support me in breaking ground on this front, for which I was grateful. I arranged for my half-hour public presentation and public questions to be livestreamed on the web, with some of my questions coming in on Twitter. I did ask that whole three-hour event be streamed, including the committee questioning after the public presentation and questions, but that request was not granted. Still, the opportunity to present my dissertation openly and to engage the community that I'd studied was important to me: a way of opening the cloister of the defense to abundance, and leaving a public, accessible record of my experience for other scholars to consider. More than 100 people tuned into the defense live, and nearly 300 engaged with it on Twitter in some way, through comments, likes, or retweets.

One of the benefits cited by participants in my study was that cultivating open, public audiences for their ideas allowed them to 'contribute to the conversation' (Stewart, 2015b) in their field and in higher education generally, even when they did not have status positions in the academic hierarchy. That sense of meaningful contribution and resulting validation is exactly what my open dissertation process gave me: being open enabled me to lead a public conversation through my work, and to experience value and belonging within a broad community of scholarship even when I felt illegible within my face-to-face environment.

My experience cannot be universalized. The topic of my dissertation study was particularly well-suited to the reflexive process of working in the open: the idea of influence within academic Twitter was, unsurprisingly, of interest *to* academic Twitter, and that created benefits for me in terms of community, audience, and opportunities. As a long-term blogger and tweeter comfortable in participatory networked spaces, I was also well-positioned to take advantage of those opportunities when they arose, and as a white woman, I did not face the sanction or risk many people of colour experience when expressing opinions in networked spaces (Gardiner, 2018). That said, even as Twitter in particular has become a more fraught and bot-ridden space since 2015, there remain vibrant academic and educator communities there, and there are also alternate platforms by which digital presence can be cultivated and shared in the open. My path to the open dissertation is only one of many paths possible.

That said, what I learned during the process of completing and sharing my own mostly-open dissertation was that programs can make it easier for graduate students to reap the benefits of networked engagement with their topics of study. Gogia's (2016) identification of the granularities of the PhD makes visible specific decision points where institutions, programs, and supervisors could encourage open dissertation practices: under the three key areas of Process, Hearing, and Document, she notes opportunities for opening each to new audiences, beyond the scarcity model of 'committee only' that has tended to be most programs' default. In my own case, I opened the process both through blogging and tweeting about it, was permitted by my committee to open the hearing in part, through the livestream of my defense presentation (though not the examination), and opened the document by licensing it CC-BY and making it searchable online. There are compelling reasons to consider opening dissertations: Willinsky (2006) frames the case for open access and open research in general as a matter of the affordable spread of valuable human knowledge, while McKiernan et al. (2016) confirm that open research practices benefit individual researchers through increased citations, media attention, and greater collaboration, funding, and job opportunities. But given the hierarchical nature of academia, few students who aren't already embedded in open or networked practice may be likely to risk advocating for opening their dissertations if those options aren't presented to them by their programs or their senior mentors.

Conclusion

The open dissertation process enabled me to scale my research inquiry into a public conversation, and to engage the open community in an otherwise often closed process. It also opened up the question of what, and *who*, the dissertation is *for*.

When it comes to preparing scholars for the pinnacle of higher education – the doctoral degree – the emphasis often is on having PhD students spend years of their lives preparing a very long, format-focused piece of writing primarily for a defence committee of three to five people plus whomever decides to check the tome out of the library in ensuing decades. Certainly, scholars often adapt their dissertations for academic books or papers, but these separate publications usually involve another few *years* of rewrites and edits from Reviewer #2 before they ever see the light of day.

This status quo does not help us make a case for the value of higher education and expert knowledge. Already we lock away much of our research in expensive, inaccessible, and increasingly unnecessary journals because we're attached to our own prestige economies. We miss the opportunity to get that research – knowledge that takes years and, often, public funds to develop – *to* the public via policy and media and open channels.

Yet outside continental Europe, most senior scholars' concept of the dissertation defence or viva seems to be a tradition of intimate questioning behind closed doors, structured as a rite of initiation, almost. We need to ask, initiation into what?

We are no longer training for the professoriate. The pretence that this is what the PhD dissertation and defence processes are *for* needs to be challenged with real talk about both casualization *and* contemporary scholarly practices. There are few tenure-track lines or permanent positions remaining, even for those with the highest degrees. Graduate students should be cultivated and fostered as scholars, absolutely, and as full contributing participants within their field of inquiry, but those of us who guide them through the PhD need to open up our own narrow concepts of their journey, so we can help them be prepared for the distributed and digital scholarly world as it exists now. Research and teaching roles are found in government and the private sector as well as in higher education, and even formal scholarly conversations demand the digital literacy to navigate disparate platforms, audiences, and public collaborators. Funders demand open publication, in Canada, and from 2013 on, the US National Science Foundation actively called for projects to 'contribute more broadly to achieving societal goals' (NSF, 2013). Yet PhD candidates who don't learn open, public practices and approaches in their doctorate implicitly get the message that they don't really matter. Our closed systems operate on premises that higher education can no longer fulfil: graduate students trained to be replicas of their supervisors without the broad input of open audiences and a distributed network of colleagues are not being set up for success. They need to be initiated into the broader world of scholarship for abundance and opening the dissertation can and should be a key part of this learning curve, both for faculty and for PhD candidates today.

Ultimately, in a time of knowledge abundance, it's time to consider making open rather than closed dissertation work the default. Many PhD candidates could benefit from networked relationships and audiences, and society would benefit from more accessible, open dissemination of graduate research. If graduate students embarking on a dissertation could make informed, supported, meaningful choices about audience(s) for their dissertations, and one of the prime responsibilities of supervision were helping students select, understand, and reach – to some scaffolded extent – those audiences, we could go a long way to moving scholarship away from scarcity and make a far more compelling case for public funding for the work we all do.

References

Boellstorff, T. (2008). *Coming of age in Second Life: An anthropologist explores the virtually human*. Princeton, NJ: Princeton University Press.

boyd, d. (2011). Social network sites as networked publics: Affordances, dynamics, and implications. In Z. Papcharissi (Ed.), *A networked self* (pp. 39–58). New York: Routledge.

Eye, G. G. (1974). As far as eye can see: Knowledge abundance in an environment of scarcity. *The Journal of Educational Research*, 67(10), 445–447.

Ellis, C. & Bochner, A. (2000). Autoethnography, personal narrative, reflexivity: Researcher as subject. In N. K. Denzin & Y. S. Lincoln (Eds), *Handbook of qualitative research* (2nd Ed.) (pp. 733–768). Thousand Oaks, CA: SAGE.

Friedman, T. L. (2005). *The world is flat: A brief history of the twenty-first century*. New York: Farrar, Straus and Giroux.

Gardiner, B. (2018). It's a terrible way to go to work: What 70 million readers' comments on the Guardian revealed about hostility to women and minorities online. *Feminist Media Studies*, 18(4), 592–608. doi:10.1090/14680777.2018.1447334

Gogia, L. (2016, October 29). Granularities of the open dissertation. Retrieved February 27, 2020 from https://googleguacamole.wordpress.com/2016/10/29/granularities-of-the-open-dissertation/

Hayano, D. (1979). Auto-ethnography: Paradigms, problems, and prospects. *Human Organization*, 38(1), 99–104. doi:10.17730/humo.38.1.u761n5601t4g318v

Husu, L. (2004). Gate-keeping, gender inequality, and scientific excellence. European Commission, Gender and Excellence in the Making. http://citeseerx.ist.psu.edu/viewdoc/download?doi=10.1.1.106.2670&rep=rep1&type=pdf#

McCoy, L. (2013). Institutional ethnography and constructionism. In J. Holstein & J. Gubrium (Eds), *Handbook of constructionist research* (701–714). New York: Guilford Publications.

McKiernan, E., Bourne, P., Brown, C.T., Buck, S., Kenall, A., Lin, J., MacDougall, D., Nosek, B., Ram, K., Soderberg, C.K., Spies, J., Thaney, K., Updegrove, A., Woo, K. & Yarkoni, T. (2016, July 7). Point of view: How open science helps researchers succeed. *eLife*. Retrieved February 27, 2020 from https://elifesciences.org/articles/16800

McMillan Cottom, T. (2015). 'Who do you think you are?': When marginality meets academic microcelebrity. *Ada: A Journal of Gender, New Media, & Technology*, 7. Retrieved July 30, 2019 from https://adanewmedia.org/2015/04/issue7-mcmillancottom/

Mewburn, I. & Thompson, P. (2013). Why do academics blog? An analysis of audiences, purposes, and challenges. *Studies in Higher Education*, 38(8), 1105–1119. doi:10.1080/03075079.2013.835624

National Science Foundation (NSF) (2013). Revised NSF merit review criteria effective for proposals submitted or due on or after January 14, 2013. Retrieved July 30, 2019 from www.nsf.gov/bfa/dias/policy/merit_review/overview.pdf

Stewart, B. (2014, November 4). Networks of care and vulnerability. Retrieved July 30, 2019 from http://theory.cribchronicles.com/2014/11/04/networks-of-care-and-vulnerability/

Stewart, B. (2015a). In abundance: Networked participatory practices as scholarship. *International Review of Research in Open & Distributed Learning*, 16(3).

Stewart, B. (2015b). Open to influence: What counts as academic influence in scholarly networked Twitter participation. *Learning, Media, and Technology*, 40(3), 287–309. doi:10.1080/17439884.2015.1015547

Stewart, B. (2015c). In public: The shifting consequences of Twitter scholarship. *Hybrid Pedagogy*. Retrieved July 30, 2019 from https://hybridpedagogy.org/in-public-the-shifting-consequences-of-twitter-scholarship/

Stewart, B. (2015d, April 6). Contributions and connections: What counts as academic influence on Twitter. *Inside Higher Ed*. Retrieved July 30, 2019 from www.insidehighered.com/blogs/higher-ed-gamma/contributions-and-connections

Stewart, B. (2016). Collapsed publics: Orality, literacy, and vulnerability in academic Twitter. *Journal of Applied Social Theory*, 1(1), 61–86.

Stewart, B. (2018). Identity at the core: Open and digital leadership. In A. Zorn, J. Haywood, & J.M. Glachant (Eds), *Shaking the brick and mortar: Moving higher education online* (139–156). Cheltenham: Edward Elgar.

Veletsianos, G. & Kimmons, R. (2012). Assumptions and challenges of open scholarship. *International Review of Research in Open and Distributed Learning*, 13(4).

Willinsky, J. (2006). *The case for open access to research and scholarship*. Cambridge, MA: The MIT Press.

Willinsky, J. (2010). Open access and academic reputation. *Annals of Library and Information Studies*, 57, 296–302. Retrieved July 30, 2019 from www.researchgate.net/publication/267714876_Open_access_and_academic_reputation

2 Doctoral candidates' experiences of social media

I don't think I could do the PhD without it

Liz Bennett and Sue Folley

Introduction

This chapter started life as a journal article based on our experiences as two doctoral candidates who made use of social media during our doctoral journey (Bennett and Folley 2014). In the article we concluded that social media offered us a great deal, in particular by providing connections to people and communities that offered both guidance and advice. It also offered a way to share the experience of undertaking a doctorate. We suggested that, if used with an informed awareness, it might be effective in helping to support doctoral candidates as they traverse the doctoral journey with its challenges of isolation, feelings of bewilderment, stuck-ness and confusion (Kiley 2009; Carter et al. 2013; Barry et al. 2018). When we wrote our article, we were both part-time doctoral candidates and in full time employment within a university in Yorkshire, UK, and found the task of managing our online identity particularly challenging, given the conflicting status of these roles. On the one hand as doctoral candidates we felt that we were novices, yet on the other as professionals we were being paid for our expertise. We theorised this experience using the notion of dual identities (Orr and Simmons 2010). As we approached writing this chapter, we were interested in whether others experienced these same conflicts of identity. We also wanted to use the opportunity to investigate if our experiences applied to other doctoral candidates, and to establish how experiences might have changed over the decade since 2007 when Twitter was still in its infancy and when we started our doctoral journey.

In this chapter we use the term social media to refer to two particular tools – Twitter and blogs. Of course social media includes an array of services and tools, some of which are well established, for instance Facebook, but many others come and go – fashions of the online world. We restricted our focus to Twitter and blogging because both tools have been in existence over the last ten years, and both offer particular affordances which support online communities. For instance, both Twitter and blogs are generally public facing, and text based. Blog posts tend to be a more developed form of writing whereas in contrast Twitter is limited in terms of the length of posts (tweets) and so tend to be more informal and conversational. Both platforms offer the

DOI: 10.4324/9780429274749-3

doctoral student a medium for presenting themselves to a much wider audience than is possible to meet face-to-face. However, alongside this possibility the medium invites behaviours which carry challenges and risks, for example the intimacy of Twitter can lead to being overly informal and simplistic. The challenge of how to handle a personal and professional online identity is something that doctoral students need to navigate as they engage in social media.

This chapter draws on data from a qualitative online survey which aimed to understand doctoral candidates' experiences of Twitter and blogging. Throughout the chapter we use the terms 'PhD' study or 'PhD student' for simplicity but the discussion is likely to apply to those working on any doctoral programme (including professional doctorates such as EdD, DBA) which are characterised by autonomous study and which takes place over an extended period of time.

The chapter starts by outlining how we gathered the opinions of our sample of doctoral candidates. Then the discussion is structured around the three questions that we set out to answer:

- What choices do doctoral candidates' make about whether to use social media whilst studying, and what are their reasons for making these choices?
- In what ways do social media help doctoral candidates' learning?
- What advice would you give to other doctoral candidates regarding their use of social media?

Whose voices are represented here?

Our original paper, Bennett and Folley (2014), was an auto ethnographic account based on our reflections of the experience of studying for our doctorates. We were doctoral candidates between 2007 and 2012, a time when Twitter was emergent (it launched in March 2006 and by December 2012 had 200 million monthly active users). As part of our professional roles we needed to keep abreast of these technological changes, so we were keen to experiment with them to evaluate how they might work for us as doctoral candidates. In this chapter we draw on our own experiences from 2007–2012, and update this using contemporary experiences that reflect the situation now that social media is so much more mature (Stewart 2017).

We distributed an online questionnaire, in spring 2019, consisting of open-ended questions and gathered views of 24 participants who were current doctoral candidates or had completed recently (within the last two years). In keeping with small scale qualitative research, our aim was to understand the particular ways that social media was experienced. The questionnaire was circulated via email to doctoral candidates at one higher education institution and also via Twitter, using relevant hashtags e.g., #phdchat, #phdforum. Our 24 participants were self-selecting and so they are not representative of all doctoral candidates, rather they illustrate the perspectives of those most engaged in using social media. We did not ask our participants to identify their location nor about their demographic characteristics.

What choices do doctoral candidates' make about whether to use social media whilst studying?

Engaging with social media

Participants were varied in terms of their use of Twitter and blogs with the majority who read blogs (19, around 80%), although fewer wrote their own blog (7, around 30%). Twitter was a popular tool: 17 participants (70%) reported that they used it. Reasons for using Twitter fell into three types of activity: keeping up to date, being a part of the doctoral community and developing their personal profile.

Keeping up to date was commented on in the following ways:

> Following key individuals and organisations to see what they are writing.

> I've made a lot of connections with people I would never have expected to or potentially been able to find without Twitter.

Those who valued being a part of a community reported that it enabled them to feel connected which also helped reduce the feeling of isolation:

> Twitter allowed me to engage in an online community of people who are going through a similar experience, to overcome isolation at times and to seek advice.

> I've used Twitter for discussions about PhD struggles to gain and provide support.

> Knowing there's a whole army of support out there if needed. Wisdom. Caring.

> It does make you feel less isolated, knowing there are others out there experiencing the same thing.

Typical comments from participants who used social media to build their professional profile:

> In final phase of PhD to get to know people, [I] advertise myself and get into contact with future PIs [principle investigators].

> I used it to post a call for research participants on my in-depth interviews and for a workshop/focus group which garnered a big response. I also

requested to have my research call for retweeted on other Twitter accounts related to my research.

I've met both virtually and physically with people I admire in my research field, and I have, to some extent, promoted my research and writing.

The potential of social media to reduce isolation and connect candidates to other peers and experts working in the same area has been noted by other studies (Spezi 2016). We also know that there is a high level of dropout of doctoral candidates and particularly international candidates, and a key reason for this was that the candidates did not understand the cultural traditions and norms of the context and therefore felt very isolated (Laufer and Gorup 2019). Hence Twitter has the potential to offer candidates other avenues for support beyond their local community. The meaning and significance of the way that our participants used Twitter and blogging is discussed through the rest of this chapter, but first we explore the response from those that did not use social media.

Choosing not to engage

Only one of our participants reported choosing not to engage with either Twitter or blogging, seven (29%) didn't engage in Twitter, five (21%) did not read other people's blogs and 16 (70%) chose not to blog about their doctorate. Twitter, in particular, was felt to be distracting with its 'always on' stream of a flow of tweets. For doctoral candidates, who are often juggling paid work and study, this can feel like an additional burden. Some participants spoke of preferring to engage in networks with greater subject specialism rather than the more generic debate via social media, whilst some participants commented that the depth and quality of the online interactions had limitations, where there might be a tendency for simplistic answers to complex questions:

I have lurked but find them confining and a little exclusive – concerned with categorisation rather than exploring new approaches: 'this is how you do things' I find #wiasn helpful if sometimes irritating.

I used to follow various PhD networks, but did not find them particularly useful – too generic and quite a low level of discussion, too many irrelevant or trivial tweets cluttering up my timeline.

I have enough to worry about without adding to the 'to do' pile! That sounds glib, but if I'm going to be writing, it needs to be of help/use to me, and blogging about my research isn't something I find useful.

The choice of whether to engage or not resonated with our experience (Bennett and Folley 2014) in that we both valued Twitter as a way to keep up-to-date with our subject area and to connect with other researchers, particularly by engaging with the #phdchat community. We realised the importance of starting to build a professional profile and developed this through our networking opportunities like conferences. We sometimes found the engagement with Twitter distracting or a tool for procrastination, but on balance felt that the benefits, outweighed these issues. We both also enjoyed reading blogs from experts and novice researchers but chose not to blog ourselves as discussed below.

Hence, we suggest that although awareness of social media has developed in the last ten years, and although doctoral candidates might be keen social media users in their personal lives (Procter et al. 2010; Gu and Widén-Wulff 2011; Bolton et al. 2013) they aren't universally drawn to using these tools in connection with their doctoral studies. This conservative attitude of doctoral candidates to uptake of social media, despite its potential value has been noted by Spezi (2016) and similarly our participants spoke of the time commitment and the distractive nature of social media as being the main reasons not to engage.

Choosing whether to blog

During our doctoral studies we were reluctant to blog because we were unwilling to open ourselves to critique and feelings that we had nothing to say (Bennett and Folley 2014). Only two of our participants were regular bloggers, but these two appreciated the value of sharing their ideas publicly because it was a way of helping them to develop their thinking:

> It's a public blog that I use to reflect, practice writing, shape my ideas by having to commit then to screen, and use to capture notes and quotes.

> Always public. Intensively in early days (separate blog) and now my studies are entwined with nomadic practice it all gets wrapped up together.

Given that doctoral study is judged by one's ability to write, we might have anticipated that more people would make use of blogging to practice this skill and to gain feedback from readers. Blogging has potential for doctoral candidates to develop in a range of ways: creating a scholarly persona; 'slow thinking'; pleasure seeking; and knowledge sharing (Mewburn and Thomson 2017 p. 24). They suggest that a professional academic self occurs in and through the writing process 'when researchers make writing choices, they conform, adapt, reframe or resist dominant academic textual genres' (p. 20). Our bloggers illustrated elements of these four practices and their quotes provide evidence to support the variety of online writing that blogging supports. For some it might be for note taking, for others a way of engaging publicly, for developing their scholarly profile. Thus it appears to be a part of the repertoire that some doctoral candidates engage, but given the small numbers that we discovered it appears to be a marginal rather than a dominant practice.

Those who did not blog expressed concerns, similar to our own, to explain their reasons for not blogging about their research:

I'm not sure I had anything valuable to say.

I'm planning to – but am waiting till I have something to say!

The decision to blog appears to depend in part on one's willingness to open up emergent ideas to public scrutiny, as well as to having sufficient time. None of our participants reported any negative impact from this public form of writing, yet from our experience comments that we received via Twitter had an impact on our confidence. We were aware that it would be easy for doctoral candidates who blog to receive critical comments on a blog post, which may feel unwelcome and damaging to one's confidence. Being resilient to such critique is probably a useful skill to develop, hence our suggestion is to engage in blogging about one's doctoral studies only after thinking though how this public medium may affect self-esteem.

In what ways does social media help doctoral candidates' learning?

The doctoral journey is one that is often understood as an identify transformation process whereby, over the course of study, the student moves into a transformed state as they become a more confident researcher. This has been described as a socialisation process that involves enculturation (Parry 2007) and acceptance into the 'academic tribe' of one's discipline (Becher and Trowler 2001). It involves recognising the rules which are both covert and hidden (Parry 2007). As Carter et al. note 'This doctoral game is about negotiating entry to a culture; acceptance there entails identity shifts' (2013 p. 339).

Our earlier paper analysed the doctoral journey and used the notion of identity formation to understand the ways that social media can affected this process. We focused on three aspects of identity formation: *mimicry*, the idea that we learn to become through 'copying' or 'trying out' the new identity (Kiley, 2009); *stuckness,* the notion of not being able to move into the transformed new state of being (Kilcy, 2009); and *oscillation*, that is moving repeatedly between feeling like a novice and transformed identity (Jazvac-Martek 2009). We revisited these notions to enable us to illustrate how social media affected our participants' learning.

Mimicry

Mimicry is a strategy adopted by candidates as they try out their new identity and involves copying the language and behaviours of those they aspire to be like (Kiley, 2009). Our experience was that the use of PhD related social networks allowed us, as doctoral candidates, to build up relationships with candidates and experts as part of our discipline community, to engage and participate with the norms and ways of speaking and writing. Social media allowed us to 'try on' or 'try out' these behaviours as we experimented with their new identity. We experienced feelings of being an imposter in that our participation in online communities was just an act and that our knowledge was not adequate. We sometimes felt that our contributions were not an authentic expression of ourselves but instead that we were merely 'trying on language' (Bennett and Folley 2014).

It was difficult to illuminate this with our survey because mimicry is a subconscious practice, so it is largely unrecognised and hence it was not specifically articulated by our survey participants. However there were some replies that were suggestive of the mimicry process. For instance the idea of observing how something is done and benefiting from exposure to the norms and practices in a discipline community:

> [I] observe some hashtag timelines first related to PhD in general, related to your topic.

> [I] like to see how blogs are shaped.

Similarly Otterbacher, Ang, Litvak and Atkins (2017) identify the practice of mimicry as a social strategy that is adopted, often subconsciously, to build acceptance and rapport within the online social media communities. So participating in online networks appears to offer doctoral candidates the opportunity to observe and mimic the discourse and practices that characterise behaviours in their academic discipline and this process supports the developing academic identity.

Stuckness

'Being stuck' refers to a stage which many doctoral candidates experience during their journey. There is often part of the process which is very challenging, and the student feels a sense of hopelessness, perhaps as though they are going round in circles (Kiley 2009). As Kiley (2009) notes, communities of learners can play an important part in both recognising this 'stuckness' and helping one another through it. These communities can be face-to-face but are also present on social media, for instance, the use of #phdlife, #phdchat provide a mechanism for sharing experiences online, and these networks can offer such support, empathy and advice to help candidates work through stuck feelings. Our participants talk about finding the online community valuable for helping to overcome stuckness:

> Doctoral research is hard, and you can feel very alone. Twitter helps ease that feeling, gives you networks that remind you there are other people who feel as stuck as you can feel, and who are there to celebrate the positive moments and excitement.

> It's nice to get replies to my tweets, especially if I am freaking out a little.
>
> Consolation with others stuck in similar situations like myself.

Similarly Johnson, Roberts, Stout, Hill & Wells (2017) reported that the doctoral candidates made more use of social media when they were having trouble moving forward, in that they were able to get both practical and emotional support via social media that was also more immediately available than from official sources. Twitter provides a space to hang out with others who similarly are feeling stuck, to participate in what Mewburn (2011) calls 'troubles talk', or the expression of challenges of doctoral study, which she argues is a necessary part of doctoral study in that they help the candidate to work through emotions as well as being a process of 'making us legible to ourselves as well as others, telling stories about troubles' as a part of coming to terms with an altered identity (Mewburn 2011 p. 323). Hence social media offers a place to help candidates work with and move through these periods of stuckness.

Oscillation

Oscillation is the movement between the novice student identity and the established persona of a 'doctor' characterised by expertise in one's field. Being a doctoral student involves this 'constantly shifting perceptions of roles in relation to others' (Jazvac-Martek 2009 p. 259). It is a process that we observed in ourselves in that when feeling confident we were keen to participate in Twitter's communities, but on other occasions our confidence dipped and we were cautious in part because of the vast audience that social media provides (Bennett and Folley 2014). Our participants commented on this process of oscillation moving between practices as they experiment and try out different ways of engaging:

> As with Twitter I used to blog a lot. I stopped. Then I started again. And then I stopped. This was about 3 years ago. I have written two blog posts since starting my EdD 6 months ago. Time will tell if it becomes a regular habit again.
>
> I suffer from imposter syndrome in both [work in study and in professional work]! Actually I think the perspective of a student has helped improve my teaching through empathy.

Intermittent use of social media was also reported by Johnson et al. (2017) who found the use increased and decreased several times depending on where they were in the doctoral process and if they were experiencing any difficulties. It is difficult to be precise about the way that this social media behaviour reflects the internal identity work, however what is suggested is that our participants' identities were being challenged and changed by doctoral study – they talk about feeling an imposter in the academic world and understanding things from other people's points of view. These perspectives are suggestive of an identity journey that involves moving from being an outsider and developing identity through participation in a community which can be experienced as 'support ... wisdom and caring' (see earlier quote).

Digital identity within a discipline community

Digital identity, the idea that we create a digital footprint in the online world, has particular significance for doctoral candidates as many are hoping that their studies will help to bring about change in their professional status. For academics, developing an online identity is a part of maintaining a professional profile which has numerous benefits, for instance supporting cross institutional partnerships, facilitating research collaborations and promoting their work to wider audiences (Lupton et al. 2017). Building an academic digital identity from an early stage was a priority for many of our participants who showed a detailed understanding of their digital identity, what it means, the work involved in its maintenance and its significance:

> I would be a little careful about what I posted, to ensure that I am presenting a professional and thoughtful image – but do that on any form of social media anyway. Wouldn't indulge in personal attacks – but I wouldn't do that in any form of media or in real life. I'm aware of what I'm responding to or posting is saying about me – but am comfortable with that so far.

> Most people that follow me work in my professional field – so I re-tweet interesting links that might be of use. However I tend not to comment.

> I embrace that Twitter is public and don't think any more about it.

> I mostly stay away from controversial or personal topics.

Online media has ways of operating that are different from the face-to face-world. As doctoral candidates make use of social media, they need to understand how these networks operate and to manage engagement in scholarly way. Understanding the new norms and values in the online medium comes about through exposure within a community and can be understood theoretically using notions of legitimate peripheral participation (Lave and Wenger 1991). This notion refers to joining a community as a novice, so at first the novice lurks on the outskirts (periphery) of the group and observes the behaviours of those who are fully engaged in the community and in particular, the experts. In this way the novice learns that norms, behaviours, rules and values on which the community is built. As they become more confident, they move from the periphery to become a more active community member. They move towards the inner circle of experts by observing and mimicking their behaviours and practices. Similarly, Lemon and McPherson (2017) argue that academic communities develop online and form a valuable way of engaging in professional networks.

During our doctoral studies we experienced a conflicted sense of our identity as both experienced professionals and also novice researchers. The public nature of social media makes managing these different identities more complex. One way we might have done so would have been to set up separate accounts for professional, personal and student accounts for our different identities, but we chose not to do this because we did not want to spend the time and effort managing different accounts. More significantly we also wanted to demonstrate through our engagement with social media, the human and real challenges of studying, rather than to present a well-groomed identity. This reflects our personalities as people who like to be open and engaged in communities and is common on Twitter where we see others sharing aspects of their professional lives alongside more personal dimensions of their life (e.g., health, family, holidays).

We were particularly challenged by being connected on Twitter to our external examiners (Bennett and Folley, 2014). We were aware of the way that posting about feeling vulnerable or nervous may affect how they judged our work. Similarly, our participants experienced some of the same conflicted sense of identity in studying whilst also being in a professional role. In the following quotes they discuss how they managed their dual identities as professional and student working in places that were not supportive or valuing of their doctoral studies:

> I taught in an FE college whilst doing my PhD. People often questioned whilst I was doing it and its value. I was considered relatively expert in my professional life but I was a beginner at research. That was sometimes difficult to manage.

> I left my employment to work as a nomad and my doctorate was a significant element in accelerating a 'too big for her boots' misinformation campaign against me. At the same time, I'd become more critical of the org[anisation] through the reading and thinking I'd been doing. FE is anti-intellectual and doctoral studies can increase vulnerability.

> I am careful not to become involved in compromising controversial discussion – I guess this partly underlies my reluctance to post, as I only re-tweet interesting, quite safe topics.

> I have to be cognizant of the fact I am researching for a university therefore it is not a neutral entity.

Managing the work associated with studying for a doctorate can be challenging, and candidates' mental and physical ill health during PhD study is becoming more widely recognised (Wisker and Robinson 2018; Waight and Giordano 2018). On the one hand developing an identity as a doctoral student can be associated with positive feelings of esteem and provide a sense of purpose (Alexander et al. 2014), but in contrast it is often experienced as challenging (McAlpine and Amundsen 2009; Kimmons and Veletsianos 2014). For instance, we wrote about our experiences of feeling like an imposter in the academic world, and similarly our participants mentioned this too. Social media provide another way in which our scholarly identity is enacted but, given its particular characteristics of being massive and open, it has a potential to be a magnifier, amplifying and heightening experiences. Whereas an embarrassing moment face-to-face is transitory, online experiences are available for all to see and are permanent.

The quotes from our participants above demonstrate their nuanced and sophisticated understanding of these issues and on how they translated this understanding to managing their online identity. Indeed none of our participants reported any particular 'horror stories' where they felt put down or diminished through its use (we asked them particularly about this). We conclude that in the intervening years since our studies the more widespread adoption of social media by academics has helped to make social media more familiar including a better understanding of the significance of maintaining an online digital identity and greater awareness of its limitations and pitfalls and more widespread and nuanced approaches to the way it is used (Fox and Bird 2015; Faris and Moore 2015).

What advice would you give to other doctoral candidates regarding the use of social media?

The overriding message from our experience which was echoed from our participants was that there is much to be gained from making use of these tools. We asked them what advice they would give to doctoral candidates who haven't yet used social media. Their responses emphasise how participation in online communities helps to reduce isolation, offers support and the potential for learning:

> It's an incredibly powerful tool for learning from peers around the world. Particularly valuable at conferences for being in the backchannel.

> Use a 'Twitter client' app like Tweetdeck. Learn to use Twitter Advanced Search – it is amazing what it will return to you about your topic.

> It is also nice to Twitter chat with people and then meet them at conferences for example. This enhanced the experience of attending conferences for me.

> I would not want to write, research or think without collaboration.

This optimistic encouragement was tempered by cautionary advice about the challenges of managing time, and of managing one's digital identity:

> It's probably useful, worth investing in developing a following, but not at the expense of spending time doing good research.

> Be selective. If you are inclined to rant – probably have separate accounts. Really useful to network and learn about what is happening in your field.

> Go ahead, just be careful as there can be issues. I am really just learning about Twitter, but I would say to only post things you are fully happy for the world to know.

> Use professionally, with caution and confidently.

> Make sure that you would be happy for a current or future employer to see what you write!

> Great idea to do both [Twitter and blogging] – as long as they do not take over your life!

> Can be a distraction at times and a way to procrastinate and delay writing.

Conclusion

The chapter provides an examination of a number of recent doctoral candidates' experiences of using Twitter and blogging including reflections on our own experiences as doctoral candidates from ten years ago. It has shown that tools such as Twitter and blogs, which were in their infancy little over a decade ago, have become familiar and well-established adjuncts that provide doctoral candidates with much that supports their studies. The chapter has presented some first-hand experiences of doctoral candidates and illustrated how they navigate these tools and the impact of these choices on the practices of using social media.

For many current doctoral candidates, social media was very valuable and a practice that they would recommend, or even find invaluable. The platforms bring doctoral candidates into contact with others, those who are travelling the same journey, who can support and empathise with each other, and also experts in research and scholarly practice who may offer advice and act as role models. They offer candidates a platform to establish themselves as researchers and thus offer them a place where they may build their own research networks and profile.

Social media platforms, and the networks they facilitate, are able to support the doctoral candidates' learning in terms of their academic identity development. Our discussion focused on three aspects of this identity formation:

overcoming stuckness, the process of mimicking the behaviour and language of the more experienced sophisticated researchers and the process of oscillation between developing identities along the way, to illustrate how social media can support these processes (Kiley 2009).

There are a number of key messages that are relevant for graduate educators and doctoral candidates to consider when thinking about whether to engage in social media. Firstly, Twitter in particular is a very powerful online medium for connecting to other candidates and to discipline communities but candidates need encouragement to explore its possibilities, to identify appropriate communities. Some may be resistant to allocating time to this because Twitter may not be perceived as an academic medium, and supervisors may be sceptical towards or unfamiliar with digital research and communication tools (Dowling and Wilson 2015). However the value of an additional support network that might help to overcome the challenges and isolation of study is one that we argue is worth promoting as a way of supporting student retention.

Second, doctoral candidates may need encouragement to learn to navigate the online communities, to recognise their potential and to help candidates to develop practices that are right for the individual. In particular we point to the value to support doctoral candidates' understanding of their discipline community and its discourse (through mimicry), of reducing isolation and helping doctoral candidates over the challenges of studying (stuckness), and of the ways that engaging online opens up new possibilities of enquiry, or understanding and of being. We suggest that exposure to Twitter might be appropriate at induction so that the candidates explore this platform and consider its value. The quotes form our participants in this chapter might help to role model the experiences of those more experienced.

Thirdly supervisors could be encouraged to model involvement in Twitter and to write for online media so that they support the message that developing an online identity has merit. They can then scaffold adoption of practices as they would do with other aspects of doctoral study. Gouseti (2017) reported that the digital practices and tools used by PhD candidates were highly influenced by their supervisors, so if the supervisor was enthusiastic about the benefit of Twitter or other social media then the student was likely to engage in the same practices.

Although our participants reported no 'horror stories', clearly such a public forum as social media has some risks, so doctoral candidates need to apply common sense. As we might expect, doctoral candidates are generally thoughtful about their engagement with social media and weigh up its potential, and this is something to be encouraged.

So our final words go to one of our participants whose response to our final question: Are there any other comments you would like to make about using Twitter and/or blogging while being a doctoral student?, replied:

> I don't think I could do the PhD without either.

References

Alexander, P., Harris-Huemmert, S., & McAlpine, L. (2014). Tools for reflection on the academic identities of doctoral students. *International Journal for Academic Development*, 19(3), 162–173. doi:10.1080/1360144X.2013.817333

Barry, K. M., Woods, M., Warnecke, E., Stirling, C., & Martin, A. (2018). Psychological health of doctoral candidates, study-related challenges and perceived performance. *Higher Education Research & Development*, 37(3), 468–483. doi:10.1080/07294360.2018.1425979

Becher, T., & Trowler, P. (2001). *Academic tribes and territories: Intellectual enquiry and the culture of disciplines* (2nd edn). Buckingham: The Society for Research into Higher Education & Open University Press.

Bennett, E., & Folley, S. (2014). A tale of two doctoral students: social media tools and hybridised identities. *Research in Learning Technology*. doi:10.3402/rlt.v22.23791

Bolton, R. N., Parasuraman, A., Hoefnagels, A., Migchels, N., Kabadayi, S., Gruber, T., ... Solnet, D. (2013). Understanding generation Y and their use of social media: A review and research agenda. *Journal of Service Management*, 24(3), 245–267. doi:10.1108/09564231311326987

Carter, S., Blumenstein, M., & Cook, C. (2013). Different for women? The challenges of doctoral studies. *Teaching in Higher Education*, 18(4), 339–351. doi:10.1080/13562517.2012.719159

Dowling, R., & Wilson, M. (2015). Digital doctorates? An exploratory study of PhD candidates' use of online tools. *Innovations in Education and Teaching International*, 54(1), 76–86. doi:10.1080/14703297.2015.1058720

Faris, M., & Moore, K. (2017). Emerging scholars and social media use: A pilot study of risk. *Communication Design Quarterly Review*, 4(2), 52–63. doi:10.1145/3068698.3068703

Fox, A., & Bird, T. (2017). The challenge to professionals of using social media: Teachers in England negotiating personal-professional identities. *Education and Information Technologies*, 22(2), 647–675. doi:10.1007/s10639-015-9442-0

Gouseti, A. (2017). Exploring doctoral students' use of digital technologies: What do they use them for and why? *Educational Review*, 69(5), 638–654. doi:10.1080/00131911.2017.1291492

Gu, F., & Widén-Wulff, G. (2011). Scholarly communication and possible changes in the context of social media. *The Electronic Library*, 29(6), 762–776. doi:10.1108/02640471111187999

Jazvac-Martek, M. (2009). Oscillating role identities: the academic experiences of education doctoral students. *Innovations in Education and Teaching International*, 46(3), 253–264. doi:10.1080/14703290903068862

Johnson, K., Roberts, J. M., Stout, M. W., Hill, M. S., & Wells, L. (2017). What educational leaders should know about social media, collaboration and doctoral learning. *Research on Education and Media*, 10(2), 32–39. doi:10.1515/rem-2017-0012

Kiley, M. (2009). Identifying threshold concepts and proposing strategies to support doctoral candidates. *Innovations in Education and Teaching International*, 46(3), 293–304. doi:10.1080/14703290903069001

Kimmons, R., & Veletsianos, G. (2014). The fragmented educator 2.0: Social networking sites, acceptable identity fragments, and the identity constellation. *Computers & Education*, 72, 292–301. doi:10.1016/j.compedu.2013.12.001

Laufer, M., & Gorup, M. (2019). The invisible others: Stories of international doctoral student dropout. *Higher Education*, 78(1), 165–181. doi:10.1007/s10734-018-0337-z

Lave, J., & Wenger, E. (1991). *Situated learning: Legitimate peripheral participation*. Cambridge: Cambridge University Press.

Lemon, N., & McPherson, M. (2017). Intersections online: Academics who tweet. In Lupton, D., Mewburn, I., & Thomson, P. (2018), *The digital academic: Critical perspectives on digital technologies in higher education*. London: Routledge.

Lupton, D., Mewburn, I., & Thomson, P. (2017). *The digital academic: Critical perspectives on digital technologies in Higher Education*. London and New York: Routledge. doi:10.4324/9781315473611

McAlpine, L., & Amundsen, C. (2009). Identity and agency: Pleasures and collegiality among the challenges of the doctoral journey. *Studies in Continuing Education*, 31(2), 109–125. doi:10.1080/01580370902927378

Mewburn, I. (2011). Troubling talk: Assembling the PhD candidate. *Studies in Continuing Education*, 33(3), 321–332. doi:10.1080/0158037X.2011.585151

Mewburn, I., & Thomson, P. (2017). Towards an academic self?: Blogging during the doctorate. In Lupton, D., Mewburn, I., & Thomson, P. (2018), *The digital academic: Critical perspectives on digital technologies in higher education*. London: Routledge.

Orr, K., & Simmons, R. (2010). Dual identities: the in-service teacher trainee experience in the English further education sector. *Journal of Vocational Education and Training*. doi:10.1080/13636820903452650

Otterbacher, J., Ang, C., Litvak, M., & Atkins, D. (2017). Show me you care: Trait empathy, linguistic style, and mimicry on facebook. *ACM Transactions on Internet Technology* (TOIT), 17(1), 1–22. doi:10.1145/2996188

Parry, S. (2007). *Disciplines and doctorates: Higher education dynamics*. Dordrecht: Springer.

Procter, R., Williams, R., Stewart, J., Poschen, M., Snee, H., Voss, A., & Asgari-Targhi, M. (2010). Adoption and use of web 2.0 in scholarly communications. *Philosophical Transactions: Mathematical, Physical and Engineering Sciences*, 368(1926), 4039–4056. doi:10.1098/rsta.2010.0155

Spezi, V. (2016). Is information-seeking behavior of doctoral students changing?: A review of the literature (2010–2015). *New Review of Academic Librarianship*, 22(1), 78–106. doi:10.1080/13614533.2015.1127831

Stewart, B. (2017). Academic Twitter and academic capital: Collapsing orality and literacy in scholarly publics. In Lupton, D., Mewburn, I., & Thomson, P. (2018), *The digital academic: Critical perspectives on digital technologies in higher education*. London: Routledge.

Waight, E., & Giordano, A. (2018). Doctoral students' access to non-academic support for mental health. *Journal of Higher Education Policy and Management*, 40(4), 390–412. doi:10.1080/1360080X.2018.147861.

Wisker, G., & Robinson. G. (2018). In sickness and in health, and a 'duty of care': PhD student health, stress and wellbeing issues and supervisory experiences. In E. Bitzer (Ed.), *Spaces, journeys and new horizons for postgraduate supervision*. Stellenbosch, South Africa.

3 It started with a tweet
How doctoral researchers become social media savvy

Julie Sheldon and Victoria Sheppard

Introduction

In recent years digital academia has become a topic of scholarship (Lupton et al., 2018) albeit with a focus on staff (Weller, 2011; Carrigan, 2016; Veletsianos, 2016). Explorations of doctoral researchers' social media usage are revealing that they, too, are increasingly harnessing social media to develop their professional/research personas (Ford et al., 2014; Gouseti 2017; Guerin et al., 2019). Piqued by the palpable interest of our research students, we set out to find out more about their online affiliations, with a view to understanding their motivational affordances. From the outset, our conversations wandered away from itemising their motivations and into discussions about their online presence more widely. We soon uncovered varying levels of digital savoir faire (savvy), revealed in tales of self-confessed lurking, netiquette caution and identity construction. This chapter presents our findings as part of a broader discussion about the role of the institution in helping doctoral students to become social media savvy.

Research design

The bedrock of our study is a survey of our postgraduate research students undertaken in 2017 and 2019 as part of the UK's national Postgraduate Research Experience Survey (PRES). We wanted to unpack the types, motivations and benefits of online communities for our current Postgraduate Researchers (PGRs) at LJMU and so we added a set of institution-specific questions on online resources and social media to consecutive PRES surveys (April–May 2017 and April–May 2019). In 2017 the survey was completed by 483 researchers (61% of the postgraduate research community), and in 2019 it was completed by 430 (57% of the community). As well as responses to the social media questions presented below, we also isolated the responses from the most active social media users to see if there was any correlation with satisfaction levels in other aspects of the doctoral experience. Analysis of the survey data helped us to identify prominent themes.

DOI: 10.4324/9780429274749-4

The survey findings were augmented by a small-scale series of six interviews with PhD students conducted during the academic years 2018–2020. A combination of self-selection and purposive sampling was used to recruit participants. Half of our participants were self-selecting, identifying themselves as actively engaged with doctoral related social media, in response to a call posted on Twitter. The remaining participants were selected using purposive sampling, in order to increase the diversity of the group. Again, these were all PhD students actively engaged in social media. The participants were predominantly female (five female, one male), home students (five home, one international) and mainly studying full time (five full time, one part-time). They represented a range of stages on their PhD journeys: three were in their second year, one in the fourth year, one writing-up, and one had just completed their viva. The range of disciplines covered psychology, education, public health, English literature, and the built environment. Although we took steps to make sure we had diversity amongst our participants, we do not claim that the group is representative of the whole student body. The recorded interviews lasted between 30 and 60 minutes, and were subsequently transcribed and analysed thematically. Finally, we acknowledge the shortcomings of our approach, and we have been cautious about generating confirmatory results from structured questionnaires and semi-structured interviews (Harris and Brown, 2010). However, the coupling of participant responses generated through PRES or through semi-structured interviews here is an illustrative rather than a scientific alignment.

Survey results

The question set we added into PRES focused on the type of online support PGRs were making use of, the online communities they participated in, how they engaged with them and the motivations for doing so. In retrospect, our questions in 2017 yielded rather crude data, as they conflated digital resources, online communities, and social media requiring different levels and modes of engagement. However it gave us an early glimpse of PGR practices and motivations and inspired the present study. In 2019 we updated and expanded the questions to distinguish between three main types of online activity – viewing websites, blogs or vlogs, actively participating in online communities and using research networking sites. While the change in questions meant that we could not make a direct comparison over time, it enabled a richer understanding of modes of online engagement among the PGRs questioned in 2019.

Types of online engagement

Social media engagement was still in the minority when surveyed in 2017, with 41% of respondents reporting that they made use of websites, blogs or social media to support their research journey. Of these respondents (n=197),

Table 3.1 Online communities' questions added into PRES

2017 Questions: Online communities and support	2019 Questions: Social media and online communities
Do you make use of any websites, blogs, or social media to support your research journey?	Do you refer to any doctoral-related websites, blogs or vlogs to support you with your research journey?
If yes, which ones?	If you answered yes, which of the following do you read/follow?
How often, on average, do you engage with these websites and/or social media?	Do you actively participate in any online communities as a researcher?
What are your main reasons for using them?	If you answered yes, which platforms do these communities use?
	Do you use any research networking sites?
	If you answered yes, which ones do you use?
	What are your main reasons for engaging with online content and social media as a postgraduate researcher?

40% used Twitter, 27% Vitae resources, 26% Facebook groups, and 24% used *The Thesis Whisperer*, but there was a diverse range of websites, forums and online groups cited beyond these, including ResearchGate and LinkedIn grouped into the other category. 64% of those who used doctoral related online resources used them regularly (30% daily, 34% weekly).

By distinguishing more precisely between types of resources in 2019, the data suggest that a majority of PGRs were in fact involved with some form of online doctoral resources or communities. A total of 86% of respondents said they either consulted websites, or participated in online communities, or used research networking sites in relation to their doctoral journey (15% did all three of these activities). 27% consulted doctoral-related websites, blogs or vlogs, 45% said they actively participated in online communities while 78% used research networking sites – mainly ResearchGate (77%) and LinkedIn (69%), with a smaller number citing Academia.edu (25%).

Motivations

The main motivations for engaging with online content and social media in the PRES 2017 results were tied to a sense of community, peer support and personal development. To a lesser extent, some respondents used social media and websites to supplement their supervision. Motivations in 2019 were very similar, with an even greater emphasis on community and networking rather than working strategies. Some motivation options were rephrased or added for the 2019 question set. The top six motivations are listed below.

Table 3.2 Motivations for engaging with online content and social media as a postgraduate researcher

PRES 2017	PRES 2019
50% said one of their main reasons was to see how other researchers have tackled certain issues	52% said one of their main reasons was to see how other researchers have tackled certain issues
45% used them to find strategies for working more effectively	39% said it was a way of making and sustaining contact with other researchers**
44% said they helped them to feel part of a wider community of PGRs	36% said it helped them to feel part of a wider community of researchers
35% used them for additional advice to enhance supervisory advice*	36% said it was to help them to promote their research**
17% used them for advice on areas they felt unable to ask their supervisors about	29% used them to find strategies for working more effectively
4% selected other (which included self-development, finding participants, finding data, and keeping up to date with research and HE)	18% used them to get advice and guidance on areas they didn't feel they could ask their supervisor(s) about

* = option removed from 2019 survey
** = option added to 2019 survey

Other survey patterns (isolating regular users)

In addition to the specific question set we added to PRES, we also isolated the most active social media users as a group, to see if there was any correlation with satisfaction levels in the other areas that PRES asks about: supervision, resources, research community, progress and assessment, skills and professional development, well-being and career aspirations. For the PRES 2017 data, we isolated the group who said they used websites and social media daily to support their research journey. For the PRES 2019 data, we isolated the group who said that they actively participated in online communities. For the majority of areas, the most active social media users had equal or higher satisfaction in comparison to the institutional average. Areas where there was a more significant difference of 5% or more are listed here.

The most active social media users were:

- *More likely to be female*: daily users in 2017 included 9% more females; active online participants in 2019 had 5% more females than the survey average. This was the only significant demographic difference.
- *More satisfied with their professional development*: in both 2017 and 2019, these groups were 8% above the average for developing contacts or professional networks during their programme; in 2019 8% more of this group felt they had increasingly managed their own professional development (+5% in 2017).

- *More likely to have taken up development opportunities*: these include developing a training plan, taking part in research and transferable skills, seeking careers advice, attending and presenting at conferences (+10% in 2019) submitting a paper for publication and communicating research to a non-academic audience (+9% in 2019).
- *More likely to consider an academic career*: 5% more of this group said they had an academic career in HE in mind for when they had completed their research degree.

Satisfaction with *research culture* was more mixed. The more engaged social media users tended to be less satisfied with the access to a seminar programme (–10% in 2017, –1% in 2019), and with opportunities to discuss their research with other research students (–6% in 2017, –1% in 2019), but they were more positive about a stimulating research community in their research field (+1% in 2017, +4% in 2019), and with opportunities to become involved in a wider research community beyond the department (+5% in 2017, +4% in 2019).

The 2019 data showed those more actively involved in online communities rated their overall satisfaction with their research degree experience more highly (+4%). They also scored higher on well-being questions: they were 3% more satisfied with their work-life balance, 5% more likely to feel their research was worthwhile, and 5% more knew how to access well-being support within the university. This suggests an upward trajectory from 2017 where there was no noticeable difference in overall satisfaction or most of the wellbeing questions, with the exception of work-life balance, where social media regulars were 10% more likely to be satisfied with this than average.

Interview results

The survey results revealed some broad trends about the type of online engagement among postgraduate researchers, the level of engagement, and the motivations. The data show that most PGRs were using some form of online communities or networks, and that this was most commonly linked to a desire to learn from peers, and to feel part of a wider community of researchers. Isolating the most active social media users suggested there may be a compensatory element at work here, that online networks may be sought by those who felt a lack of immediate face-to-face research culture within the local environment of research group or department. However, active engagement with online communities may also have increased the sense of belonging to a wider research culture, and this has offered opportunities too. There is a correlation between research-related social media use and aspirations for an academic career. Those most actively engaged in online research communities or social media appeared to be highly motivated in their professional development, and more likely to have been involved in researcher development activities beyond the production of the thesis, such as skills training, conference presentations, publishing and outreach. All of these broad trends suggest that online communities are important to the development of an academic identity.

The interviews gave us a chance to build on this, and to focus more on the specifics of how PGRs might be using social media to construct an academic identity. Participants were first asked about their route into postgraduate research, and their experience of face-to-face PGR/research communities before talking about their engagement with doctoral-related online resources and social media. They were asked what platforms they used, to explain the different types of support they sought, and to describe their levels of engagement, and typical behaviour. They were also questioned about their supervisors' social media practices and whether they thought that universities had any role to play in supporting PGRs use of social media. The participants are represented in this chapter as 'PGR 1, 2, 3 4, 5 and 6'. Naturally, their distinctive personae emerge from the interviews and we present quotes illustrative of their usage of social media and online platforms.

The interview findings, combined with the survey data, allowed us to identify five ways in which PGRs demonstrate their social media savvy through the use of Twitter. Let us be clear, we are not thinking of social media savvy to mean having a brand, getting lots of followers and even being an influencer, but an understanding of the rules of engagement, having confidence in an online voice, and a general canniness about developing an academic persona.

1. PGRs use Twitter to self-consciously construct a professional academic identity, which is distinct from other online identities they have.

Although the PGRs we interviewed talked about consulting different websites, and most had profiles on research network sites, the social media platform that they seemed to use most actively to engage with academic communities was Twitter. All of the PGRs we interviewed had Twitter accounts and kept these separate from other social media identities used for more personal interactions (such as Facebook), tending to see it as 'purely an academic thing' (PGR5). In two cases, PGRs also used Twitter for personal networks too, but maintained two separate Twitter accounts – one personal and one for research; PGR2 had no crossover between these personal and professional Twitter identities, acknowledging that none of her friends would appreciate her tweeting about her PhD.

All were guarded about what they posted, self-conscious about their tone, and were wary of seeming too personal or 'over-sharing'. This is unsurprising given that the PGRs we talked to conceived of their Twitter personae as professional identities. PGR4 was very aware that her Twitter profile could easily be looked at by potential employers, and this influenced what she felt able to say. She noted that staff with permanent academic posts were more likely to be critical about their institutions on Twitter than PGRs or those working on less secure contracts. Furthermore, although PGR4 was a very active Twitter user herself, an early adopter (since 2009) who felt she had developed her own 'Twitter voice', even a 'brand', she remained guarded about saying anything that exposed vulnerability. She noted that there had been a lot of helpful Twitter activity and hashtags around mental health in academia, but felt that she would not want to post anything about mental health herself for fear of it being too exposing. For PGR5, Twitter caution was connected to a fear of the permanence of online discussions, and the worry that even if you changed your mind about something that you had posted in public, someone else would remember. A fear of getting something wrong in public also prevented PGR5 from responding to questions asked on Twitter. Growing up with online communities, and having acted as a moderator for an online forum, he had observed a lot of social media fights, felt that Twitter could be a 'hellscape' at times, and all of this had led him to be particularly 'circumspect' about what he posts.

Previous studies of researchers' use of social media emphasised the cautious approach of postgraduates, noting that while digital practices were widespread for seeking and managing information, using social media for interaction and collaboration was less prevalent (Procter et al., 2010; JISC, 2012). Even Gouseti's more recent study (2017) suggested that PGRs are more likely to follow the work of established academics than contribute content themselves. So we asked the PGRs in interviews if they tended to use social media in a more consultative way (following others/ reading advice) or if they got more actively involved in conversations or even initiated conversations themselves. Half of the PGRs (1, 2 and 3) said they felt happier 'lurking', and if they wanted to know the answer to questions, they were more likely to search other peoples' posts, rather than pose a question themselves. PGR1 said that she follows others who would themselves ask high profile academics questions directly, even though she didn't feel able to. While it is tempting to read this as a passive mode of engagement, this quiet or circumspect approach is not necessarily down to a lack of confidence or inexperience as an academic. Two PGRs implied that their Twitter interactions simply reflected their offline social interactions. PGR3 said she generally favoured consulting over posting not just on academic Twitter but on more personal social media platforms too, preferring not to draw attention either to her own achievements or problems. PGR5 meanwhile felt that he brought the same circumspection to Twitter that he exercised in real life conversations:

> It's not so much that I don't feel confident posting opinions. [...] Sometimes I prefer to listen – that's just who I am as a person, and I'd rather just sit back and see what's going on and then maybe occasionally engage with a conversation.

His cautious approach is not indicative of any passivity, rather it stems from a hesitancy about how best to maintain his authenticity (wanting to 'be me' whilst learning the mannerisms of his new group).

2. The way in which PGRs use social media can change during their research programme, moving from a consultative to a more active mode of engagement.

The passive follower vs active participant distinction is further complicated when considering how modes of engagement change during the course of the PhD. This shift is summed up by PGR6 who felt that as she was still relatively new both to Twitter and her PhD, the balance of activity was tilted towards retweeting, gathering information and asking questions, rather than posting her own material just yet (although she had also used it to recruit participants successfully). During the early years of postgraduate research, most of the PGRs we spoke to had consulted blogs, vlogs or followed Twitter accounts that focused on the experience of doing a PhD or provided how to advice, all of which were helpful and reassuring (favourites included Write That PhD, Hugh Kearns, the Thesis Whisperer, James Hayton, Simon Clark vlogs, @PhDForum, @AcademiaObscura, #PhDChat, #AcademicTwitter, #AcademicChatter). These shed light on perceived mysteries of doctoral research, provided practical guidance on writing, publishing and motivation, and reassured PGRs that they were not the only ones feeling overwhelmed or suffering from imposter syndrome. The PGRs we interviewed seemed to value the ways in which social media personalities humanise the processes of research. PGR1, an international PGR, felt that social media was 'really closing the gap' and made established, high profile academics much more approachable.

The PGRs we spoke to who were in the later stages of their PhD had moved away from the self-help/how to sites and more towards making their own research visible. They had also narrowed down their field of interest and felt that they had honed their social media practices. They talked with hindsight about their early attempts to construct their online identities – tweets that took hours to compose and were then deleted, in an effort to find the right voice, or practices that restricted visibility – such as using a protected Twitter account or an ID unconnected to the PGR's name. In the process of refining their Twitter practices, the later stage PGRs described how they had become more selective over time about who they followed, with an increasing focus on their research interests. PGR4 started off following celebrities, but stopped, and now mutes other researchers she follows if she is not so interested in their subject area. PGR5 goes further than this, is very focused on using Twitter for academic purposes and unfollows people if they are using it in a more personal way – sharing baby photos, for example. Certain moments mentioned by the later-stage PGRs encapsulate this journey towards a more visible online academic identity, moments that may be described as Twitter milestones. PGR4 described the flattery of certain people ('academic celebrities') following her back on Twitter, particularly when they are big in her field of research, while being tweeted by others is 'quite fulfilling, to see that people know about your research'. PGR5 posted on Twitter about passing his viva on the day it took place, partly to mark the occasion, to make it 'seem a little bit more real', partly as a way of thanking his supervisor and examiners. He also quickly changed his Twitter handle to include the 'Dr' title, something that a few months earlier, many women had done using the #ImmodestWomen hashtag (Riddell,

2018). While this movement was not directly mentioned by PGR5, there was, it seems, a shared motivation to use Twitter to celebrate expertise in the public domain.

These examples suggest that social media use among doctoral researchers involves a degree of trial and error. But even those who have reached certain levels of recognition may continue to be cautious; engagement in online communities cannot easily characterised as either active or passive, but frequently hesitates between the two. Bennett and Folley, in this volume, describe this relationship building within the tribe as a process of trying on or trying out the disciplinary norms and conventions.

3. *PGRs' online presence is informed by critical readings of others online personae and interactions.*

PGRs learn a lot about how to interact online through readings of others, and are quick to critique the kind of behaviour they want to avoid. As well as unfollowing or muting people who are not using Twitter in the same way and avoiding involvement in fractious debates, the PGRs we spoke to were also savvy about reading Twitter interactions and profiles. PGR4 was conscious of gaining more Twitter esteem once your followers outnumbered those you followed, was aware of Twitter behaviour such as 'subtweeting' (getting attention of someone in particular without naming them), the 'coward ratio' of controversial posts (gaining likes but not retweets) and also of tools that allow you to track anyone who has unfollowed you on Twitter. The interviewees were sceptical of those who used social media in what they saw to be a perfunctory way (two of our PGRs were put off by James Hayton's impersonal automated tweets to his blog posts), and some were uncomfortable with the slippage between self-promotion and academic bragging on Twitter.

The reassuring element of doctoral-related social media that PGRs found useful, especially in the early days of the PhD, was tempered by a sense that sharing the lows of the PhD could sometimes be self-indulgent. While Mewburn (2011) has shown that there is often valuable identity work and community building going on when PGRs engage in 'troubles talk' online, some of our interviewees found the negativity became a barrier. PGR5 felt that on Twitter, 'people will often frame personal issues as political or social issues', for example, interpreting an individual set of circumstances as a problem with academia as a whole. He felt that while Twitter was useful for bringing up important points for discussion, sometimes it's 'just people moaning'. PGR3 similarly felt that some of the forums and blogs were a bit negative:

> 'Quite often [...] they present a problem, but they never really give you a solution. I know that everyone has worries and doubts when they're doing a PhD, but if you've had quite a positive experience, there's nothing really there for you to relate to, which is why I like those vlogs more [Simon Clark and Tara Barazabon], because they're practical people getting on with it day by day'.

4. For those most actively involved in them, online communities not only provide an extension of face-to-face communities but a real alternative to them.

A third of our interviewees viewed the communities offered through social media in a subsidiary or ancillary light. Two PGRs who said they wouldn't use social media to ask questions or find solutions to problems, both preferred to talk to people face-to-face to do this, and felt that they had strong peer communities on campus to enable this. But in both their cases, social media had offered a way of maintaining contact with other researchers they had met at conferences and events. For PGR3, Facebook and Twitter were now being used by 50 PGRs who had met at a summer school in Australia who 'wouldn't be able to keep in touch otherwise'. In contrast, the remaining two thirds of our interviewees were more invested, to differing degrees, with PGR4 confessing that she 'lives on Twitter', and PGR2 describing how she actively preferred it to face-to-face interactions, which require more time and more motivation to engage with. As someone living outside of her university city, she valued the accessibility of online communities, and being able to interact from anywhere, though wondered whether this was down to an introverted nature.

For these PGRs, in addition to maintaining contact with researchers they had already met, social media provided a means of meeting new people, with the advantage that they were more likely to approach academics at face-to-face events such as conferences if they already knew them from Twitter. This was seen as a positive means for overcoming shyness, and both PGR4 and PGR6 said that it was much easier to meet on Twitter. Before starting her doctorate, PGR1 used PhD forums to ask advice about undertaking postgraduate research in the UK; she still keeps in touch with a poster who provided detailed help and support, and who works in a similar area of research.

Those who were more invested in their online communities were more likely to have used them proactively to progress their research, and were also more likely to have been offered opportunities as a result of their online presence. Both PGR4 and PGR6 had asked their networks to participate in their research and PGR6 had received a better response by calling for participants on social media than through email campaigns, reaching people she wouldn't have come into contact with otherwise. PGR4 had been offered writing jobs, guest blogging roles, and teaching at another university, reflecting that 'I can't emphasise enough how many opportunities I've had through Twitter'.

For most of the PGRs we interviewed, then, social media does not just sustain face-to-face, offline communities, it actively creates new academic networks too. More recently, during the pandemic, social media has also been a valuable space to enact an academic identity, when the physical spaces normally associated with this identity were suddenly no longer accessible. While the majority of our interviews were conducted before the pandemic, the final one took place three months into the UK's first lockdown in June 2020. In this context, Twitter took on the role of reaffirming her academic self, which may otherwise have been lost.

She noted how much more she was using social media now that she was no longer socialising with peers in her postgraduate office:

> you are part of this academic community that's on Twitter and you feel a bit more of an academic, and especially now in lockdown, you get, not stripped of that, but you think where do I fit into it I'm just at home now? but when you log into Twitter you think oh I'm still in that community.
> (PGR6)

5. Social media role models are important. If the supervisor is not providing any social media steer, PGRs felt that the university had a role to play in promoting good practice.

Half of our PGR interviewees had found their own way through online support and communities, learning how to navigate them by observing others, and by trial and error. The other half, however, were encouraged either by their main supervisor (PGR6), their co-supervisors (PGR5), or had another role model within their department who offered advice and guidance (PGR4). The advisory functions of these role models varied – from directly recommending getting on Twitter, suggestions of who to follow, what to call yourself, through to more indirectly providing a template of how to engage with others. It is perhaps significant that those PGRs with role models who encouraged Twitter use were the ones who seemed most confident in using it to make their research more visible.

All of the PGRs we spoke to were overwhelmingly positive about the opportunities social media had offered them as researchers. Twitter, in particular, had helped them to get an idea of what was going on in their field, to reach out to participants, get practical advice and tips, feel part of a supportive community, maintain connections and make new ones. Those who had benefitted from role models were conscious that other PGRs may miss out on these opportunities if they were not so fortunate, with some saying they would not have used Twitter without this push. The most active Twitter users we spoke to had taken advisory or leadership roles themselves – one wrote a guest blog post guiding aspiring academics on how to use Twitter, while another set up a Facebook group to help PGRs connect with one another during lockdown. The PGRs who had benefitted from social media mentoring felt that the university could provide the kind of encouragement that their role models had. All of the PGRs we spoke to felt that universities had a light-touch role to play in providing guidance on effective use for conducting and promoting research, etiquette, ethics, signposting what/who to follow and the use of hashtags.

Conclusion

To sum up, our research confirms that social media are significant tools for doctoral researchers. As anticipated, and this was amplified in the context of a global pandemic, we found online communities functioning principally as a means of peer support, compensating to some extent for a diminished physical research environment. What was unexpected was that, regardless of their prior experiences of social media, forming their academic online persona was one of learned astuteness. We found that doctoral researchers typically enter their social media research sphere as lurkers, trying out their affiliations with likes, comments or repostings, and developing their academic voice with refinements and adjustments of pitch. They search for an authentic voice, one that gives them a credible online academic persona, through a process of trial and error. And the academic voice is incompatible with their private voice, often requiring a conscious separation from their pre-existing online personae.

References

Carrigan, M. (2016). *Social Media for Academics*. London:Sage.
Ford, K.C., Veletsianos, G., and Resta, P. (2014). The structure and characteristics of #PhDChat, an emergent online social network. *Journal of Interactive Media in Education*, 2014(1). doi:10.5334/2014-08
Gouseti, A. (2017). Exploring doctoral students use of digital technologies: what do they use them for and why? *Educational Review*, 69(5), 638–654. doi:10.1080/00131911.2017.1291492
Guerin, C., Aitchison, C., and Carter, S. (2020). Digital and distributed: Learning and teaching doctoral writing through social media. *Teaching in Higher Education*, 25 (2), 238–254. doi:10.1080/13562517.2018.1557138
Harris, L., & Brown, G.T. (2010). Mixing interview and questionnaire methods: Practical problems in aligning data. *Practical Assessment, Research and Evaluation*, 15, 1–19. doi:10.7275/959j-ky83
JISC (2012). Researchers of tomorrow The research behaviour of Generation Y doctoral students. Available at: www.jisc.ac.uk/reports/researchers-of-tomorrow
Lupton, D., Thomson, P. and Mewburn, I. (eds) (2018). *The Digital Academic: Critical Perspectives on Digital Technologies in Higher Education*. London: Routledge. doi:10.4324/9781315473611
Mewburn, I. (2011). Troubling talk: Assembling the PhD candidate, *Studies in Continuing Education*, 33(3), 321–332. doi:10.1080/0158037X.2011.585151
Procter, R., Williams, R., and Stewart, J. (2010). If you build it, will they come? How researchers perceive and use web 2.0. London: Research Network Information. Available at: http://wrap.warwick.ac.uk/56246/
Riddell, F. (2018, June 8). We need #ImmodestWomen when so many men are unable to accept female expertise. *New Statesman*. Available at: www.newstatesman.com/politics/feminism/2018/06/we-need-immodestwomen-when-so-many-men-are-unable-accept-female-expertise
Veletsianos, G. (2016). *Social Media in Academia: Networked Scholars*. London: Routledge. doi:10.4324/9781315742298
Weller, M. (2011). *The Digital Scholar: How Technology Is Transforming Scholarly Practice*. Basingstoke: Bloomsbury Academic.

4 Intersubjective reflections of @PhDForum

A doctoral community on Twitter

Donna Peach

Concerns about the welfare of doctoral students have continued for some time (Pearson, 1999), with issues regarding mental health, motivation and attrition rates most highlighted. As such, there is a growing body of knowledge that aims to develop an understanding of the needs of people undertaking a doctorate and the ways in which they can be best supported. There are multiple reasons why supporting doctoral students is important, including the benefit their research brings to themselves, their university and society (Schmidt & Hasson, 2018). Of equal importance, is that no discussion about doctoral students and their well-being should occur without recognition of neoliberal policies that create a competitive academic community with increased expectations and pressure to perform. A balance in work and life commitments is often asserted to be of benefit, and the converse can form the basis of poor mental health (Barry et al., 2018; Mackie & Bates, 2019). However, many doctoral students are balancing multiple demands on their time, including the challenges that come with everyday life, poverty, isolation, self-doubt and a lack of resources (Bryan & Guccione, 2018; Corcelles et al., 2019). In response, universities are increasingly aware of the need to offer supportive measures (Eisenberg, Lipson, & Posselt, 2016). Additionally, postgraduate research students are also reaching out in social media platforms and creating their own and shared online spaces. One of these latter spaces is the Twitter feed @PhDForum that I began in 2012, and which at the time of writing this chapter has more than 92,000 followers. This chapter reflects on the origins and development of @PhDForum through the intrasubjective view of my role and experience within this online community.

    A desire to understand the needs of people undertaking doctoral studies has slowly developed over the last thirty years, with a predominant focus on students in the UK, but also inclusions from USA, New Zealand and Australia. John and Denicolo's (2013) review of the literature, notes the developing interest from the UK government in this precious resource, which in part prompted the reconfiguration of higher education bodies, leading to the development of the UK Council for Graduate Education (UKCGE) and the Higher Education Academy (HEA). In 2006, the HEA review of postgraduate students was undertaken by Leonard, Metcalfe Becker and Evans (2006), who report universities lacked

DOI: 10.4324/9780429274749-5

the direct knowledge emanating from postgraduate students' experiences. Although some further research has been undertaken since the Leonard review, John and Denicolo (2013) find there remains an absence of understanding of the qualitative experience of postgraduate students. Consequently, there is also a paucity of collective knowledge about how the experiences of doctoral students relate to that of academic staff (González-Ocampo & Castelló, 2018). Undoubtedly, the categorical data that has been collated to date will serve some of the needs of higher education institutes, for example in their ambition to gain research funding and influence public policy. However, a predominant focus on categorical factors suggests the postgraduate researchers' outputs and the funding they bring into universities, outweigh the appreciation of their whole contribution and the negative effects this experience can have upon them.

Time management is crucial to the successful completion of a doctorate. Once you start your PhD, the clock is ticking. Full-time students typically take four years to complete their doctorate, for those with studentships this translates to three years with funding and an unfunded 'writing up' year. There is variation, in Australia most students complete in four years (Jiranek, 2010), whereas students in England take an average of seven years (Jump, 2013) and those in the humanities can take approximately nine years (Ehrenberg et al., 2007). Smith et al., (2006) suggest contemporary doctoral students are different to those in the past, as they actively explore the factors which contribute to their (in)ability to complete their studies. While that may be true, approximately half of all doctoral students fail to complete. A plethora of social media apps and websites emerged to support doctoral students. However, inherent in the design of social media platforms is they serve to both ignite and retain your attention. It can be difficult to switch attention back to our studies. That difficulty led to the creation of applications (apps) providing a barrier to the use of other apps and websites.

One social media platform which has an ever growing and dynamic academic community is Twitter. The Twitter account I curate, @PhDForum launched in 2012 and since that time, more than 92,000 people have connected with this 'supportive, knowledgeable and dynamic higher education community'. What began as an attempt to develop a doctoral support group in preparation for my own PhD, has grown into what Jack Grove at the *Times Higher Education* described in 2016, as 'one of the world's largest PhD-related groups'. The evolution of @PhDForum was organic. It developed via its engagement with a range of doctoral student experiences, from contemplation of a proposal, through to thesis submission, viva voce and post-doctoral advice. I am consistently aware that the activity of curating the content of the @PhDForum involves multiple facets of engagement, both within the functionality of the platform and the lives of those who engage with @PhDForum. My ability to interpret the experience of others who use @PhDForum is of course limited. However, I have a longstanding relationship with this transient population; I value my personal insights into the nature of my relationship with other people over the last eight years, both in and out of the public gaze. Drawing on those perceptions, this intrasubjective examination of the relationship between myself as curator and the @PhDForum community, arguably illuminates the transcendent experience of guardianship in online communities of practice (Massa, 2017).

In many ways @PhDForum is limited by the infrastructure of the popular micro-blogging platform. However, as a curator I recognise its potential to foster collaborative communities (Gruzd, Wellman & Takhteyev, 2011). In 2012, I was completing a master's degree with a view to starting a doctoral programme. Previously, as an undergraduate and distance learner with the Open University, I valued a peer-to-peer Facebook group and wanted to repeat that experience as a doctoral student on Twitter. However, being new to Twitter, I did not understand how its function differed from Facebook. I became familiar with #phdchat which is used to connect with other doctoral tweeters. However, I did not feel the use of it engendered the same sense of community that I was hoping for (Nistor et al., 2015). I started the account imagining it would be like a Facebook group. I now realise that had I understood the intended functionality of Twitter, I may not have created @PhDForum. Our understanding can be both facilitated and limited by the discourses available to us and our experiences. To better understand @PhDForum, I will now examine how it might be viewed through cybercity, and community of practice paradigms.

@PhDForum as a cyberstreet

People using Twitter often differentiate between their 'real world' experience as opposed to the 'Twittersphere'. Gruzd et al. (2011), examined the concept of real and imagined Twitter communities and drew on Jones's (1997) idea of a 'virtual settlement', suggesting that a cyber community can be said to be established if it met four conditions; interactivity, two or more communicators, a common meeting space, and sustained membership (Jones, 1997). The @PhDForum meets each of those conditions. Indeed, Jones' reflections on cyber communities itself draws on what he terms Rheingold's technological determinism, suggesting communities will inevitably develop wherever people and communication technology intersect (Rheingold, 1983 cited in Jones 1997). In their research on the networking of information for the major cities of New York, Tokyo, London and Paris, Förster and Mainka (2015), suggest Twitter could be viewed as a mirror of the society using it.

However, it remains a challenge to extend the language of community structures within our 'real' world to those of the cyber spaces we inhabit. If Twitter is a cybercity, @PhDForum could be considered a cyberstreet, a space accommodating multiple simultaneous interpersonal relationships which co-exist within and via a cyber communication network. The portrayal of a street is useful as it provides a view of a bounded space but not one that is as limited as say, a house. The cyberstreet is public and can be visited without engagement with any of the residents or other visitors. If @PhDForum is a cyberstreet, it would reside in what could be described as a ubiquitous Twitter learning environment for doctoral students, early career researchers and academics. Thus, the information highways of communication from the higher education community on Twitter, could be viewed as a district within the @PhDForum cyberstreet that is open to all travellers. Notably, there are limits to engagement. Those who pass through @PhDForum are limited by the geographical time-zone and dominance of English language speakers within its curation. Although apps can be used to share tweets across a 24-hour time zone, scheduling tweets is not the same as the immediacy of engaging with someone who is present.

The embryonic notion of this academic cyberdistrict and associated streets could extend the binary typology of resident-visitor, a concept developed for tourism research and adopted by White and Le Cornu (2011) for use in understanding online community behaviours. As the founder and curator, I comply with the construct of a 'resident' but over time there is a permeability which sits more comfortably with that of a visitor, I might stop for a while, call in regularly for a cup of coffee and a chat, but move on without much of an announcement. Although, my role differs from others who pass through, observing, but not talking, occasionally leaving a 'like' note or following so to make their presence visible. I reflect that those who participate in this cyberstreet have other places to visit, other roads to travel, which may sit in the academic cyberdistrict and beyond. Therefore, a person may reside in the cybercity but only visit a district when there is a need to do so, as with our non-cyber lives we have multiple identities which simultaneously co-exist.

My identity and engagement with the @PhDForum have developed as my own doctoral journey came to an end. To make sense of this I will use the concept of the street to reflect on what my identity is as a curator. I could be considered a postal worker, amplifying news from the district to those visiting and resident in the cyberstreet. I, as the postal worker, need to continue to play a role, conscious that if I stop, there will be a void in the communication structure. So many people now associate with this cyber-street, I feel a sense of responsibility to its maintenance. I recognise that my contribution brings some value to the cyberdistrict. As I began my time on Twitter seeking community, it is natural for others to do the same. Indeed, the growing function of @PhDForum is to support others in developing their tribes and emboldening the whole community. There are several ways this has occurred in its history. The success or longevity of these activities are generally linked with my own time and the free availability of tools that could be adopted to facilitate what I perceive to be the needs of the community.

Whatever concept we draw on, essentially @PhDForum activity is the formation of tweets. Anything beyond the actuality of communicating in no more than 280 characters, originates from the meaning constructed by the people who are actively posting, reading and responding to tweets, myself included. In the process of active engagement with Twitter via @PhDForum I learned that I needed to be active in sharing the contributions of those who engaged with the forum. Although tweets were sent to @PhDForum, other members of the community would have a greater chance of seeing them if I retweeted them. I viewed each tweet as being sent to the community and as such I post them onwards. From my perspective the sense of community is facilitated by the sharing of these communications.

@PhDForum cyberstreet as a community of practice

There are multiple definitions and methods of understanding behaviour in groups and within online communities. Communities of Practice (CoP) are comprised when a group of people share goals, knowledge and activities (Lave & Wenger 1991; Wenger, 1999). As described above, @PhDForum is part of a wider Twitter academic community, and as such its CoP domain is permeable. Those who engage with @PhDForum are individuals, and representatives of groups and organisations, who may engage with many topics separate to the @PhDForum. However, @PhDForum provides a domain that supports the doctoral learning process. CoP for doctoral students in the form of small groups are important to their experience of the learning environment (Lahenius (2012). At other times, when concerns rose with regard to 57% doctoral student attrition rates, researchers focused on the influence of the subject discipline in relation to the doctoral experience of socialisation (Gardner, 2010). In response higher education institutions seek internal responses to the personal and organisational factors that affect attrition (Smith et al., 2006). The compilation of networks constructed between Tweeters support @PhDForum being perceived as a CoP (Wenger, McDermott & Snyder, 2002). Arguably, an external CoP such as @PhDForum might improve a student's sense of socialisation.

Notably, the informal social interactions provide opportunities for peripheral, active and core members. Most of the followers of @PhDForum are peripheral as they do not actively tweet to the forum but may occasionally reveal their presence 'liking' or 're-tweeting'. Using a CoP analogy, those who tweet could be positioned as 'active' and those who do so regularly could be considered 'core' members. As the curator, I am a core member as my presence is relatively constant. However, what I have observed over time is that 'core' members are transitional in accordance with the life of their own doctoral studies, some move from core members to being on the periphery and others become inactive. Importantly, I, as an active member, perceive a sense of community and that not only facilitates a willingness to share knowledge (Nistor et al., 2015) but to sustain a changing COP over time.

Borzillo, Aznar and Schmitt (2011), examined how and why members of a CoP move from the periphery to the core. They suggest five phases which depict the existence of an ongoing process, which they define as awareness, allocation, accountability, architectural, and advertising. Their discussion focuses on a CoP leader; as the curator, I would take up a position of 'leader'. Although, drawing on the earlier construction of myself as a postal worker who shares content between core and peripheral members, any leadership role is one to facilitate collaboration. That perception accords with Borzillo et al. (2011) who found leaders were instrumental in stimulating participation of the members. Within the Twitter cyberdistrict, there are people who position themselves as 'leaders' in the academic community, and those more specifically, in the doctoral community. Such individuals are visible and at times they identity with a cohort of assistants, who by default become leaders by their curation of certain Twitter accounts. However, we know much less of the relationship between research students and their perceptions of their CoP (Sala-Bubaré & Castelló, 2017).

Although I assert a position of collaboration, I recognise the curation of @PhDForum is subjective. There is no consensus on what content is shared. I, as the only curator can choose what is retweeted. Although others within the community can tweet to the forum and their posts will be available for others to see, they become amplified when I retweet because of the number of followers @PhDForum has. Curating a CoP on Twitter is time consuming and requires a commitment of one's self to the community. That said, until recent changes, which I will detail in a later section of this chapter, I have separated my personal identity from the forum. I do not include my name in the @PhDForum 'bio' information as I did not want who I am to disrupt the engagement between members of the community. However, who I am is core to the principles underpinning @PhDForum. I want the forum to promote collaborative engagement, simply for the good that it brings.

Therefore, I am resistant to promoting Twitter accounts and activities that seek financial engagement or who I am concerned might skew the doctoral experience. For example, I do not endorse organisations or individuals who offer supervisory, writing, transcribing and proof-reading services. These types of services can be helpful to doctoral students, but I cannot verify their quality. I am also mindful of the tone of my tweets and the ways in which a positive, supportive and collaborative community can be encouraged. Within @PhDForum competition is not encouraged, I am cautious about promoting those who I perceive to be self-publicists and whose tone could make others feel inadequate. However, I balance that with knowing the success of others is inspirational for those who are striving to reach their goals. People love to see someone who has successfully defended their thesis as it brings hope that the goal they have set themselves is achievable.

Curating equality within an online community

I am also conscious of Marwick and boyd's (2010) construct of an imagined audience and the function of tweets to draw in the members of that audience who might have an interest in its content. As the @PhDForum curator, I recognise the process of imagining the audience as I compile a tweet, but there are also ways in which the audience has become visible to me and to each other. I intentionally describe @PhDForum as a community and define those who engage with it as members, rather than the Twitter terminology of followers. This language is intended to promote the premise of mutual engagement, that is arguably important to the success of a CoP (Gau, 2014). Traditionally, academe has not been a CoP based on mutual engagement, at least not for everyone, as it privileged White western wealthy men. Those traditional biases remain inherent. Although there is now greater diversity of gender, race, ethnicity and class the dominance of historic privilege continues to limit the perceived value of intersectional representation (Story, 2016; Young & Hines, 2018).

Higher education has always been dominated by a White western male populous. In the USA, only 4.4% of Americans with doctoral degrees are Black (Barker, 2016). In the UK, Advance HE (2016), report only 25 of 19,000 professors in 2016–2017 were Black women, and 90 were Black men. This race bias limits the perceived value of intersectional representation, which is a grave concern, when perpetuated at the core of where knowledge is co-constructed and disseminated. Sorensen et al. (2009), propose a critical-dialogic model to explore communication to understand intergroup relationships. To consider policies for higher education interracial groups they focus on reviewing what is understood by the communication processes on campus. Sorensen et al. (2009) suggest that a sustained facilitation of intergroup dialogue can encourage positive relations across groups. Curating @PhDForum, I make a conscious effort to tweet and share matters of racial inequality, and discrimination both in society and within academia, including class and gender. That activity is facilitated by Twitter accounts such as @BlackWomenPhDs who support the visibility of black women with PhDs and current doctoral students.

I am a White woman, who was born into poverty and late to access higher education. I recognise the importance of talking about the power structures that create notions of difference, knowing those who are the majority will not share my perceptions (Saguy, Dovidio & Pratto, 2008). One way, this difference revealed itself via @PhDForum was in response to one of its #phdweekend tweets. As a part-time doctoral student, weekends provided the time for me to study. My personal experience was of being sat alone at my desk, huddled away from other activities in the house. To break the sense of isolation, I used my personal Twitter account as a place to report in, to the audience I imagined was also busy with academic writing over the weekend. I then began to use @PhDForum to send out a message that doctoral students studying over the weekend were not alone. My personal tweets often encouraged those I connect with on Twitter to send encouraging messages. And this was mostly the same response for the tweets from @PhDforum, but there were occasions when I was challenged. On one occasion the challenge from someone on Twitter caused a significant reaction.

The exchange started when I tweeted about support for those studying at weekends, using #phdweekend. The tweeter called for a halt in my endorsing a view that PhD work is ceaseless and accused me of expressing a dangerous attitude. I replied how I always supported time away from study, but there was also a need to recognise that many doctoral students work full-time and study part-time. Often the weekend is their time to study. The individual never replied, but the popularity of the tweet demonstrated that their view was widely shared. Positively, the exchange prompted a dialogue about the normalisation of and necessity to study at the weekend. It was apparent that many doctoral students had not perceived the broader identities of other doctoral students. Although the issue focused on the rights and wrongs of studying at weekends, the context of each viewpoint embedded concepts of 'worthiness', 'stigma', 'mental health' and 'choice'.

I realised that particular @PhDForum #phdweekend tweet had not catered for all of its potential audience. Thus, a tension arose with competing views being expressed about the role and function of what @PhDForum represents and the multiple, complex effects of its communications when tweets are contextualised differently by a diverse audience. Sorenson et al. (2009) suggest the experience within dialogue is influential for some time and as the curator of a tweet, which led to criticism, I support that view. On reflection, I was upset about the criticism as one of the dimensions of @PhDForum as an academic community of practice is to support early career researchers (Nistor & Fischer, 2012). I felt I had failed to represent the whole community.

Contribute to an inclusive academe

Behaviour on social media platforms and particularly on Twitter is frequently described in negative terms. Language such as cyber-terrorism, threats, and trolling are used to reflect the harmful dynamics that can abound when communication is less meditated by conventions that are imposed by 'in-person' exchanges. How we as academics chose to exercise, or not, our moral responsibility to others, in my view is as applicable in online settings, as elsewhere (Miller et al., 2019). Regrettably, intimidation in academic institutes is problematic, with up to 27% of respondents reporting recent experience of bullying (Meriläinen et al., 2019). Putting aside the online bots and those who are paid to troll, Twitter is full of people and we collectively share many of the same challenges in life, illness, bereavement, stress, joy and hope. One of the things I love about the @PhDForum community is that it not only has the capacity to share understanding and bridge difference; equality is fundamental to its existence. As its founder and curator, my moral code is certain and the messages I share aim to convey a sense of togetherness and respect. Twitter provides an opportunity to hold court about one's view of the world and for others to be willing to listen and learn that their own world view might be limited by the narrowness of their own experience. I want the @PhDForum to be experienced as a safe cyberstreet, which might have some challenges, but where the space is well lit and inclusive.

Although research has sporadically been completed since 2006, there remains much which is unexamined about the experience of doctoral students (John & Denicolo, 2013). Hunter and Devine's (2016) study of 183 doctoral students from nine different countries, reports a need to lessen the emotional demands placed on students. They note that students' well-being can be affected by the learning and social environment they experience, and these vary greatly across both disciplines and universities (Gardner, 2010; Golde, 2005). More recently, research has begun to explore the social space provided by Twitter. An example of this is Hernández (2015), exploration of the experiences of minority Latina/o students in USA universities. Hernández (2015) suggests the relationships constructed within academia are formal and thereby limit the formation of interpersonal relationships. She suggests Twitter serves as what Solórzano, Ceja and Yosso (2000) define as 'counter-spaces'. Counter-spaces are environments which can encourage and maintain a positive racial climate which is both collegiate and can challenge racial tropes and ideology (Solórzano et al., 2000). They regard Twitter as such a counter-space, viewing it as both a support system and a means of social change.

Isolation is a feeling reported by many doctoral students and Twitter is seen as a platform that facilitates greater visibility, although, loneliness can also be experienced in virtual environments (Usta, Korkmaz & Kurt (2014). One means of increasing visibility to locate the community you identify with, is by using the follower lists of other Tweeters as you might a telephone directory. Who is in the cyberstreet your visiting? (Solórzano et al., 2000) comment on the visibility of follower lists enabling Latina/o students a sense of community even if they are as White and Lecornu (2011) suggests just 'visitors'. As these formative constructs that conceptualise online behaviour are applied, interesting questions arise such as – does the relative permanence of a follower list suggest residence within a community, even if individuals only visit that counter-space? The concept of what constitutes residence and visitor status might be limiting when as with the global reach of Twitter, one's community is also geographically broad. Twitter's international academic community allows doctoral students to extend their perception of belonginess beyond regional barriers and include national and international members (Solórzano et al., 2000). However, the academic community does not exist in isolation and supportive tweets can originate from to anyone visiting that cyberspace, unless your account limits who can view them.

As with all communication, tweets impact people's feelings both in positive and negative ways. We as humans need and desire connection with others, it has been and remains part of our survival as a species. With increasing online activity, the computer screen becomes not just a work device but a portal into a supportive community, filled with many people you have never met, but whom you feel you have come to know, and who know you. At its best Twitter content nurtures our humanity, which reflects the best of academic practice.

Metzger, Petit and Sieber (2015) suggest mentoring graduate students who represent the future generation of academics can diminish bullying within the humanities, using Metzger's model of connection–cultivation–integration (CCI). The three staged model suggests a developing relational based model within which social behaviours such as bullying or being collaborative are learned and embedded via a process of negative and positive conditioning and modelling. The social learning of hierarchy, power, and inequalities transfer into social media spaces and @PhDForum could be viewed as a cyber counter-space. Thus, it can be used to disrupt oppressive academe constraints permitting the sowing of collaborative seeds, without needing to seek permission.

The cyber-embodiment of connectedness

Our use and construction of 'self' in social media platforms is a complex, mediated process of curation and modification (Kasch, 2013). Whether we are a visitor or a resident, we are, at any one time inhabiting the experience of a counterspace, where verbalised and pictorial communications are shared and processed across time and place (Tripathi, 2005). Some of my favourite activities on @PhDForum are when people share photographs of their experiences. The perceived value of viewing the photographs of others adds weight to Tripathi's (2005) consideration of the value of Merleau-Ponty's ontology of embodiment. A sense of connection is experienced even when the photographs do not contain the presence of a body to view, because the person is present in the activity of taking and sharing the photograph. Thereby, we see the view of the world they had in that moment and can imagine their experience.

An example of how connectivity through photographs could be contagious occurred one night after I had tweeted a photograph of my desk. Prior to that evening, I had seen tweets containing photographs of doctoral students' workspaces, usually tidy with a neat pile of books and a statement about the writing they were about to embark on. My photo occurred in the middle of the night when I was full of a cold. I wanted to show how my desk was chaotic and questioned if that should prompt a feeling of imposter syndrome. There were an initial few comments and shared photographs in reply to that tweet. Those germinated #stateofmyphddesk, which developed its own momentum.

Over the course of the next few days/weeks people shared photographs of their workspaces, which included, desks, sofas, chairs, floors and beds. Also, popular inclusions were of academic pets, including cats, dogs and rabbits. Some pictures were taken in universities, some in cafes, on holiday (by the swimming pool), libraries, most were taken at home and one of the most memorable was posted by someone during a flight.

I have since tried to rekindle the #stateofmyphddesk, but I have been unable to ignite the energy it embodied. I reflect there was something special about the unstructured organic way it grew, dynamically between strangers across the globe. My attempts to repeat its success are in some way forced and do not incite the same original interest. However, others' photographs are continually shared, and these are a great inspiration to others and often mark the key milestones in the doctoral journey namely, submission, viva completion and graduation. These landmark events are important not only to the individual, their family, friends and supervisory team but also to the wider community. They let people know it can be done, and that they too will be able to share their success. I have learned that @PhDForum and those who constitute this community deserve to have a recognised collective presence, but equally they have the right to self-define what that means for each of them.

Not all of the @PhDForum communication occurs in the public space of its Twitter feed. I will occasionally receive direct messages asking me to anonymously request information from the community. I will often support this, to help the identity of the individual. However, it can also be a means of offering support out of the view of the rest of the community. I recall providing support to a doctoral student and @PhDForum member who had a few weeks to rewrite their PhD following a viva voce which concluded major corrections were required. I had not met (and have never met) this person but I had kept track of their re-submission date and would message occasionally to let them know they were not alone. Sadly, they failed that resubmission, which was heart breaking, but I was glad I had been there to support them. As Wright et al. (2014) argue, it is difficult to underestimate the value of social networks for students. I reflect there is something special that extends beyond the functionality of a tweet in cyberspace, which shows an insight into the valuable connectedness, which brings people together. In doing, so we reveal our humanity in that collective virtual space, and in the process of a shared sense of common purpose, we contribute to and thereby co-produce our community.

Until recently, my insights into how other people perceive or experience the @PhDForum community have been limited. I was delighted to accept an invitation from Dr Michelle Ryan of Exeter University, to deliver the keynote at their doctoral college summer event. It was inspiring to experience how others valued the @PhDForum as a means of supporting doctoral students. At that point in time, my awareness of its value to others remained somewhat opaque. As the curator of @PhDForum I perceived the cyber community 'through the looking-glass' (Cooley, 1902). However, as discussed above, I am essentially related to the interpersonal world of the @PhDForum, although other people's relationship with that community bears no relationship to who I am. Indeed, I suggest there is a reciprocal interdependence between my personal self and the @PhDForum environment (Bandura, 1978). My self is ever present, but I choose to hide my identity to facilitate reciprocal determinism which requires members of @PhDForum to actively create their experience of community (Bandura, 1986).

There has been some transition in my activity and use of self, following the imposition of social distancing during the COVID-19 pandemic. For some time, I had been contemplating what I could do via @PhDForum to support the mental health and well-being of students. I had been particularly struck by tweets detailing academics who had died by suicide and I wanted to make a difference. During some annual leave, I decided to open a free to use online study room, one day a week. It soon became apparent that the UK friendly schedule of that day did not suit everyone and so I extended the day to 12 hours, starting at 6am. I then added on a Saturday morning session for the part-time doctoral students. People in Australia started to enquire if there were any times to suit them. I was concerned that the room had to be moderated and that there had to be some means of monitoring who had the access code. I set up each session as an individual event with a separate code and advertised it. Some days there were more than 100 people in the room.

However, it was unsustainable to maintain that level of activity once I returned to work. After several weeks of being in the online room, I decided to open the space up, so it was freely available to access 24/7. I created an access code that people can easily obtain and can use whenever it suits them. I was worried that the space would feel unsafe, that people would be disturbed by imposters, and stop using what could be a useful space. However, my worries to date have been unfounded. The room has now been running since June 2020 and like the Twitter feed, people collate in the space that is created but they develop their own individual relationships within it.

Unlike other study groups that provide a place to talk about work, this study room does not. There is a chat box facility where people do connect, and they have begun to develop other groups while they are in the room to share productivity apps where they plant virtual trees, together. There is banter, fun and encouragement, people quickly seem to be included if they want to engage. You can simply be in the room without your camera or using chat, some describe it like being in a library. I continue to host the scheduled sessions on Wednesdays and Saturday mornings, as some people find them useful. I am uncertain how long that usefulness will remain, but it appears to be welcomed and as such I will maintain that commitment. The difference in the @PhDForum tweets is that now I am seen, by some. People use my name when tweeting the forum as they know of my connection to the forum. It is a natural progression from the activity of the online study room and subject to change as the community continues to evolve.

Conclusion

The completion of postgraduate research is a means to develop ourselves both intellectually and personally (Golde, 2005). However, the challenges, isolation, and sacrifices experienced while undertaking a doctorate are can affect the mental health of those working and/or studying in higher education. My own experience as a part-time doctoral student meant the regular use of weekends to further my studies. It is important to recognise the normalisation of working in the week and studying at the weekends is also indicative of the postdoc experience. Too many academics find the sheer amount of work required to be perceived as successful, comes at the expense of personal time. Therefore, the investment required to complete a PhD extends beyond ourselves and includes our families, friends, academic supervisors, and examiners. As relational beings we seek socialisation and a sense of belonging to a community both via our 'in-person' connections and online. Often our families and friends may not understand the complexity and demands of a PhD and as such we need to find a social group or other support that can understand and meet our needs (Waight & Giordano, 2018).

Attempts to analyse and articulate what constitutes a shared understanding of an online community is evolving, alongside the rapid development of our technological capabilities. Importantly, we want to retain our sense of self and understand how we can transfer our sense of the 'real world' into 'online spaces' (Förster & Mainka, 2015). We seek to adapt everyday concepts and human behaviour into cyberspace activities, such as White and Lecornu's (2011) resident-visitor typology. Although, the application of these binary concepts can have some limitations, they facilitate a discourse that is premised on factors that we historically understand, such as what it means to be resident or to visit.

Importantly, the foundational research which has taken place over the past three decades has provided a foundation from which we can build. Research, often led by the needs of universities and their pressure to perform, has guided the focus of much of the research to date. Arguably, our knowledge of the doctoral community is poor and the means by which the community grows and communicates is ever changing. The @PhDForum is a community and my role as curator provides a privileged but subjective standpoint to their collective experience and to respond to their needs. I have no idea how the community will evolve. There is no strategy, but I have learned to listen to and observe their needs and think about what I can sustain that will make a difference. It is a huge privilege and I feel blessed to be a member of this community.

References

Advance, H.E. (2016). *Equality in higher education: Statistical report 2016*. Retrieved from www.advance-he.ac.uk/knowledge-hub/equality-higher-education-statistical-report-2016

Bandura, A. (1978). The self system in reciprocal determinism. *American Psychologist*, 33(4), 344–358.

Bandura, A. (1986). *Social foundations of thought and action: A social cognitive theory*. Englewood Cliffs and London: Prentice-Hall.

Barker, M.J. (2016). The doctorate in black and white: Exploring the engagement of black doctoral students in cross race advising relationships with white faculty. *The Western Journal of Black Studies*, 40(2), 126–140.

Barry, K.M., Woods, M., Warnecke, E., Stirling, C., & Martin, A. (2018). Psychological health of doctoral candidates, study-related challenges and perceived performance. *Higher Education Research & Development*, 37(3), 468–483. doi:10.1080/07294360.2018.1425979

Borzillo, S., Aznar, S., & Schmitt, A. (2011). A journey through communities of practice: How and why members move from the periphery to the core. *European Management Journal*, 29(1), 25–42. https://doi.org/10.1016/j.emj.2010.08.004

Bryan, B., & Guccione, K. (2018). Was it worth it? A qualitative exploration into graduate perceptions of doctoral value, *Higher Education Research & Development*, 37(6), 1124–1140. doi:10.1080/07294360.2018.1479378

Cooley, C.H. (1902). *Human Nature and the social order.* New York: Charles Scribner's Sons.

Corcelles, M., Cano, M., Liesa, E., González-Ocampo, G., & Castelló, M. (2019). Positive and negative experiences related to doctoral study conditions, *Higher Education Research & Development*, 38(5), 922–939. doi:10.1080/07294360.2019.1602596

Ehrenberg, R.G., Jakubson, G.H., Groen, J.A., So, E., & Price, J. (2007). Inside the black box of doctoral education: What program characteristics influence doctoral students' attrition and graduation probabilities? *Educational Evaluation and Policy Analysis*, 29(2), 134–150.

Eisenberg, D., Lipson, S.K., & Posselt, J. (2007). Promoting resilience, retention, and mental health. *New Directions for Student Services*, 87–95. https://doi.org/10.1002/ss

Förster, T., & Mainka, A. (2015). Metropolises in the Twittersphere: An informetric investigation of informational flows and networks. *ISPRS International Journal of Geo-Information*, 4(4), 1894–1912.

Gardner, S.K. (2010). Contrasting the socialization experiences of doctoral students in high-and low completing departments: A qualitative analysis of disciplinary contexts at one institution. *The Journal of Higher Education*, 81(1), 61–81. doi:10.1353/jhe.0.0081

Gau, W.B. (2014). A study on mutual engagement in communities of practice. *Procedia – Social and Behavioral Sciences*, 116, 448–452. https://doi.org/10.1016/j.sbspro.2014.01.238

Golde, C.M. (2005). The role of the department and discipline in doctoral student attrition: Lessons from four departments. *Journal of Higher Education*, 76(6), 669–700. doi:10.1353/jhe.2005.0039

González-Ocampo, G., & Castelló, M. (2018). How do doctoral students experience supervision? *Studies in Continuing Education*. doi:10.1080/0158037X.2018.1520208

Gruzd, A., Wellman, B., & Takhteyev, Y. (2011). Imagining Twitter as an imagined community. *American Behavioral Scientist*, 55(10), 1294–1318. https://doi.org/10.1177/0002764211409378.

Hernández, E. (2015). #hermandad: Twitter as a counter-space for Latina doctoral students. *Journal of College and Character*, 16(2), 124–130.

Hunter, K., & Devine, K. (2016). Doctoral students' emotional exhaustion and intentions to leave academia. *International Journal of Doctoral Studies*, 11, 35.

Jiranek, V. (2010). Potential predictors of timely completion among dissertation research students at an Australian Faculty of Sciences. *International Journal of Doctoral Studies*, 5, 1–13.

John, T., & Denicolo, P. (2013). Doctoral education: A review of the literature monitoring the doctoral student experience in selected OECD countries (mainly UK). *Springer Science Reviews*, 1(1), 41–49.

Jones, Q. (1997). Virtual-communities, virtual settlements & cyber-archaeology: A theoretical outline. *Journal of Computer-Mediated Communication*, 3(3). doi:10.1111/j.1083-6101.1997.tb00075.x

Jump, P. (2013). PhD completion rates, 2013. *Times Higher Education*. Retrieved from http://wvAv.timeshighereducation.co.ul/news/phd-completion rates-2013/2006020. article

Kasch, D. (2013). Social media selves: College students' curation of self and others through Facebook. *UCLA*. Retrieved from https://escholarship.org/uc/item/04259791

Lahenius, K. (2012). Communities of practice supporting doctoral studies. *International Journal of Management Education*, 10(1), 29–38.

Lave, J., & Wenger, E.(1991). *Situated learning: Legitimate peripheral participation.* Cambridge:Cambridge University Press.

Leonard, D., Metcalfe J., Becker R., & Evans J. (2006). Review of literature on the impact of working context and support on the postgraduate research student learning experience, *Higher Education Academy and UK GRAD Programme.*

Mackie, S.A., & Bates, G.W. (2019). Contribution of the doctoral education environment to PhD candidates' mental health problems: a scoping review. *Higher Education Research & Development*, 38(3), 565–578, doi:10.1080/07294360.2018.1556620

Marwick, A.E., & boyd, d. (2010). I tweet honestly, I tweet passionately: Twitter users, context collapse, and the imagined audience. *New Media & Society*, 13(1), 114–133.

Massa, F.G. (2017). Guardians of the internet: Building and sustaining the anonymous online community. *Organization Studies*, 38(7), 959–988. https://doi.org/10.1177/0170840616670436

Meriläinen, M., Käyhkö, K., Kõiv, K., & Sinkkonen, H. (2019). Academic bullying among faculty personnel in Estonia and Finland. *Journal of Higher Education Policy and Management*, 41(3), 241–261.

Metzger, A., Petit, A., & Sieber, S. (2015). Mentoring as a way to change a culture of academic bullying and mobbing in the humanities. *Higher Education for the Future*, 2(2), 139–150.

Miller, G., Miller, V., Marchel, C., Moro, R., Kaplan, B., Clark, C., & Musilli, S. (2019). Academic violence/bullying: Application of Bandura's eight moral disengagement strategies to higher education. *Employee Responsibilities and Rights Journal*, 31(1), 47–59.

Nistor, N., & Fischer, F. (2012). Communities of practice in academia. *Learning, Culture and Social Interaction*, 1(2), 114–126, DOI:doi:10.1016/j.lcsi.2012.05.005

Nistor, N., Dascălu, M., Stavarache, L.L., Serafin, Y., & Trăușan-Matu, Ș. (2015). Informal learning in online knowledge communities: Predicting community response to visitor inquiries. *Design for Teaching and Learning in a Networked World*, 9307, 447–452.

Pearson, M. (1999). The changing environment for doctoral education in Australia: Implications for quality management, improvement and innovation. *Higher Education Research & Development*, 18(3), 269–287.

Saguy, T., Dovidio, J.F., & Pratto, F. (2008). Beyond contact: Intergroup contact in the context of power relations. *Personality and Social Psychology Bulletin*, 34, 432–445.

Sala-Bubaré, A., & Castelló, M. (2017). Exploring the relationship between doctoral students' experiences and research community positioning. *Studies in Continuing Education*, 39(1), 16–34.

Schmidt, M., & Hasson, E. (2018). Doctoral students' well-being: A literature review, *International Journal of Qualitative Studies on Health and Well-being*, 13(1), 1–14, doi:10.1080/17482631.2018.1508171.

Smith, R., Maroney, K., Nelson, K., Abel, A., & Abel, H. (2006). Doctoral programs: Changing high rates of attrition. *Journal of Humanistic Counseling, Education and Development*, 45(1), 17–31.

Solórzano, D.G., Ceja, M., & Yosso, T. (2000). Critical race theory, racial microaggressions, and campus racial climate: The experiences of African American college students. *Journal of Negro Education*, 69(1/2), 60–73.

Sorensen, N., Nagda, B. (Ratnesh) A., Gurin, P., & Maxwell, K.E. (2009). Taking a hands on approach to diversity in higher education: A critical-dialogic model for effective intergroup interaction. *Analyses of Social Issues and Public Policy*, 9(1), 3–35. https://doi.org/10.1111/j.1530-2415.2009.01193.x

Story, K.A. (2016). Fear of a Black femme: The existential conundrum of embodying a Black femme identity while being a professor of Black, queer, and feminist studies. *Journal of Lesbian Studies*, 21(4), 407–419.

Tripathi, A. (2005). Computers and the embodied nature of communication: Merleau-Ponty's new ontology of embodiment. *Ubiquity*. ACM Digital Library.

Usta, E., Korkmaz, Ö., & Kurt, I. (2014). The examination of individuals' virtual loneliness states in Internet addiction and virtual environments in terms of interpersonal trust levels. *Computers in Human Behavior*, 36, 214–224. https://doi.org/10.1016/j.chb.2014.03.072

Waight, E., & Giordano, A. (2018). Doctoral students' access to non-academic support for mental health mental health. *Journal of Higher Education Policy and Management*, 40(4), 390–412. https://doi.org/10.1080/1360080X.2018.1478613

Wenger, E. (1999). *Communities of practice: Learning, meaning, and identity*. Cambridge: Cambridge University Press.

Wenger, E., McDermott, R., & Snyder, W. (2002). *Cultivating Communities of Practice. A Guide to Managing Knowledge*. Boston, MA: Harvard Business School Press.

White, D.S., & Le Cornu, A.(2011). Visitors and residents: A new typology for online engagement. *First Monday*, 16(9). https://doi.org/10.5210/fm.v16i9.3171

Wright, F., White, D., Hirst, T., & Cann, A. (2014). Visitors and residents: Mapping student attitudes to academic use of social networks. *Learning, Media and Technology*, 39(1), 126–141. https://doi.org/10.1080/17439884.2013.777077

Young, J.L., & Hines, D.E. (2018). Killing my spirit, renewing my soul: Black female professors' critical reflections on spirit killings while teaching. *Women, Gender, and Families of Color*, 6(1), 18–25.

5 Online communities that support postgraduate well-being

Kay Guccione and Chris Blackmore

Introduction

This chapter considers how online communities can support the well-being and mental health of postgraduate students, with particular focus on the role of peer support, and the ways that technology can be used to facilitate and enhance connections. We present two case studies – special interest networks for researchers and a specific project using photography for well-being – which illustrate how different kinds of online communities can be initiated within the PGR learning community, and the impact they can have. Both case studies pre-date the COVID-19 pandemic which began in early 2020, and which necessitated the rapid shift online of much teaching, research, supervision and other contact which would previously have taken place face-to-face. This has highlighted the potential value of online communities and also brought into focus some of the problems inherent with online interaction, including the impact on individual PGR well-being which can be both positive and negative.

Supporting the early phases of the doctoral journey

> I spent ages not really sure what was meant to be happening with the PhD, and I should have said something sooner but I was too embarrassed, honestly, I felt too ashamed, like I should have known.

In our work with PGRs, we often encounter people in the above keenly felt situation. They may be mid-way through their program of doctoral study and have realised something feels wrong. They may be closer to the end stages and feeling the pressures of time as they head towards thesis submission date with significant fears about how they will get the thesis written on time. Over time, uncertainties that go unresolved from the earliest stages of the doctorate, escalate into prolonged worrying, and a feeling of 'never having found your feet' may escalate into anxiousness, anxiety and panic. Not knowing 'the rules' of academia, and having never experienced the researcher-supervisor relationship before, postgraduate researchers can find it difficult to transition

DOI: 10.4324/9780429274749-6

to the demands of doctoral study. The process of transition to university undergraduate study has received significant attention in the literature but the transition to the doctorate has not been characterised to the same extent. There has been a tendency to assume that the transition to postgraduate study is taking place in a similar educational environment, and so will be less problematic (Tobbell & O'Donnell, 2013).

In working with researchers in coaching or mentoring settings, we invite them to reflect on the events, relationships and study strategies that led them to be experiencing their doctorate in a stressful way. In doing so, they express a set of common regrets. They may feel that they wasted time by waiting too long to take action to resolve the unknowns, or that they had their time wasted by hands-off supervisors and would like to have been guided more firmly in the early stages, or that they got lost in the middle and weren't as proactive as they might otherwise have been. Importantly, it's very common that these researchers feel that being behind, making slow progress or under-performing is not their usual mode of operating.

> Being a rubbish student is way out of character for me, I've got top marks before in literally everything else. This works differently though, no-one is really helping you. The landmarks of modules and deadlines are gone you know, and instead it's just one long slog where you're thinking, am I doing this right?! It's been one long and confusing experience.

This is a matter of importance because when people who have a prior track record of high performance and success start to feel lost and fall behind, we can infer that the cause is not a simple matter of not having high enough intellectual capability. Transitions to doctoral education are complex, demanding and emotional and can be hampered by out-of-date narratives of success that position transitioning as an objective, academic progression, that comes easy to intellectually capable students. The progression into postgraduate doctoral study may in fact be the most significant transitional leap for a student due to higher workload, unscaffolded self-directed study, less support and an incomparable learning environment (McPherson et al., 2018). Our own work with students struggling to transition, and data collected through our Thesis Mentoring programme, reveal an expectation mismatch rather than a failure to recruit the 'right' students to doctoral programmes, as university rhetoric can often imply. The tools of study and hard work that these high-achieving students had spent years honing, suddenly no longer serve them well – not on this bigger, more complex project for which they find themselves responsible. The doctorate is usually associated with a transition from dependence to independence, as the learner becomes the professional researcher or academic (Laudel & Gläser, 2007) and the strategies they developed through their prior experience of more structured university study, don't transfer to doctoral level study in a straightforward way. Study strategies require examination and adaptation but can be slow to re-normalise in a culture where the 'norms' are hidden because solo projects are the primary structure for doctoral study and isolated working reigns. It's no wonder then that, amidst this confusion, early-stage doctoral students have been identified as a group that are at specific risk of withdrawing (Lovitts and Nelson, 2000).

Leveraging informal learning for researcher well-being

Doctoral students experience significant stress and anxiety (Garcia-Williams et al., 2014). Contributing factors include time pressures, uncertainty about doctoral processes, sense of belonging in scholarly communities, and financial pressures (Cornwall et al., 2018). Working within researcher communities, we speak often to people who describe feeling lost, isolated and confused. As old study strategies fall away, researchers' confidence, self-belief and enthusiasm can be eroded, and insecurities and a fear of falling behind, or not being 'good enough', arise. Previous research reports that 80% of postgraduates find their first year overwhelming (Cluett & Skene, 2006) and feelings of isolation and 'imposter syndrome' are not uncommon. Doctoral students can expect some pressure from the challenges of new learning, and do accept that some stress is a normal part of work life. However, in an unfamiliar work environment, postgraduate students can find it hard to know whether they are experiencing the 'healthy' stretch and pressure of being intellectually challenged or the 'unhealthy' chronic stress that impacts on their well-being (Metcalfe, Wilson & Levecque, 2018). Developing good professional strategies that enable a researcher to stay buoyant through new challenges and uncertainties, and to cope with taking on higher responsibility, is a necessary process in the maintenance of academic well-being (Schmidt & Umans, 2014; Stubb, Pyhältö, & Lonka, 2012). We know that making sense of transitional experiences can be supported by good professional relationships, and that the supervisory relationship is a large part of this process. Supervisory relationships play a large role in facilitating transitions to doctoral study (McAlpine and McKinnon 2013; Wisker and Robinson 2013). We also know from an emerging body of work on the hidden curriculum of doctoral education, that the range of supportive and influential relationships in doctoral learning can be broad, complementing and expanding on a researcher's academic development through supervisory relationships (Wisker et al., 2017). Doctoral learners are often sustained by unseen, rarely recognised informal structures, social support systems and extra-curricular activities (Hopwood, 2010).

If our new postgraduate researchers had opted to enter into a graduate job or training scheme instead of enrolling in further study, their first and formative understanding of their role and responsibilities within a new workplace culture would have been informed by a job description and a contract of employment. Perhaps these basic guidance documents would have been supplemented by an induction to the organisational structure, culture and values, scaffolded by accountable line management, and complemented by networks of wider colleagues and perhaps even a mentor. All of these ways of supporting and enhancing transitional learning can be adopted for doctoral programmes. They can be introduced into doctoral support structures as accessible inclusive practices, or empty promises, depending on how they are conceptualised, and how they are positioned within the institution. Our own role in supporting the development of new doctoral researchers has been to leverage the informal relationships and learning opportunities as well as the more traditional PGR learning spaces. We strive to add value to early doctoral learning processes and to adapt good practice examples of the above ideas for busy researchers who may not come on to campus very frequently, and who may be located across vast disciplinary areas. Questions arising for us as practitioners are: How can we build accessible and responsive online systems that support transition, and network building? And, how can online communities encourage the building of professional relationships between peers, that allow for the exchange of knowledge and also facilitate emotional support between peers?

Use of technology in well-being

The rapid increase in the availability of high speed, compact digital processors has led to a huge increase in the use of computers, laptops and mobile devices in many areas of life. Technological solutions have, throughout the ages and in many forms, been proposed as ways of improving lives, beating illness and cheating death. The current incarnation of this is the plethora of apps which jostle for attention on the screens of mobile phones around the world. With the huge processing power that can now be contained within our pockets, we have small supercomputers which can be used to monitor health states and diagnose illness, connect us with other people all over the planet, and access immeasurably large archives of information. Online therapy is now a reality in which 13 different web apps and 35 different smartphone apps for depression, anxiety or stress are available through either referral services or the online NHS Apps Libraries (Bennion et al., 2017). Computer-based self-help programmes are increasingly common, for example, Beating the Blues, MindGym, and Living Life to the Full (some of which have been recommended by NICE, 2006). With the move towards Artificial Intelligence, a new era of interaction by voice, facial recognition and quasi-intelligent agents is dawning, with an increase in personalisation across health and education. Virtual and augmented reality are providing immersive experiences with therapeutic potential. Thus, the tools we consider to be 'new technologies' give us new powers for us to harness, and whilst these innovations are presented to consumer markets packaged in utopian messaging, they also open up new questions to be answered. What role can they play in helping us to live well?

For the postgraduate researcher embarking on the doctorate, it is likely that digital technology will play an important role, not only in the practicalities of research (such as retrieval and organisation of information, searching for useful resources, use of technical equipment and computer software) but also in the promotion and maintenance of psychological well-being. The PGR experience can be a solitary one, and there is evidence that this social isolation is a factor in low levels of well-being (The Conversation, 2019; Belkhir et al., 2019); digital and online technologies offer many solutions to this isolation, and whilst there is an increasing awareness that social media can have some drawbacks (Kross et al., 2013; Lin & Utz, 2015; McDool et al., 2016; Steers et al., 2014), the ability to connect with other communities of interest is potentially very useful for doctoral students, and these same tools can facilitate valuable contact with family and friends.

Use of online platforms in learning

With the development of the hardware, software and infrastructure which have made the information revolution possible has come the potential to reimagine the whole process and experience of education. The capacity for connection, so efficiently harnessed by social media platforms, has had huge implications for education. We now live in a world where the answer to a particular question can be rapidly found online and where opinions about the answer can be discussed with numberless other people. There have also been huge changes in the ways in which teachers and learners interact, and in how students relate to their learning communities. While face-to-face lectures and tutorial groups persist, much of this interaction is now mediated by an online learning environment, usually hosted by the educational institution (and provided at great expense by a technology company). Access to education has been transformed through exclusively online courses and MOOCs, with their challenge to existing economic models of learning and teaching, while attending students can now access online resources (including 'flipped lectures' and 'lecture capture'). Thus electronic communication is becoming an ever more important component of the student learning and teaching experience.

The doctoral journey is one which now wends its way through a digital landscape, where online reference management software provides the underpinning structure for academic outputs to grow, and where social media platforms bloom to allow sharing of ideas, opinions and results. Communities of practice spring up around methodological areas; demonstrations of research and analytical techniques colonise video platforms. The 'sage on the stage' teacher, trainer or conference presenter comes back to life and freezes under the control of their students. Doctoral study is also mediated through technological affordances which have their own emotional flavour. Immersed in a social media platform, we may detect the polished sheen of selectively presented academic lives, with successful research and carefree down-time in a virtuous cycle of mutual appreciation. Underneath, we may get glimpses of the Sisyphean, often solitary work involved in doctoral study, the tense relationships and the sacrifices which seem to be demanded of health and well-being in completing the task. Whatever the lived experience of researchers may be, online spaces can be powerful instruments that enable sharing and community support.

Case study 1: special interest networks for researchers

Rationale for special interest networks

We were approached by a postgraduate researcher seeking to access conversations around managing her stressful research topic, and seeking some logistical support to organise a meet up for other researchers in similar situations. Speaking to her, it became immediately clear that she wasn't talking about issues common to all postgraduate researchers, for example the stresses of project management, or of needing help with academic writing or keeping up motivation for doctoral study. The issue she raised was that her research topic itself involved working with sensitive and upsetting materials related to rape narratives. Her work also involved presenting research outcomes on these sensitive issues that others could find inflammatory, and so she had encountered verbal abuse when presenting in person, and also in online spaces. Clearly, a high emotional load was required in considering and navigating such issues which, without regular debriefing, the researcher was experiencing as chronic stress. Although engaging in traumatic or sensitive research themes can be exceptionally rewarding for a researcher, it is important to be mindful of how well-being may be affected. Research has shown that exposure to traumatic research without adequate support or coping strategies, may lead to vicarious trauma (O'Halloran and O'Halloran, 2001; Dominey-Howes, 2015). Vicarious trauma is the negative change in our thoughts, perceptions and interpretations of events as a result of repeated engagement with sensitive, traumatic or upsetting materials and experiences (Jenkins and Baird, 2002).

Together with the researcher, we hosted a face-to-face scoping meeting to design the online Emotionally Demanding Research Network, inviting all interested postgraduate and early career researchers across the university. The first meeting was face-to-face in order to facilitate open discussion and to build trust and confidence from the outset. We welcomed 22 people to a series of facilitated discussions where small groups considered: how a researcher's relationship with their research topic and materials can impact on their health and well-being; what measures they take, or boundaries they set to mitigate their exposure to the upsetting materials or experiences; and what support, events or conversations they'd like to receive through the network. The results of our first collective mapping of the issues and enablers were written up as a blog post and circulated to all postgraduate researchers for further anonymous input through a Google form, which enable wider access to input into the design of the online Google+ community.

Following this first consultation and design process, we set up a Google+ community space and the new network was announced with around 50 researchers joining in the first few weeks. Key online activities included sharing experiences, resources, and ideas, requesting information, and setting up online chats or smaller face-to-face events.

The underpinning principles of special interest networks

The popularity of this format meant that two more subsequent special interest networks were created, again due to researcher interest in co-leading a peer support group. The Disabled and Ill Researchers' Network, and the Parent-PGR Network followed the same process of consultation (What are the issues? What works well? What needs to change? How would the ideal network help you?), co-design and online space development. Through each of these three network scoping processes, it was clearly articulated that the resulting communities should have the following underpinning principles:

1 The community should be accessible and open to all researchers whether they were on campus or remotely located. We seek to be inclusive to people with different mobility and access needs, and to ensure that busy researchers managing different working patterns, family lives and health conditions can enjoy full access to the conversations, support and resources offered through the network. Isolation plays a role in a person becoming overwhelmed by exposure to traumatic materials and so researchers engaged in fieldwork can be particularly vulnerable, being both immersed in their work, and geographically remote from their personal and professional support networks. We pledged to write up blog posts that detailed the discussions and outcomes of any face-to-face sessions, and to develop spaces and resources that could be accessed online.

2 The community should be responsive at the point of need. Researchers and researcher developers felt that it was important that members should be able to interact with their peers on their own schedule, asking questions and sharing resources as the need or opportunity arises. Due to the organisational integration, and the ability to set private spaces and monitor membership and discussions, we set up a Google+ Community as our primary online space. This, while initially intended as a discussion space, became more of a resource and links repository. To facilitate discussion, and requests for support, an email mailing list was therefore also created for the communities. Members are encouraged to use the lists to, for example, post articles or links, start or respond to discussions, and organise or promote face-to-face events.

3 The community should be co-led and consultative. To prevent the networks from being just another channel for promoting organisational messages, it was keenly felt that researchers themselves should own the content, and set the tone for each of the networks, and should decide which issues or activities to prioritise. Each network benefits from co-leaders who are researchers, and who interact with the group in order to, for example, consult the members on key issues, or to organise events. The network leads seek support from researcher development staff as needed, and make suggestions or raise issues on behalf of the group. This means that the networks each have their own unique member needs, and

Supporting postgraduate well-being 73

their own ways of working, and developers would benefit from avoiding the trap of trying to work with each in precisely the same way, in favour of building control and ownership within the membership.

4   The community should be strategically driven, and work in partnership with university teams and services. The supporting role of the researcher developer should be strategic, in linking the aims and activities of the network with other important individuals, teams, services, and groups with shared interests or remits – both inside and beyond the university. Good partnership working can enable researcher groups to seek data, clarify guidance or regulations, press for changes to structural blocks, or to help define or enhance processes that affect them as researchers. It can also facilitate consultation with interested groups of researchers, when universities are seeking to design or reshape programmes or processes. Further, it can help researchers connect to other researchers and opportunities across organisations. The University of Sheffield Emotionally Demanding Research Network works in partnership with the University Counselling Service, and the University Research Ethics and Integrity Team. Our Disabled and Ill Researcher's Network works in partnership with the Disability and Dyslexia Support Service and the Counselling Service. The Parent-PGR Network works in partnership with the University Staff Parents' Network and the Postgraduate Scholarships Officer. The role of the researcher developer is paramount in facilitating this dynamic flow of information and in building strong partnerships.

Examples of activities and impact from the networks

As discussed above, each of the fledgling networks sets its own priorities and preferred activities. Common to all is the instinct to combine occasional face-to-face activities with online responsive sharing. The pace of working has also differed between the three communities. Now, at the 18-month stage, summaries of each network's key activities and outputs are below:

The Emotionally Demanding Research Network

Working with the University Counselling Service to design two workshops covering self-care in emotionally demanding research, and strategies for researchers focusing on marginalised experiences. Each was made available in text (blog) format after the face-to-face session. These facilitated sessions complement group debriefing – reflective sessions in which creative methods are employed to help researchers.

Collaboration with the University Research Ethics Committee to create a Specialist Research Ethics Guidance Paper (University of Sheffield, 2019a) related to Emotionally Demanding Research. This is designed to help individuals designing research projects to assess the emotional load and risk to the people who will be conducting the research. It is complemented by amendments to the

Ethics Application System for all research projects; the 'Risks to the Researcher' section now lists 'emotional load' and 'vicarious trauma' as prompts to the applicant. The group has also suggested wording its amendments to the university's 'Grant Costing Tool' which will enable the risks of emotional load and vicarious trauma to be flagged at an earlier point, when applying for funding.

The Disabled and Ill Researcher's Network

Collaboration with and sponsorship by the Academic Leads of an institution-wide review of PGR Processes, and PGR Well-being, to design an online questionnaire on engagement with Leave of Absence (a period of unpaid leave from study) processes. The anonymised summary data covers reasons for taking an LOA, experiences of taking an LOA, and barriers to taking an LOA, and will feed into process improvement through redesign.

The creation of a series of blog stories, written by members (University of Sheffield, 2019b). This growing resource is a way of sharing experiences, advice, ideas, and guidance, and works to raise the profile and voice of our disabled and ill researchers.

Working with the University Disability and Dyslexia Support Service to inform the design of a new peer mentoring programme for new disabled postgraduate researchers.

The Parent-PGR Network

Working with the researcher development colleagues to begin to design an online learning resource and workshop for doctoral supervisors, covering how to work with researchers who have children, or who take parental leave during the course of their studies.

Limitations and considerations for practice

As is noted throughout the online learning literature, online discussion spaces cannot be expected to automatically engage members who do not know each other well (who frequently have not had the opportunity to meet each other in person) in disclosure about their health or concerns. The topics covered in the networks above can be sensitive, and in order to share openly researchers must feel that they are in empathetic company, with people who share their experiences and understanding. It is worth being mindful of the fact that even if facilitators don't see the value to participants demonstrated through the online space, it doesn't mean that value is absent.

The role of facilitator (in this case, a researcher development staff member) is paramount in helping to establish ground rules, and to help participants to feel safe to share, through setting clear expectations, offering guidance, and monitoring online behaviour. We strongly recommend that other institutions seeking to replicate these types of network should assign resource to the groups in the form of a facilitator who is accountable for progress and available to encourage and support busy researchers. The workload is considerable, and we should not rely on the unpaid labour of early career researchers to run such initiatives. Further facilitator duties will include:

- Setting ground rules for confidentiality and behaviour and monitoring the community for signs of distress, conflict, or requests for help. Signposting members in need of help to a support service, or alerting an individual or team at the institution.
- Keeping networks informed of institutional process and policy issues, opportunities, articles and upcoming events;
- Making sure the groups are consulted on issues that affect them and championing their voice to senior leaders in the university and nationally;
- Ensuring that networks are identified in funding allocations and connecting them to other funds sources to support their work;
- Ensuring that mailing lists are up to date, online spaces are facilitated and keeping up momentum by organising events and meetings;
- Making sure that networks are cross-linked to key university support services with shared agendas, connecting us to external groups working on similar issues, and making sure that our voices are heard in national or sector debates and dialogues.

Linking the researcher-led networks to senior partners who champion and sponsor the work (e.g., Heads of Service or Academic Leads) gives any project outcomes or findings an interested and invested audience, which increases accountability for the networks to complete work, and encourages issues to be driven into actions.

Case study 2: the STEP project

Rationale for the initiative

As discussed, the transition to doctoral study can be problematic, and the early stages of the PhD are often particularly challenging. The possibility of a link between support during transition to postgraduate study and outcomes (including retention and mental health) for doctoral researchers, led us to design a way to enable postgraduate researchers to reflect on their transition. Self-reflection is an important practice in doctoral learning as '[A] process of a continual internal dialogue and critical self-evaluation of researcher's positionality as well as active acknowledgement and explicit recognition that this position may affect the research process and outcome' (Berger, 2013, p. 220). Self-reflection also has therapeutic value wherein externalising a problem (e.g., through reflective writing) can relieve distress. Indeed, significant subjective and objective health improvements have been reported when individuals write or talk about personally upsetting experiences (Pennebaker &

Chung, 2011). Given that writing is the medium through which the doctoral degree is assessed, and that writing is also a success measure in research careers, it seemed important to offer researchers a different medium through which to personally reflect on and make sense of their experiences, thereby avoiding mental associations between reflection and judgement. A growing acceptance that creative expression can be beneficial for mental health and well-being (Clift, 2012) and healthy human development (Heenan, 2006), led us to favour a creative approach. Researchers' familiarity and high engagement with social media (sharing image-based stories to represent their daily activities or emotional states), and the increasing accessibility of digital photography, led us to choose smartphone photographs as our mode of reflection, adapting a photo elicitation approach (Harper, 2002). Creative use of photography for therapeutic benefit is not without precedent; expression through photography has been shown to facilitate empowerment (Teti et al., 2016; Mizock et al., 2015; Wang & Burris, 1994) and self-reflection (Breen, 2006; Mizock et al., 2015; Teti et al., 2016; Wang & Burris, 1994), enabling participants to process trauma (Teti et al., 2016) and better understand how their emotions were influenced by the world around them (Lane, 2015).

To facilitate a sense of belonging in scholarly communities and to help PGRs to overcome experiences of isolation, we designed the pilot initiative as a series of face-to-face and online group activities. Returning to our intention to separate reflective and judgemental learning experiences, we used a cross-disciplinary peer group approach rather than anchoring the idea within supervisory relationships. Indeed, the relationship with the supervisor may, in itself, be a factor in researchers experiencing the transition as problematic, and supervisors naturally differ in the extent to which they recognise, empathise with and respond to the confusion experienced during doctoral transitions.

Learning design

For the 'Student Transitions through Engaging with Photography' (STEP) pilot project, first year (six-month stage) doctoral researchers were invited to attend two face-to-face workshops to learn the skills of reflection and photography, and between workshops, to take and share a series of photographs representing their early doctoral experiences. The two workshops were facilitated by the lead authors and a professional photographer (who was also engaged in PhD research at a separate institution).

In workshop one, the rationale and framework for the project was introduced, the ideas of reflection and sensemaking were discussed in the context of the doctorate, and participating researchers (19 people) were provided with introductory practical skills in capturing images through digital (phone or camera) photography. The workshop included time to put learning into practice, taking photos on the topic of 'transitions' and sharing those photos in a pop-up gallery, discussing each in turn as a whole group. In the final part of the workshop a Padlet board was demonstrated (www.padlet.com) and

Supporting postgraduate well-being 77

Figure 5.1 The STEP Padlet board

researchers were invited to join the board, choose pseudonyms, and to share and annotate their photos (Figure 5.1). A number of considerations were applied to the Padlet design concerning board privacy, participant anonymity, group size, whether liking and commenting should be enabled, and whether the facilitators commenting could be conflated with 'assessment'.

The second workshop was four weeks later, and between the two workshops, participants were set the task of taking and sharing one photograph each on the theme of 'In Between'. This was intended to relate to the core theme of Transitions, signifying the 'in between' time when one is not sure what has started and what has ended (Bridges, 2003). As facilitators, we modelled reflective commenting on participants' shared photos, and invited them to do the same. All 19 participants engaged with the online photo-sharing task.

Ten of the original group attended workshop two, in which participants learned about the relationship between images and text, and that choosing a title and caption was a reflective act. To promote creativity, they used both freewriting, and text cutting techniques to title and caption their photographs. The chosen photo titles were both literal and metaphorical, and reflected doctoral practicalities and priorities; transitional themes concerning unknowns, uncertainties and concerns; and community and relational themes. The Padlet board remained in place post-workshops, with all participants indicating their intention to continue to share, caption and comment on photographs.

Outcomes of the pilot project

In total, the Padlet board gained 48 photo posts on the two set themes, with researchers who participated indicating informally that they had gained new skills and understanding, and would continue to use reflective photo-taking and photo-sharing as a transitioning tool. To gain a deeper understanding of the postgraduate researcher experience and the role of photo-reflection, all researchers who attended one or both workshops were invited to be interviewed by the research team which comprised the two facilitators (academic researchers) and four medical undergraduate students undertaking a research placement. Six postgraduate researcher participants agreed to take part in semi-structured interviews which allowed for a flexible approach in collecting the data while enabling the researchers to address a clear set of concepts (Denscombe 2007, p. 176). Audio recordings were transcribed for qualitative thematic analysis to identify both commonalities and individual differences in experience (Braun and Clarke, 2006).

Evaluating photography as a means for doctoral self-reflection

Most interviewees reported that creating, captioning and sharing photos helped them to make sense of their doctoral transitions. Some favoured other methods of self-expression such as drawing or journaling, but none rejected photography as an option. The main concern participants held was that they were 'too practical' or 'not artistic enough' to use this format effectively. One participant didn't think that photography helped them personally, but felt that participation in the workshops prompted them to find other more pragmatic forms of reflection. Participants valued the opportunity to join an online space, through the Padlet board, and to share their resources openly. They responded positively to the use of monthly themes for photography, rather than an open brief.

Three main areas of reflective change were identified from the data, with researchers who participated reporting that they had increased their awareness of, or taken action to resolve issues of:

1   Belonging to a researcher community: Four of the six participants interviewed discussed their feelings of isolation and loneliness, and all participants talked about the importance of community during the study process. The STEP project was found to have reduced feelings of loneliness by providing opportunities to connect with doctoral researchers outside disciplinary networks using the virtual community of the Padlet page. In keeping with the idea of image-based rather than verbal or written reflection, the online environment was set up as a reflective gallery, rather than a space for dialogue. However, at participants' request, we enabled functionality allowing them to comment on, or 'like' one another's' photographs. We as moderators, modelled good practice in commenting and responding to comments. Participants valued the variety of responses to their own contributions, which ranged from technical issues to academic questions and emotional responses.
2   Alleviating stress in the early stages of the doctorate: Several participants reported feelings of stress and pressure during their doctorate, with one

person actively seeking specialist counselling support. The STEP project was reported to provide time away from the pressures of doctoral study, where the researchers could relax, have time to think, share experiences and support each other to bring about some change.

3   Awareness of organisational services that support mental health: All participants mentioned learning about a variety of other institutional support services and teams, with varying opinions being expressed about how useful, appropriate and accessible these were for different people and different challenges. None of the participants had utilised these institutional support services, but all thought that knowing about the range of support services was a positive gain from the project. A project like STEP could provide a feed-in route to specialist services.

Limitations and considerations for practice

Although this was a single cohort, with a limited number of interviews, and an attenuated time-span, the results nevertheless suggest that doctoral researchers do find the transition to postgraduate research study difficult, and that there is value in offering them a creative opportunity to reflect on their own early experiences of the doctorate, and to share that with peers. Sustained engagement requires formal facilitation and we suggest that six monthly photo-themes be developed and participants should be encouraged to engage along the course of the initiative, from the 6–12-month period. We also recommend partitioning the cohort into small groups to aid navigation of the Padlet resource.

Participants found benefit in both the self-reflection through creative activity and in the connections with others that stemmed from sharing common experience. The creation of online or webinar versions of the face-to-face workshops is essential to enable the most isolated researchers to engage with the initiative. Our pilot project did not include supervisor input, though participants were encouraged to share a version of their reflections with their supervisors. To maximise transitional learning, and drive action, new knowledge and understanding gained through the six-month programme could feed into the review at the end of the first year, and enhance process-driven reporting experiences.

Despite the many commonalities that doctoral researchers have as a group, there is great variation in their experience, skills, interests and in their transitional learning. Universities must therefore ensure that the range of support services are accessible to and relevant to research student groups, not appended onto systems created to mesh with undergraduate experiences.

Whilst a creative approach such as photography used in the STEP project may not be suited to all PGRs, resources which are tailored specifically to doctoral researchers are reported to be of great value to them. This evaluation suggests that photography for reflection could be a valuable tool for doctoral researchers as they chart their own progress through their doctoral studies.

Conclusion

The experience of transitioning to, and managing the constraints and challenges of PGR study is a demanding one. It can also be a solitary one, which – without opportunities for reflection, dialogue and sense-making – can have significant impacts on the well-being of students. The case studies presented here show that community building technologies and online environments can be used to create and support new networks and enable peers to connect with one another, and this can be a meaningful source of support for the users. For these networks to flourish, care has to be taken in how they are set up and facilitated, with adequate sustained support for building links to functions across the institution. We must also be vigilant in ensuring online communities are accessible, welcoming and useful spaces which facilitate authentic dialogues and which do not replicate unhelpful power dynamics, demand unpaid emotional work, or contribute to the social isolation which may be present elsewhere in the PGR journey.

References

Beating the Blues (n.d.) Available from: www.beatingtheblues.co.uk/

Belkhir, M., Brouard, M., Brunk, K., Dalmoro, M., Ferreira, M., Figueiredo, B., Huff, A., Scaraboto, D., Sibai, O. & Smith, A. (2019) Isolation in globalizing academic fields: A collaborative autoethnography of early career researchers. *Academy Of Management Learning & Education*, 18(2), 261–285. doi:10.5465/amle.2017.0329

Bennion, M., Hardy, G., Moore, R. & Millings, A. (2017) E-therapies in England for stress, anxiety or depression: What is being used in the NHS? A survey of mental health services. *BMJ Open*, 7, e014844.

Berger, R. (2013) Now I see it, now I don't: Researcher's position and reflexivity in qualitative research. *Qualitative Research*, (May 2003), 219–234. Available from: http://doi.org/10.1177/1468794112468475

Braun, V. & Clarke, V. (2006) Using thematic analysis in psychology. Qualitative Research in Psychology, 3(2), 77–101.

Breen, R. (2006) A practical guide to focus-group research. Journal of Geography in Higher Education, 30(3), 463–475.

Bridges, W. (2003) *Managing Transitions: Making the Most of Change*. New York: Perseus.

Clift, S. (2012) Creative arts as a public health resource: Moving from practice-based research to evidence-based practice. Perspectives in Public Health, 132(3), 120–127.

Cluett, L. & Skene, J. (2006) *Improving the Postgraduate Coursework Student Experience: Barriers and the Role of the Institution*. Proceedings of the Australian Universities Quality Forum. AUQA Occasional Publications. Available from: www.researchgate.net/profile/Sid_Nair/publication/255608482_Closing_the_Loop_Talk_the_TalkWalk_the_Walk/links/0c96053054e90801bf000000.pdf#page=76

Cornwall, J., Mayland, E.C., van der Meer, J., Spronken-Smith, R.A., Tustin, C.& Blyth, P.(2019)Stressors in early-stage doctoral students. Studies in Continuing Education, 41(3), 363–380. doi:10.1080/0158037X.2018.1534821

Denscombe, M. (2007) *The Good Research Guide: For Small-Scale Social Research Projects*, 3rd edition. Maidenhead: Open University Press.

Dominey-Howes, D. (2015) Seeing 'the dark passenger' – reflections on the emotional trauma of conducting post-disaster research. *Emotion Space and Society*, 17, 55–62.

Garcia-Williams, A.G., Moffitt, L.& Kaslow, N.J.(2014)Mental health and suicidal behavior among graduate students. *Acad Psychiatry*, 38, 554–560. https://doi.org/10.1007/s40596-014-0041-y

Harper, D. (2002) Talking about pictures: A case for photo elicitation, Visual Studies, 17(1), 13–26. doi:10.1080/14725860220137345

Heenan, D. (2006) Art as therapy: An effective way of promoting positive mental health?Disability & Society, 21(2),179–191.

HEFCE (2014) *Understanding the Recruitment and Selection of Postgraduate Researchers by English Higher Education Institutions*. Available from: www.hefce.ac.uk/pubs/rereports/year/2014/pgrrecruitment/

Hopwood, N. (2010) A sociocultural view of doctoral students' relationships and agency. *Studies in Continuing Education*, 32(2), 103–117.

Jenkins, S. R. & Baird, S. (2002) STS and vicarious trauma: A validation study. *Journal of Traumatic Stress*, 15, 423–432. doi:10.1023/A:1020193526843

Kross, E., Verduyn, P., Demiralp, E., Park, J., Lee, D., Lin, N., Shablack, H., Jonides, J. & Ybarra, O. (2013) Facebook use predicts declines in subjective well-being in young adults. *PLoS ONE*, 8(8), 1–6.

Lane A. (2015) Snapshots – A therapeutic photography group activity in Warath adult mental health unit. *International Journal of Mental Health Nursing*, 24(1).

Laudel, G. & Gläser, J. (2007) From apprentice to colleague: The metamorphosis of early career researchers. *Higher Education*, 55(3), 387–406.

Lin, R. & Utz, S. (2015) The emotional responses of browsing Facebook: Happiness, envy, and the role of tie strength. *Computers in Human Behavior*, 52, 29–38.

Living Life to the Full (n.d.) Available from: https://llttf.com/

Lovitts, B. & Nelson, C. (2000) The hidden crisis in graduate education: Attrition from Ph.D. programs. *Academe*, 86(6), 44–50.

McAlpine, L. & McKinnon, M. (2013) Supervision – the most variable of variables: Student perspectives. *Studies in Continuing Education*, 35(3), 265–280.

McDool, E., Powell, P., Roberts, J. & Taylor, K. (2016) *Social Media Use and Children's Wellbeing*. IZA Discussion Paper No. 10412. Available from: https://ssrn.com/abstract=2886783

McPherson, C., Punch, S. & Graham, E. (2018) Postgraduate transitions from masters to doctoral study: managing independence, emotions and support. *Stirling International Journal of Postgraduate Research* SPARK 4.

Metcalfe, J., Wilson, S. & Levecque, K. (2018) *Exploring Wellbeing and Mental Health and Associated Support Services for Postgraduate Researchers*. Vitae.

MindGym (n.d.) Available from: https://uk.themindgym.com/

Mizock, L., Russinova, Z. & DeCastro, S. (2015) Recovery narrative photovoice: Feasibility of a writing and photography intervention for serious mental illnesses. *Psychiatric Rehabilitation Journal*. 38(3), 279–282.

NHS Apps Library (n.d.) Available from: www.nhs.uk/apps-library/category/mental-health/#

NICE (National Institute for Health and Care Excellence) (n.d.) Available from: www.nice.org.uk

O'Halloran, M. & O'Halloran, T. (2001) Secondary traumatic stress in the classroom: Ameliorating stress in graduate students. *Teaching of Psychology*, 28(2), 92–97. Available from: https://doi.org/10.1207/S15328023TOP2802_03

Pennebaker, J. & Chung, C. (2011) Expressive writing and its links to mental and physical health. In H.S. Friedman (ed.), *Oxford Handbook of Health Psychology* (417–437). Oxford University Press.

RSPH (n.d.) #StatusOfMind report. Available from: www.rsph.org.uk/about-us/news/instagram-ranked-worst-for-young-people-s-mental-health.html

Schmidt, M. & Umans, T. (2014) Experiences of well-being among female doctoral students in Sweden. *International Journal of Qualitative Studies on Health and Well-Being*, 9(1). doi:10.3402/qhw.v9.23059

Steers, M., Wickham, R. & Acitelli, L. (2014) Seeing everyone else's highlight reels: How Facebook usage is linked to depressive symptoms. *Journal of Social and Clinical Psychology*, 33(8), 701–731.

Stubb, J., Pyhältö, K. & Lonka, K. (2012) The experienced meaning of working with a PhD thesis. *Scandinavian Journal of Educational Research*, 56(4), 439–456.

Teti, M., French B., Kabel, A. & Farnan, R. (2016) Portraits of well-being: Photography as a mental health support for women with HIV. *Journal of Creativity in Mental Health*, 12(1), 48–61.

The Conversation (2019) Overworked and isolated: The rising epidemic of loneliness in academia. Available from: https://theconversation.com/overworked-and-isolated-the-rising-epidemic-of-loneliness-in-academia-110009

Tobbell, J. & O'Donnell, V. (2013) Transition to postgraduate study: Postgraduate ecological systems and identity. *Cambridge Journal of Education*, 43(1), 123–138.

University of Sheffield (2019a) Specialist research ethics guidance paper on emotionally demanding research, risks to the researcher. Available from: www.sheffield.ac.uk/polopoly_fs/1.834056!/file/SREGP-EmotionallyDemandingResearch.pdf

University of Sheffield (2019b) Disabled and Ill Researchers' Network webpage. Available from: www.sheffield.ac.uk/rs/ecr/mentoring/dirn

Wang, C. & Burris, M. (1994) Empowerment through photo novella: Portraits of participation. *Health Education Quarterly*, 21(2), 171–186.

Wisker, G. & Robinson, G. (2013) Doctoral 'orphans': Nurturing and supporting the success of postgraduates who have lost their supervisors. *Higher Education Research & Development*, 32(2), 300–313.

Wisker, G., Robinson, G. & Bengtsen, S. (2017) Penumbra: Doctoral support as drama: From the 'lightside' to the 'darkside'. From front of house to trapdoors and recesses. *Innovations in Education Teaching International*, 54(6), 527–538.

6 Online communities of practice for academic practice and a sense of belonging

Janet De Wilde, Gabriel Cavalli and Stephanie Fuller

Introduction

In this chapter we explore the use of online communities of practice (OCoP) to support the development of academic practice, we share our experience in how they foster a sense of belonging. We suggest that not only may doctoral researchers, postdocs, and early career staff benefit from joining a community of practice to learn from experts and enhance their academic practice, but the community may also help them assimilate into an academic community and hence the wider academy. Established academic staff also benefit in communities of practice as they can share knowledge and experience to enhance practice, but they can also learn from others to develop new practice. The benefits of communities of practice being online as well as face-to-face is that the online domain reduces both temporal and spatial dependency for communication, hence OCoPs facilitate sustained dialogue and ease of sharing of information. We examine the theory of communities of practice from Lave and Wenger (1991) and its relevance for sustaining these online communities and we also examine the role of OCoPs in identity and belonging to a community.

In 2020, due to the Covid-19 pandemic, the nature of online communities for academic practice became pertinent as academics not only had to connect online for day-to-day matters, they also had to transform their academic practice for online delivery. Some academics had been involved in distance learning for many years and were more comfortable with this transition, however for others this was a new experience, and the learning journey was challenging. Several online communities emerged for mutual support, for example, on Facebook several groups emerged with the name 'Pandemic Pedagogy'. In these online communities, teachers and academics shared ideas and solutions to develop their online practice. It gave relevance to situated learning, we were learning in a new situation thrust upon us, novices learnt from those with experience, but there was also significant peer to peer learning.

Alongside the pandemic situation, Higher Education Institutions have their education and research strategies for enhancement of teaching, learning, and research practice. Blended, digital, and hybrid learning and working practices are embedded in these strategies. Online communities of practice have potential to support the development of practice and engagement with new practice to deliver change. Other authors in this book have provided examples of online communities for doctoral research practice, here we illustrate the concept and application of online communities of practice to two educational case studies of academic practice from Queen Mary University of London (QMUL). These case studies highlight the role of OCoPs in a sense of belonging.

Communities of practice

The theory of community of practice (CoP) was presented by Lave and Wenger (1991). They developed this concept based on their apprenticeship model of learning and their social situated learning theory (Lave and Wenger 1991). They explored the nurturing of newcomers into new practice by experienced masters. This provided an interpretation of how learning takes place outside of formal courses and examines the relationship of an individual's growing knowledge and experience to their position in the community and hence a greater belonging to that community. Legitimate peripheral participation was termed to explain the learning of a newcomer to a community of practice. In this model, newcomers develop their knowledge, attributes, and skills through working with and learning from established community members, termed 'old timers'.

In academic CoPs the newcomers may traditionally be recognised as early career staff such as doctoral researchers, postdocs, and teaching associates etc. However, they can also be expert staff but new to the group, who can bring in new 'ways of doing'. Furthermore, as witnessed in the pandemic situation often newcomers come with skills, for example digital dexterity, that established members may benefit from.

Wenger (1998, p. 73) identified a community of practice as having three essential components: joint enterprise; mutual engagement; and a shared repertoire. These descriptions were clarified over time to be the domain, the community, the practice (Wenger-Trayner and Wenger-Trayner, 2015). The joint enterprise, or the domain, is considered the shared learning agenda for the community of practice where members share a passion and take joint responsibility for the 'learning agenda' (Wenger 2000).

> Communities of practice are groups of people who share a concern or passion for something they do and learn how to do it better as they interact regularly.
> (Wenger-Trayner and Wenger-Trayner, 2015, p. 1)

Online communities thrive when the community finds a clearly shared and identified aim and benefit, the joint enterprise or domain, for the community. This may grow organically (as in Case study 1) or may be designed (as in Case study 2). This clarity allows for meaningful participation discussed later.

When there is no clear purpose, the group starts to realise the lack of purpose and the group engagement often falls away. The benefit of online communities of practice is that the aim of the group is clear each time members log in and the dialogue and information is built up over time and remain visible and accessible to all members. There is less segmentation of sharing compared to face-to-face communities where someone may miss out on a conversation due to not being present.

We find resonance in Eckert's (2006) statement that 'a community of practice engages people in mutual sense-making ... about the enterprise they're engaged in'. In our experience, and as demonstrated in our case studies, this is fundamental to create and sustain a sense of belonging. Coming together to 'make sense' of academic practice is critical in the development of our practice. We can see just how much there is to make sense of in our practice if we segment academic practice into educational practice e.g., how students learn, teaching, assessment for learning, assessment as learning, constructive feedback, peer-to-peer education, peer observation, student engagement, learning gain, etc, and into research practice e.g., critical reading, critical thinking, critical writing, creating hypothesis, research question, collecting data, conducting experiments, fieldwork, data analysis, conceptual analysis, assessing, writing up the findings of research, presenting findings, presenting arguments, applying for funding, and supervising/ managing, and assessing researchers etc. Tomkin et al. (2019, p. 1) provide evidence for using the community of practice approach in academic practice development, they established that 'Instructors who were members of a community of practice were much more likely to employ student-centric practices'.

Mutual engagement manifests online as peer–peer connections, sharing ideas, constructing new knowledge and understandings with others on and beyond campus (Brooks, 2010). Online communication is frequently text-based, O'Connor (2001) identified that norms are reduced enabling introverted participants to share their ideas on an equal footing with extroverts. This wider participation is also the experience of the authors. Knowledge is expanded through discussion (Bielaczyc & Collins, 1999); hence, a main function of an online community of practice is to facilitate discussion about the joint enterprise. The original model had the concept of 'old timers' as the masters within the CoP, however, an individual's position in the community of practice is more often determined by the amount of *meaningful* participation (Handley et al., 2006) rather than their experience level or time spent in the community.

A challenge in engagement in online communities is choosing a platform for the community. Any choice can inadvertently exclude people due to any political, cultural and other associations with that platform. White (2008) and White and Le Cornu (2011) introduced a residents and visitors mapping to examine and model how and where we engage online. A resident would be frequently engaging online using one or more preferred platforms whereas a visitor is someone who would visit to get the information needed and then leave. It needs to be noted that there are also those who prefer face-to-face communication and may not belong to any online community. Another consideration is the access required to the technology and devices needed for sustained engagement. This is often expensive and may exclude those from certain socio-economic backgrounds. To ensure diversity in the engagement in the community due consideration should be given to the inclusivity of any choice made. For a work-based community of practice the solution may be the university supported platform, however, in our experience, choices that can sustain a CoP might be more organically selected (for example, see case study 1). However, to reach out to a wider community and to encourage diversity in engagement the decision of which platform and its accessibility needs to be taken with care.

Online a *shared repertoire* is developed by sharing each other's experience, the highlighting of tools that are useful to solve a problem and guidance documents, videos, podcasts that have been developed by the community or sourced separately. Over time, this repertoire is expanded, and curated through commentary and 'likes' or other rating systems. Online newcomers can quickly find the highly rated sources of information and advice. They can see who contributes regularly and who engages meaningfully. This is all held within the online space. This online sharing of information and expertise in all its forms provides a huge benefit to the community and their individual and shared practice.

Identity and a sense of belonging

A community of practice is related to identity and a sense of belonging because we are identified by what we do each day, e.g., our practice. Furthermore, a sense of belonging is more than a feeling of belonging; it is developed by having skills and competences to feel at ease within a community and in our practice. The role of OCoPs in knowledge and skills development for newcomers and hence for their identity formation is supported by Gannon-Leary and Fontainha (2007). Brooks (2010) highlighted that OCoPs due to their flexibility and accessibility facilitated relationship building and becoming assimilated into the academy.

Brown and Duguid (2001) note that in situated learning e.g., being amongst other practitioners, it is about knowing or learning how to be in practice, and hence it is involved in the process of identity development for newcomers. Online, the frequency of being connected or the opportunity to be amongst other practitioners is increased and hence the identity of those in the community is enriched and the sense of belonging deepened. Here we find relevance with Wenger (2000, p. 239) where he states that identity is a 'lived experience of belonging' we agree it is defined through a level of immersion that it should also be lived. Our first case study demonstrates the lived experience of an OCoP and our second case study highlights the use of an OCoP in developing a sense of belonging.

Case studies

The case studies we have selected to illustrate how identity and sense of belonging can be forged in a CoP cannot be more different. Case study 1 describes a CoP that organically emerged as members were recruited into a transnational education (TNE) setting as 'fly-in' faculty, which also organically transitioned online. Case study 2 describes an OCoP, which was designed as such to support participants of an educational development programme. Both have functioned as successful CoPs, with evidence of members developing a strong sense of identity and belonging through their participation of the OCoP. This illustrates that there are many ways in which OCoPs and CoPs can be formed and operate, and therefore, provide identity and sense of belonging to members.

Case study 1 Forming a teaching and learning community of practice sustained online

This case study involves an academic staff online community of practice (OCoP/CoP). CoP members teach at a Transnational Education (TNE) engineering school: Queen Mary Engineering School (QMES, China). The QMES is a collaboration between Queen Mary University of London (QMUL), UK and Northwestern Polytechnical University (NPU), China. QMES started operating in August 2017. The CoP is formed by 'fly-in faculty' QMUL QMES staff spending periods of 2–5 weeks in QMES. Herein, we focus on the formation of this CoP and its online presence. The strength of this CoP, expressed on the quality and impact on student experience, will be the focus of a follow-up publication.

The 'fly-in faculty' nature of the role has been critical for the CoP to emerge. Our job, which underpins CoP elements domain and practice, (Wenger, 1998) brought us together. However, our sense of community (Duncan-Howell, 2007) quickly coalesced before becoming a distinctive CoP as members find themselves co-localised far away from home. Our primary need in forming a community was to support each other in these circumstances. QMUL QMES staff travel together, share meals, and out-of-hours' time, with most living in shared accommodation while in QMES. Originally, this was a community of learning (to live/survive in the new environment), if not of practice. This close interaction is unusual in the workplace, in particular in Higher Education (HE), where individualised character of academic work is the norm (McDonald and Star, 2006; Nagy and Burch, 2009). Consequently, the opportunities for community cohesion and consolidation of our CoP have been outstanding, unparalleled in our experience of HE. As Lave and Wenger (1991) describe, it is through informal interactions when relationships and processes that shape a CoP get imagined, proposed, established, sustained, transformed and, occasionally, discontinued.

Currently, we display all fourteen indicators that Wenger postulates would demonstrate that a CoP has formed (Wenger, 1998, p. 125). In addition to strong social cohesion, this is also because of our strong sense of identity and meaning. Part of QMES's mission, as envisaged by QMUL's leadership from QMES's inception, is to develop robust and externally recognised Scholarship of Teaching & Learning (SoTL) as a highly valued academic endeavour, rather than, as usually perceived in STEM HE, secondary to disciplinary research. As the first QMES appointments were SoTL-focused, this was enthusiastically received and central to developing negotiated identity.

Moreover, it has been extremely relevant that a new T&L setting was established. QMES is a shared QMUL-NPU space, neither fully British nor fully Chinese; therefore, innovation is enabled and supported. Consequently, core roles sought by CoP members and QMES/CoP agenda have been initially developmental in nature (e.g., school-embedded academic development roles), rather than managerial/'T&L admin' (e.g., Director of Studies/Exams). These roles emerged organically as CoP members literally negotiated their specific contribution as part of the emerging joint practice and vision in the new setting. The latter preceded the former, and this has given a shared identity within the CoP to the initial members, which has been enthusiastically embraced by new members.

Success stories in our shared practice in T&L and SoTL have been formally (e.g., awards) and informally recognised in QMUL and externally. We would argue they are the product of a combination of: 1) astrong sense of social community coupled to externally-driven mission fully embraced by initial members leading to coalescence of CoP; and 2) freedom of innovation in a new setting with enabling and enthusiastic support from institutional leadership. It is difficult to imagine such positive outcomes in the absence of this scenario. Institutional expectations of practice-share and -transfer should consider this carefully.

While the CoP started face-to-face, online presence became a necessity, and emerged organically. Most OCoPs in the established CoP literature are designed as such, and particular attention is given to platform choices (Barab et al., 2004; Sherer et al., 2003). Our transition online was rather less planned. Initially, we required social media (WeChat) to sustain our community while in China (e.g., 'Are you coming for lunch?', 'Can you show me where to buy …?', 'How did you top-up your campus card?', 'Where's the bus stop?'), while we maintained work-communication through the usual channels (e.g., email). Soon, though, as the CoP coalesced, social media use evolved into preferred communication channel for our shared *practice* within the CoP. Thus, social media (WeChat) not only sustained us socially in China/UK, but, naturally, the community started using social media for practice-related knowledge sharing and support, while email and other channels have been kept, mostly, for formal/decision matters, and/or involving staff not in the CoP.

Interestingly, this behaviour was not discussed or designed. Informal learning and critical support within the CoP is now sustained through social media (WeChat). Practice related issues are typically discussed primarily online, through social media channels (e.g., 'Has anyone come across X?',

'Does anyone know how to … (quick tips for VLE use)', 'I am frustrated with …', 'Do you have good references for topic Y?', or simply 'Help! with …'). As the CoP has grown and simultaneous face-to-face presence of specific staff in QMES is now rarer, online communication has been invaluable to sustain our CoP.

As the recent COVID-19 crisis hit China first and we had to teach from the UK, it was the strength of our CoP and flexible use of a large range of available online tools, including social media, which made our teaching online transition extremely smooth and successful. We supported each other, co-selected tools and tested them together from across the globe (UK, Malaysia and China). We were not limited in online choices from our institution, but rather used what worked, usually as combination of tools. We also sustained our social community through online socials, which have felt like a much needed catch-up, rather than the awkward artificially designed similes we have experienced in other groupings. Therefore, we were in a privileged position to support QMUL in London transition online during the crisis and prepare for Blended Learning ahead of 2020–2021.

Based on our experience a recipe for successful academic O/CoPs would be (in conjunction with Wenger et al., 2002a, and Jakovljevic et al., 2013):

1 Focus on mission beyond 'the day-to-day job' (Meaning)
2 Recruit in alignment with this mission (Identity)
3 Support and enable community building (Community)
4 Allow and support innovation from within the CoP, including role/identity negotiation and online tools.

Case study 2 Online modules in educational development at Queen Mary University of London

A communities of practice approach has been advocated as an effective method for online learning design in the literature (see for example, Baran & Cagiltay, 2010; Boulton & Hramiak, 2012; Kirschner & Lai, 2007). Distance learning courses can struggle to achieve the same sense of community, cohort identity and social relationships compared to face-to-face delivery, potentially leaving participants feeling isolated and alone. Therefore, it's particularly important to try to engender the social side of learning and to help build a community among distance learning participants.

A communities of practice approach is especially relevant for professional development courses where peer learning plays a vital role in participants' experience. The approach draws on Wenger's proposal that meaningful learning is a socially situated process. Wenger, McDermott and Snyder (2002a) define communities of practice as:

> groups of people who share a concern, a set of problems, or a passion about a topic, and who deepen their knowledge and expertise in this area

by interacting on an ongoing basis… They also develop personal relationships and established ways of interacting. They may even develop a common sense of identity. They become a community of practice.

(pp. 4–5)

While Wenger's early work on communities of practice suggested that these were not groups that could be deliberately engineered, later writings on the concept do explore ways in which communities of practice can be developed and designed which is a useful resource for seeking to develop the social side of learning online.

The educational development programmes at QMUL are offered to new academic staff, PhD students who teach and clinicians who teach QMUL students. Modules are offered in both online and face-to-face formats. The key challenge for the distance learning courses was to create opportunities and spaces in the curriculum for participants to develop common knowledge, practices and approaches as well as to establish personal relationships and a shared sense of identity.

For our curriculum design module, we wanted to develop an online course which fully supported discussion and peer learning across disciplines. Participants complete a curriculum design project across the duration of the module through interaction with and feedback from course colleagues and tutors. 'Seven Principles for Cultivating Communities of Practice' (Wenger et al., 2002b) is a valuable resource for designing this kind of community-based course, however, as an online module some of the principles for communities of practice are less appropriate than others. While there will always be different levels of participation, we want to bring all students into the active group and for everyone to actively engage in their module. Although there may still be more peripheral members, we aim to encourage everyone to be active participants, even if as 'lurkers' they would still learn a lot from the experience. An online module is therefore a very specific type of community of practice.

The basic format of the distance learning module involved weekly webinars to bring students together for group discussion, input from tutors and to give and receive feedback on their individual projects using breakout rooms. Webinars were designed to try and engage all participants through audio-video discussion (both as a whole group and in smaller breakout groups), polls, and activities such as writing on slides or a digital whiteboard and via the text-based chat. Webinars were accompanied by weekly asynchronous writing tasks which were posted to an online forum, and participants were required to give feedback to at least one colleague too. The weekly writing tasks came together at the end of the module to form the assignment. We hoped that through having space to discuss progress on their own design projects in small groups during each webinar and following this up outside of the synchronous space by providing feedback to each other through forums, we could engender an active community of practice throughout the duration of the module. Participants would be learning from and about each other's teaching practice, while gaining feedback on their work from colleagues and tutors from across a variety of disciplines throughout the course.

We believe the course moved some way towards creating a successful online community of practice. In response to a questionnaire about their experience of community online, 79% of participants of this module (and the subsequent version of it) (total respondents = 29) agreed or strongly agreed that they felt part of a community on the module. Webinars were rated as important or very important for building a community by 76% of respondents, while asynchronous activities were rated important or very important for building a community by 34%. Webinars were the key element of the design that contributed to a community, however asynchronous forums were also important for some participants and highlighted in some free text responses. When asked to identify which elements of the module most contributed to the sense of community in free text answers, respondents highlighted the webinars, and particularly the breakout groups as key. Also important was providing feedback to each other – a process through which they both learnt more about each other's work and developed their own practice. Comments included:

> By comparison to other DL modules I have done where there is only an online forum, my sense of community was much stronger for having the webinar. Both voice and image are needed, I think, and seeing the same people repeatedly also helps.
>
> Part of successfully passing the course required us to comment on other people's forum posts. This forced me to read other people's work and think about how it related to my own work, and there was a sense of reciprocity in commenting on blog posts which helped build up a sense of community.

The full results of the research across all distance learning modules offered within QMUL's educational development programmes are discussed in another publication (under submission). They suggest that aspects of a community of practice have been achieved. Colleagues are clearly able to 'deepen their knowledge and expertise' through interacting with and learning from each other across the duration of the course, and hopefully beyond it too. The space for developing personal relationships is something which perhaps needs further development. Providing more informal opportunities for participants to interact, developing group work activities or specific social or fun activities are options that we will explore.

Discussion and conclusion

As mentioned above, there are many ways in which OCoPs are formed, and how they can support identity and sense of belonging. Clearly, while our case studies are very different in this respect, both make strong references to shared spaces for transactional interaction as key to develop this sense of identity and sense of belonging. In case study 1, this emerged from a need to learn to survive in the new environment, followed by exchanging practice tips and advice online. In case study 2, this emerged mostly through webinars, as members connected to discuss their work with the whole community.

These spaces are, therefore, characterised by a sense of multi-directionality ('mutuality of engagement', Wenger, 1998), co-creation and equality, where participants feel they can both learn from others but also contribute back *into* the community. There may be newcomers and old-timers, members with more, or less, experience in the practice domain, but, above all, there is a sense of learning together, from each other. As Wenger (1998, p. 152) states,

> identity ... translates into a form of individuality defined with respect to a community. It is a certain way of being part of a whole through mutual engagement ... it is more important to give and receive help than to know everything oneself.

Interestingly, this experience shows tension with Nagy and Burch's (2009) assertion that traditional academic practice is not well aligned with community formation. Moreover, in describing identity as in the previous paragraph, Wenger (1998, p. 152) used identity in academia as an example to contrast with his own use of the term: 'This results in a definition of individuality that differs from, say, forms of individuality in certain academic circles, where knowledge is a form of personal power and not knowing is largely construed as a personal deficit'.

What is clearly different in our case studies, compared to traditional academic practice, is the fact that, in these cases, membership to the community provides *competence* in an unfamiliar environment. According to Wenger (1998, p. 153) this is central to build identity in practice. In our case, participants have a vested interest in becoming community members, to address a need and accessing competence (in case study 1, teaching and living in a literally foreign environment, in case study 2, navigating successfully a compulsory and assessed module).

In light of our case studies and experience through participation of these two OCoPs, we cannot fail to reflect that *strong* identity in relation to the CoP, 'identity in practice', is mostly forged through members' contribution *into* the community, which Wenger calls 'the identity of participation' and 'identification through engagement' (1998). On the other hand, our experience suggests that *strong* sense of belonging to the CoP emerges both from members being benefited by the community, addressing a specific need/accessing competence, as described above, coupled to being recognised for their contribution to the community; participation that is recognised by the community is legitimate participation (Lave and Wenger, 1991; Wenger, 1998).

In reference to sense of belonging, Wenger acknowledges the importance of community recognition of individual members through his concept of 'negotiability by engagement' (1998, p. 202). We find his following statement crucial to understand *strong* sense of belonging in an academic CoP: 'Members whose contributions are never adopted develop an identity of non-participation that progressively marginalizes them. Their experience becomes irrelevant because it cannot be asserted and recognized as a form of competence' (Wenger, 1998, p. 202). Moreover, Wenger (1998, p. 152) also states that 'we become who we are by being able to play a part in the relations of engagement that constitute our community'. This links to the concept of meaningful participation referred earlier. Academics derive meaningful participation from creating knowledge, therefore, in an academic OCoP this multidirectional learning co-creation (Wenger's 'mutuality of engagement', 1998) is fundamental to create academic identity and sense of belonging. The OCoP/CoP should be aware of barriers to meaningful participation and co-creation. These are often hidden and may lead to participants not becoming full members of a community and being marginalized.

To conclude, we propose that designers of effective academic OCoPs/CoPs should invest time and resources fostering spaces of interaction and exchange where all members of the community can contribute and be benefited by, as a means to instigate a strong sense of identity and belonging in community members.

References

Barab, S., Kling, R. and Gray, J. (Eds) (2004). *Designing for Virtual Communities in the Service of Learning*. Cambridge: Cambridge University Press.

Baran, B. and Cagiltay, K. (2010). Motivators and barriers in the development of online communities of practice. *Eurasian Journal of Educational Research*, 39, 79–96.

Bielaczyc, K. and Collins, A. (1999). Learning communities in classrooms: Advancing knowledge for a lifetime. *NASSP Bulletin*, 83(604), 4–10.

Boulton, H. and Hramiak, A. (2012). E-flection: The development of reflective communities of learning for trainee teachers through the use of shared online web logs. *Reflective Practice*, 13(4), 503–515.

Brooks, C.F. (2010). Toward 'hybridised' faculty development for the twenty-first century: Blending online communities of practice and face-to-face meetings in instructional and professional support programmes. *Innovations in Education and Teaching International*, 47(3), 261–270.

Brown, J.S. and Duguid, P. (2001). Knowledge and organisation: A social practice perspective. *Organization Science*, 12(2), 99–246.

Duncan-Howell, J. (2007). *Online Communities of Practice and Their Role in the Professional Development of Teachers*. PhD Thesis. Queensland University of Technology. Available at: https://eprints.qut.edu.au/16512/1/Jennifer_Duncan-Howell_Thesis.pdf (accessed: 17 August 2020).

Eckert, P. (2006). Communities of practice. In Brown, K. (Ed.), *Encyclopedia of Language and Linguistics*, 2nd edn (pp. 683–685). Amsterdam: Elsevier. http://dx.doi.org/10.1016/B0-08-044854-2/01276-1 (accessed: 1 September 2020).

Gannon-Leary, P. and Fontainha, E. (2007). Communities of practice and virtual learning communities: Benefits, barriers and success factors. *eLearning Papers*, 5(3), 54–65.

Handley, K., Sturdy, A., Fincham, R. and Clark, T. (2006). Within and beyond communities of practice: Making sense of learning through participation, identity and participation, identity and practice, *Journal of Management Studies*, 43, 641–653.

Jakovljevic, M., Buckley, S. and Bushney, M. (2013). Forming communities of practice in Higher Education: A theoretical perspective. In *Proceedings of the MakeLearn Conference*. Available at: http://uir.unisa.ac.za/handle/10500/14634?show=full (accessed: 17 August 2020).

Kirschner, P. and Lai, K-W. (2007). Online communities of practice in education. *Technology, Pedagogy and Education*, 16(2), 127–131.

Lave, J. and Wenger, E. (1991). *Situated Learning: Legitimate Peripheral Participation*. New York: Cambridge University Press.

McDonald, J. and Star, C. (2006). Designing the future of learning through a community of practice of teachers of first year courses at an Australian university. In *Proceedings of the First International LAMS Conference: Designing the Future of Learning, 6–8 December 2006, Sydney, Australia*. Available at: www.lamsfoundation.org/lams2006/pdfs/McDonald_Star_LAMS06.pdf (accessed: 17 August 2020).

Nagy, J. and Burch, T. (2009). Communities of practice in academe (CoP-iA): Understanding academic work practices to enable knowledge building capacities in corporate universities. *Oxford Review of Education*, 35(2), 227–247.

O'Connor, K. (2001). Contextualization and the negotiation of social identities in a geographically distributed situated learning project. *Linguistics and Education*, 12 (3), 285–308.

Sherer, P., Shea, T. and Kristensen, E. (2003), Online communities of practice: A catalyst for faculty development. *Innovative Higher Education*, 27(3), 183–194.

Tomkin, J. H., Beilstein, S. O., Morphew, J. W. and Herman, G. L. (2019). Evidence that communities of practice are associated with active learning in large STEM lectures. *International Journal of STEM Education*, 6(1), 1–15.

Wenger, E. (1998). *Communities of Practice: Learning, Meaning, and Identity*. New York: Cambridge University Press.

Wenger, E. (2000). Communities of practice and social learning systems. *Organization*, 7(2), 225–246. doi:doi:10.1177/135050840072002

Wenger, E., McDermott, R.A. and Snyder, W. (2002a). *Cultivating Communities of Practice: A Guide to Managing Knowledge*. Boston: Harvard Business School Press.

Wenger, E., McDermott, R. and Snyder, W. (2002b). Seven principles for cultivating communities of practice. Working knowledge. Available at: www.clearwatervic.com.au/user-data/resource-files/7Principles_Community-of-Practice.pdf (accessed: 22 June 2021).

Wenger-Trayner, E. and Wenger-Trayner, B. (2015). Brief introduction to communities of practice. Available at: http://wenger-trayner.com/wp-content/uploads/2015/04/07-Brief-introduction-to-communities-of-practice.pdf (accessed: 1 September 2020).

White, D. (2008). Not 'natives' and 'immigrants' but 'Visitors' and 'Residents'. TALL Blog: Online Education with the University of Oxford, April 23.

White, D. and Le Cornu. A., (2011). Visitors and residents: A new typology for online engagement. *First Monday*, 16(9).

7 Blending online and offline in a community of practice model for research degree supervisor development

Sian Vaughan and Geof Hill

Introduction

Research degree supervision is a specialist academic practice, and as such there is a growing discourse around what the practice is and how it can be supported. Alongside the increasing body of journal articles and books, the discourse also inhabits the online spaces of blogs and social media hashtags. The growth in online activity means that the potential communities and support available to current doctoral researchers is arguably very different to the experiences of most research degree supervisors when doing their own doctoral study. The challenge for many supervisors is in identifying, understanding and navigating these online resources to support their own supervisory practice and their doctoral researchers.

This chapter reflects on our experiences in developing a model of supervisor development based on a community of practice ethos and how in doing so we increasingly blended the online and offline. We outline the model of a Community of Practice around Research Supervision and how the structure of conversations catalysed by both questions and resources enabled awareness of the discourse on supervision. In discussing resources offline, we were able to raise awareness as supervisors shared their knowledge of online resources during conversations. This revealed familiarity and the enthusiasts, as well as creating space for concerns to be raised and reluctance to engage to be explored. Through a scaffolded practice-led inquiry approach to investigating research supervision, supervisors could then choose to personalise further investigation of online PhD resources and spaces, sharing their findings back within the community of practice group conversation. We discuss examples whereby supervisors explored social media hashtags, the use of apps, and virtual research communities to draw out lessons and plans for developing their own supervisory practice. Somewhat unexpectedly, some supervisors also choose to speak back to the discourse and its online communities through then publishing their practitioner inquiries in blog form. We conclude with some comments on the potential and the importance of linking online and offline in enabling research degree supervisors to recognise supervision as an academic practice and the support available to them through communities of practice both local and global.

DOI: 10.4324/9780429274749-8

Context

Research degree supervision is a specialist academic practice, and as such has generated a practice specific discourse aimed at deconstructing the practice as well as supporting it. Conversations about research supervision emerged in Australia and the United Kingdom (UK) in the late eighties and early nineties as research supervisors began to make their own research supervision practices transparent by publishing their research supervision experiences as guides and illuminators of the practice (for example, Phillips & Pugh, 1987; Salmon, 1992). These studies were the first in a series of practice-led inquiries contributing to an emergent discourse. The growth in doctoral candidature in the 1980s shone a light on the previously hidden or unpublished role of the research supervisor (Manathunga, 2005). Other forms of practice-led inquiry relating to research supervision were individual doctoral degrees that focused on research supervision as part of explorations into higher education practices (for example, Lovas, 1980; Francis, 1996; Hill, 2002) and practice investigation projects undertaken by university research centres such as *Journeying Post Graduate Supervision* (Aspland et al., 2002) and *The Supervisory Dialogues* (Wisker et al., 2003). These projects, as well as contributing to the discourse, encouraged the growing research focus on teaching and learning in higher education research to encompass research degree supervision as an academic practice.

The discourse was enlarged with the introduction of several international conferences dedicated to research supervision. A revival of the Society for Research into Higher Education (SRHE)[1] following a decline from its early instigation in the 1960s, coincided with emergence of practice-led inquiries into research supervision and growing awareness of the connections between doctoral completions and effective research supervision. The events in the UK coincided with the initiative of the Quality Postgraduate Research (QPR)[2] conference in Australia in 1994 and the International Doctoral Education Research Network (IDERN)[3] in 2007, which expanded the discourse with conference proceedings. Each of the networks represented by these conferences aligned with a range of journals, for example, *Studies in Higher Education, Higher Education Quarterly*, (previously *Universities Quarterly* which it had taken over from Blackwells), *Higher Education Research and Development* and the *International Journal of Doctoral Studies* that reinforced the idea of peer-reviewed research into all higher education practices and thus contributed to building the discourse surrounding research degree supervision (Bastalich, 2017).

With a rise in technology, at the beginning of the millennium, many of the already available resources became available electronically. As discussed elsewhere in this volume, several notable online resources emerged to support doctoral education, notably the blogs *The Thesis Whisperer* (Mewburn, 2010+) and *Patter* (Thomson, 2011+) which explicitly aim to support doctoral researchers with advice and guidance. Blogsites have also been established that directly aim to support research degree supervisors through sharing practices, challenges and research such as *The Research Supervisor's friend* (Hill, 2011+), *The Supervision Whisperers* (Mewburn & Miller, 2017+) and *Supervising PhDs* (Guccione, 2017+). Social media platforms such as Twitter, Instagram and Facebook have facilitated the initiation of multiple online communities for academics and doctoral researchers, for example, with the popularisation of hashtags such as #PhDChat #PhDlife and #AcWri. Universities have also developed an array of support services and online resources which contributed to understandings of the nature of research supervision (for example, University of Sydney, 2020) and later networks such as the *Research Supervisor's Network* established by the UK Council for Graduate Education and its launch in 2019 of the *Good Supervisory Practice Framework* as an online toolkit for reflection and professional development by supervisors (UKCGE, 2019). The popularity of online discussions around a range of higher education topics also coincided with the broader business agenda of creating professional networks online. In many of these networks (for example, *Academia* and *LinkedIn*) academics uploaded copies of research papers related to supervision for universal access. Thus, the online resources for supporting doctoral education are numerous and growing.

This increasingly accessible array of online resources in the discourse was beneficial for supervisors. It also presented a challenge for supervisors as readers and resource users in identifying, understanding and navigating these online resources to support their own supervisory practice and their doctoral researchers. Therefore, alongside instruction in particular institutional procedures, the professional development agenda for research degree supervisors has shifted to embrace alerting supervisors to the vast array of resources online and in the literature, and facilitating individual reflection on supervision as an academic practice which needs developing and refreshing, practising the practice.

A Community of Practice around Research Supervision model

As one university endeavouring to advance an agenda of research supervision professional development, Birmingham City University initiated a face-to-face community of practice around research supervision as an accredited supervisor development programme in 2015. In this chapter we reflect on the experience and impact of the programme, and on how the focus on face-to-face conversations and dialogues between supervisors has enabled space for engaging with online communities around research degree supervision. As such, the data on which we draw includes: our own lived experience as supervisors and as the designers and facilitators of a supervisor development programme; and the anonymised notes of each group, audio recordings generated for moderation and the programme evaluation forms.

The Community of Practice around Research Supervision supervisor development programme was initiated at Birmingham City University (BCU) in the midlands of the UK in response to a university-wide agenda to improve research supervision. As a post-1992 university with strong traditions of professional and practitioner education, BCU recognised that a quickly growing population of doctoral researchers across both PhD and Professional Doctorate programmes entailed a growing number of academics undertaking research degree supervision. Members of the university's Research Committee were keen to reflect the practitioner focus of much of BCU's research, and so instead of a didactic training model, they commissioned a dialogic approach to recognise and support supervision as an academic practice. Gaining SEDA (Staff and Educational Development Association) accreditation ensured benchmarking with sector-wide standards and provided national recognition.

The community of practice model designed involves six 90-minute discussion sessions occurring one per month, with then a two-month lead into the final session. These sessions enable discussion and sharing of experiences that scaffold the identification of individual practitioner inquiries which are then reported on in the final session. In line with the community of practice ethos, the assessment is participatory and draws on a professional dialogue models (Pilkington, 2013). Eligibility for accreditation is based on active participation in the discussions, evidence of engagement with the literature of supervision, and an action plan for ongoing development and reflection informed by the practitioner inquiry. Each of the first five sessions are initiated with catalyst questions and resources shared in advance.

1 Who am I as a participant of this community of practice?
2 What prior knowledge do I bring to the practice of research supervision?
3 What is good research supervision?
4 What resources can I use to support my aim of improving my research supervision?
5 How will I know when I have achieved my aim of improving my research supervision?

(Hill & Vaughan, 2018)

These catalysts follow a five-step process to initiate reflection and scaffold engagement with resources: firstly acknowledging what 'troubled' (Schön, 1983, p. 50) the practitioner about their research supervision practice; secondly exploring the provenance (Hill & Lloyd, 2018) of participants as research supervisor; thirdly exposure to the discourse and literature surrounding 'good' research supervision, as well as reflecting on experiences; fourthly identifying and sharing of relevant resources for advancing supervision practice; and finally planning how to undertake a practitioner inquiry (Stenhouse, 1981; Anderson & Herr, 1999) relevant to the individual's context, proposing the rationale, sources and anticipated outcomes.

The final, sixth session is structured around participating supervisors feeding back on their individual practitioner inquiries and how they envisage their findings will inform their practice going forward. The learning in each session is reinforced through the distribution of anonymised notes afterwards for review and as a prompt for individual reflection. The notes provide a summary of the discussion as well as further details of literature and resources identified during the conversation. Each of these five scaffolding steps invites different ways drawing on and talking back to the educational discourse.

The programme is based exclusively on community of practice principles. As a group of academic professionals we can come together to talk about a common practice and through this dialogue each advance our own understanding and practice. Dialogue is facilitated as open and honest, with respect for differing experiences and positions. Thus, groups are kept purposively small and each has two facilitators, experienced supervisors who have themselves been through the programme. That supervisor-participants then go on to volunteer to facilitate other groups suggests that they see the benefits in continuing to participate in the conversations and to actively being part of a supervisor community. Indeed, feedback from participants has been overwhelmingly positive and it is clear that supervisors perceived benefits in having the space for peer dialogue and of feeling part of a broader community of practice of research degree supervisors:

> The opportunity to talk to others and discuss concepts as well as being grounded in theory was fantastic.
> (Participant evaluation 2018)

> The space for reflection and sharing of ideas was both welcome and extremely valuable. The experience of others was excellent in terms of contextualising my own approaches, and the discussions aided me in thinking through next steps – some reinforcement, some positive renewal and re-thinking.
> (Participant evaluation 2017)

The sense of a supportive community of peers in which honest dialogue was possible seems to have been particularly valuable to research degree supervisors:

> You need to feel safe in an environment, so you can show your weaknesses, your vulnerabilities and understand that they are not going to be used against you in the future.
> (Participant comment in session 2017)

> It did all this in a friendly and not judgmental atmosphere that allowed the participants to reflect on their work and explore the potentials they have.
> (Participant evaluation 2017)

The benefits in creating space and time for busy academics to reflect communally on research degree supervision and the changing landscape of doctoral education have been clear. Whilst this small group, participatory and dialogic development programme has emphasised face-to-face local community connections, it has also had unanticipated benefits in increasing awareness and reflection on larger global online communities for doctoral researchers and research degree supervisors.

Discussing the online offline to raise awareness

As with any community of practice, we look at the array of sources which informed people's practice in our conversations. Perhaps expectedly, discussion on online communities and resources occurs most frequently during the fourth session which considers resources to support supervision as a practice. However, reflections on the online have also entered conversations in the other sessions. As we discussed 'troubling' we introduced aspects of the discourse that referred to the same issues of troubling. In conversations about prior experience when we discuss 'provenance', often supervisor participants would reflect on their knowledge and use of online resources including social media hashtags and blogs. Interestingly, in the communities of practice, supervisors tend to bring into the conversation online communities for doctoral researchers rather than explicitly focusing on online communities of research degree supervisors. This suggests that they are primarily considering how the online can support their supervisees, and only indirectly how this can benefit themselves as supervisors.

The anonymised notes from the conversations demonstrate that as well as raising awareness as supervisors shared their knowledge of online resources, these conversations revealed familiarity and the enthusiasts for virtual communities:

> I have used some of the blogs myself and also shared them with students. I find them to offer useful advice, information and tips for various aspects of research. But the main reason why I use them is for reflecting and reassurance – for me and for students. For me, reading a blog post on an issue I am currently grappling with, enables me to see the issue from different perspectives and it usually leaves me feeling more confident about my approach or finding a solution.
> (Group notes, 2017)

This supervisor neatly sums up the benefits from accessing online communities around doctoral education and these benefits are the same ones that participants identified in being part of our face-face Communities of Practice around Research Supervision – encouraging reflection, sharing approaches and gaining confidence. In particular supervisors identified how the different registers of discourse online could benefit themselves and their students, particular through the use of satire and humour:

> podcast on how to fail a PhD – humorous but useful.
> (Group notes 2018)

> Two participants suggested that when a student they had used the PhD comic (web and paper publications). Fun and very true.
> (Group notes 2018)

PhD comics is good for explaining institutional politics.

(Group notes 2019)

These comments also reflect the variety of online spaces and media that supervisors were aware of, encompassing audio, visual and text media online. Treating real life issues such as institutional politics and enculturation into academic life through humour was seen as beneficial in normalising experiences, and acknowledging the emotional labour of undertaking doctoral research:

> Social media can be beneficial for sharing experiences, 'normalising' to an extent the problems that PGRs can face.
>
> (Group notes 2019)

> All felt that blogs give the 'real experience' more immediately, even perhaps more useful than books.
>
> (Group notes 2018)

As well as normalising to an extent some anxieties around the lived experience of doctoral studies, supervisors have drawn attention in the conversation to how communities online can help address issues of diversity and inclusion. As well as recognising online as an increasing important mode of professional networking for academics, it has been noted that:

> Social media can be a powerful tool for young researchers as it is egalitarian and can be beneficial for those with social anxiety around face-to-face networking.
>
> (Group notes 2019)

> This supervisor (& team) has a WhatsApp group for students & supervisors which mitigates potential issues about physical distance from the university.
>
> (Group notes 2018)

> We also discussed how online there are supportive communities for older students, students who are parents, students with disabilities, students with mental health problems.
>
> (Group notes 2018)

From such anecdotal evidence, it is clear that some supervisors do perceive online communities generated through hashtags, Facebook groups and apps as providing useful additional support to doctoral researchers.

As the designers of the programme, it is interesting for us as authors to reflect on how supervisors have revealed they are deploying such online resources in their supervisory practice. Signposting seems to be the main mode in which these online communities and resources are utilised, and there do appear to be particular academic issues and stages in which the online is being drawn upon. Issues around supporting academic writing has emerged as the most common arena in which online resources are called upon:

> [Pat Thomson's] posts about grappling with theory ('theory fright') useful.
> (Group notes 2018)

> Another useful resource was *Explorations of Style* [website] ... in providing this reference she also recommended Patrick Dunleavy's Write for Research Twitter feed as useful.
> (Group notes 2017)

> Writing advice via social media/blogs is sometimes received better by PGRs who won't turn to textbooks.
> (Group notes 2019)

'Useful' tends to be the most common phrase used to describe the various online discussions of academic writing, with supervisors commenting on how they have seen benefits from signposting to particular techniques and strategies in contextualising their feedback to supervisees. The perception is that the online resources provide tools that enable them to act on feedback in constructive ways. It is also notable that supervisors identified a reluctance amongst some doctoral researchers to engage with the books on academic writing, with more than one supervisor reflecting that their supervisee seemed reluctant to admit to struggling to the extent of borrowing a text book from the library but were more likely to engage with blog posts online on the same issues. Whether this is because of the relative invisibility of engaging online compared to being seen with a book can only be speculated. Supervisors have also commented on how these discussions have drawn their attention to techniques that they were not personally aware of and have used in their own academic writing practices, such as pomodoros, reverse-outlining and topic sentences. The other common stage of the doctoral journey at which supervisors noted signposting to online resources was around the viva voce, a frequent cause of anxiety in doctoral researchers in the UK:

> Viva Survivors – particularly useful if you have doctoral researchers approaching the examination stage. There is a whole archive of podcasts – interviews with people about their doctoral viva (they are not primarily horror stories!); range of blog posts and other resources focusing on examination issues and preparation.
> (Group notes 2018)

Again, it appears that the online communities are valued by supervisors for providing emotional reassurance, not 'horror stories', and an implicit recognition that such reassurance may be better received from peers than by the supervisors themselves.

Blending online and offline 103

Not all supervisors express positive thoughts about online communities and resources. It is key to our community of practice ethos that we enable safe spaces for concerns to be raised and reluctance to engage to be explored in a non-judgement environment. Several strands of more negative concerns around online doctoral education have emerged across differing groups. There are concerns that social media becomes another expectation of and pressure on doctoral researchers, adding to the competitiveness of the current doctoral landscape:

> Danger that too much emphasis is put on the construction of a profile on media, where is the substance?
>
> (Group notes 2019)

There has been detailed discussion in some groups of concerns around the substance and depth of self-declared online expertise, particularly around issues of peer-review or lack thereof for blogs.

> I find the opinionated nature of blogs very difficult.... Social media can tend too much to just bragging and/or moaning!
>
> (Group notes 2016)

Some supervisors are cautious of trusting the online environment. This mistrusting response has also appeared in relation to the potential negative consequences of the sharing of emotional lived doctoral experience online:

> Another said that blogs, and other students, tend to relate their own positive or negative experiences, and reading the latter may throw you off balance; e.g., 'my supervisor is a devil' ... and this may be misleading or even hurtful if the relationship with students is all one way. So perhaps seminars and books may give a more balanced view.
>
> (Group notes 2018)

Here a supervisor was expressing concern that blog posts might influence doctoral researchers to interpret or reinterpret supervisory relationships negatively. The concern appears to be that trauma and negative experiences would be read into situations and anxieties could be magnified rather than resolved through reading about others' experiences. There has also been open discussion that the active use and promotion of online community platforms by supervisors might lead to inflating the expectations of supervisors. For example, when a supervisor reflected on how they use WhatsApp to enable a sense of cohort amongst their supervisees, the group then:

> discussed how this makes the supervisor(s) potentially available to handle queries 24/7 and not all supervisors would be comfortable with that arrangement.
>
> (Group notes 2018)

This issue of comfort appears to be of key importance to how supervisors engage with online communities and resources. Whilst potential benefits are shared, there are undercurrents of mistrust. In our view as authors it is important that our community of practice programme enables space for supervisors to honestly share reservations as well as developing understanding through shared examples of the online doctoral landscape which in the majority of cases is very different to that of their own doctoral study.

Personalising the investigation of online PhD resources and spaces

The individual practitioner enquiries that scaffold the community of practice sessions enable supervisors to focus their reflection on an area of research degree supervision that has personal resonance and relevance for them. Thus, there is the opportunity for supervisors to choose to explore online resources and communities in more depth. Our experience however, is that a minority of supervisors choose to do so.

Our experience has been that where supervisors have chosen to investigate online support for doctoral researchers, their interest has been on the socio-emotional support available amongst peers for their supervisees rather than particular supervisory tools that they might personally engage with in their academic practice. For example, a supervisor participant in 2017, had initially proposed a practitioner inquiry into how social media enabled support mechanisms for students, prompted by how in the conversations

> We also discussed how social media facilitates connections between PhD students and can act as a support network for candidates across different disciplines, as a form of *Networked Participatory Scholarships* (Veletsianos & Kimmons 2012; Cooper 2016).
> (Participant presentation slides, December 2017)

At his presentation, he reported that when using the Twitter hashtags #PhDlife and #PhDsupervisor he looked at what doctoral researchers were tweeting about and noticed that most were about stress, not the research itself. Whilst he did share examples of the tweets he had found, his practitioner inquiry had evolved into a focus on supporting doctoral researcher well-being. Whilst there was implicit recognition of the support role played by online doctoral communities in the initial proposition, the supervisor's individual reflection and action planning to enhance their own practice was focused very much on face-to-face interactions, and a supervisor's role in recognising the need for, and signposting other support services. Whilst the group then shared knowledge and experience of local resources, the initial focus on online communities was not returned to in the discussion.

In 2018, another supervisor chose to undertake a practitioner inquiry to enable them to think about the pastoral role of a supervisor by investigating how doctoral researchers experience the PhD. They did this via an interrogation of

Twitter posts using the hashtag #PhDlife, scraping seven days of tweets to explore the topics and tone of tweets in conjunction with looking at literature on social media in doctoral education and academia. The tweets revealed the hashtag provided a space for playfulness, the exploration of precarity and the realities of doctoral study. Interestingly, the supervisor concluded that, in the sample, this was not a space where expertise was played out; instead it was a space where anxiety and humour were enacted in comments on the emotional labour of performing the particular identity of doctoral researcher. One supervisor wondered if in doing so, the tweeters were:

> playing out online the expectations of the supervisor: you aren't quite there yet, I told you it would be hard.
> (Participant, audio recording 2019)

Mirroring the discussions in other groups, discussion of this practitioner inquiry focused on the potential of online communities to combat loneliness and offer support for the emotional lived experience of doctoral study. The group also discussed the supervisor's role in reproducing tropes of isolation and procrastination and the potential for consciously countering this by signposting and helping their supervisees find their own online communities.

To date, out of nearly 150 practitioner inquiries, very few supervisors have chosen to explicitly focus on investigating online tools that they could use for supervision meetings, rather than as signposting to support beyond supervision. In 2019, this supervisor investigated which online tools might enable and enhance the sense of community amongst distance-learning doctoral researchers and in doing so support them in a group supervision approach. The supervisor discussed a number of potential platforms with their three current supervisees and discovered that the doctoral researchers had already created and/or found their own online communities. In response to the presentation, supervisors discussed how different platforms might encourage different behaviours and relationships:

> There is a need for boundaries and to balance the personal with moments of authority, if too personal then the PGR can perceive /misuse relationships to avoid conflict and deadlines.
> (Group notes 2019)

The group acknowledged that some platforms seem to encourage a more informal, personal mode of communication – the chats and gifs – and that this could challenge establishing a more professional supervisory relationship. The group agreed on the need to use appropriate technology with a degree of critical awareness of the types of relationship and interaction that a supervisor wishes to foster. As with any supervisory practice, the group concluded that flexibility and reflection would be required of a supervisor trying to create and foster cohorts online.

Feeding back into online communities

Whilst relatively few supervisors chose to investigate online support for doctoral researchers in their individual practitioner enquiries, several have chosen to contribute to online resources for research degree supervisors. This suggests both a community-minded approach that values their experiences in the development programme, and a presumption that supervisors do use such tools and resources.

For example, a supervisor in the Law School used a strengths-based inquiry approach to reflect on her first year of being a research supervisor. The outcome of her inquiry was a model of supervision that she shared with other first-time research degree supervisors in our university, and that she contributed to *The (Research) Supervisor's Friend* blogsite: 'to offer guidance to new research supervisors' (Cooper 2016). Her explicit intention – to offer a supportive touchstone for other new supervisors – can be seen as characteristic of the 'gift economy' of academic blogging (Mewburn & Thomson, 2013). In the same year another supervisor's practitioner inquiry took the form of a reflection on their supervision practice analysed through a framework that they devised from the supervisory literature (Bøgelund 2015), again sharing both their approach and findings on *The (Research) Supervisor's Friend* blogsite (Feldman 2016).

It is interesting to note that later participants in the communities of practice programme went on to reference these contributions to the online discourse – for example, the supervisor initially looking at Twitter hashtags in 2017 discussed earlier in our chapter themselves referenced Cooper and Feldman's blog posts in their own practitioner inquiry report. Thus, the blending of offline and online by the communities of practice is brought full circle, as oral reports and conversations within face-to-face sessions are then disseminated online, and the online publications are later discussed within subsequent face-to-face conversations.

Conclusions and a pandemic postscript

Our experience has demonstrated the importance of linking online and offline in enabling research degree supervisors to recognise supervision as an academic practice and the support available through communities of practice both local and global. Research degree supervision is an academic practice with communities plural; it is not just a singular community of practice amongst local colleagues in one institution. Through online supervisory spaces, subject and disciplinary communities both online and in other networks, supervision is an academic practice that is shared and can be reflected upon and continuously learnt through an individual academic's participation in multiple communities. As supervisors we are always in the process of learning and refining, of becoming-supervisor as Grant (2018) puts it. This is why, in our view, it is also crucial to not just facilitate awareness of such online resources and communities. It is important to provide space for supportive dialogues of open reflection amongst supervisors in which anxieties around online communities for doctoral education can be honestly raised, experiences shared and the potential of such online communities critically evaluated in relation to the particular contexts of individual supervisory practices. Just as online spaces can enable the 'troubles talk' of doctoral researchers (Mewburn 2011) which can be cathartic and supportive for them and their peers, as indeed many of our supervisor participants noted, it is as important for research degree supervisors to also have trusted spaces in which their troubles can be shared and interrogated, including supervisors' concerns around online practices. Whilst there may not be many surprises amongst the views shared by our anonymous supervisor participants, it is important that their voices can be heard and that conversations take place between research degree supervisors about their academic practices of supervision.

At the time of writing, March 2020, higher education is facing unprecedented challenges and the question of online support for doctoral researchers and their supervisors has taken on a new urgency. Whilst for many supervisors the occasional supervision meeting by telephone, Skype or other online platform has become commonplace over recent years, the current situation requires all supervisory contact to be via remote means. In the UK, as with many countries, universities are physically closed in response to the Covid-19 global pandemic and doctoral research and its supervision have to take place online by participants who are socially-distancing and only having face-to-face contact with members of their own household. We have thus moved our Community of Practice around Research Supervision development programme to online delivery, as arguably creating space for supervisors to share experiences, anxieties and ideas about online supervision practices is more relevant and urgent. Whilst it is relatively early in conditions which are currently envisaged to exist for at least the next six months, early indicators are that the use of video-conferencing (in our case Microsoft Teams) whilst a change in platform, does not fundamentally change the nature of the experience and quality of the conversations between supervisors. Meeting virtually, our supervisors are still forming supportive and reflective communities of practice.

Notes

1 The Society for Research into Higher Education is a UK-based international learned society concerned to advance understanding of higher education, especially through the insights, perspectives and knowledge offered by systematic research and scholarship. The Society aims to be the leading international society in the field, as to both the support and the dissemination of research. Established in 1965, and revitalised in the 1990s, it holds annual conferences see www.srhe.ac.uk/downloads/ShattockSRHEfirst25years.pdf
2 The Quality Postgraduate Research (QPR) conference was established in Australia in 1994 as a way of biannually bringing together research degree supervisors,

postgraduate students, academic developers, university decision makers and administrators, governmental representatives and those who conduct research in postgraduate education and associated areas to discuss, debate and make sense of the complex and changing area of HDR policy and practice. See www.qpr.edu.au/whatisqpr

3 The International Doctoral Education Research Network (IDERN) is a network of scholars and practitioners established in 2007 and actively engaged in researching doctoral education and hosting a conference every two years to three years. See www.mun.ca/educ/research/idern.php

References

Anderson, G. and Herr, K. (1999). The new paradigm wars: Is there room for rigorous practitioner knowledge in schools and universities? *Educational Researcher*, 28(5), 12–21. doi:10.3102/0013189X028005012

Aspland, T., Hill, G. and Chapman, H. (Eds) (2002). *Journeying Postgraduate Supervision*. Brisbane: Queensland University of Technology.

Bastalich, W. (2017). Content and context in knowledge production: a critical review of doctoral supervision literature. *Studies in Higher Education*, 42(7), 1145–1157. doi:10.1080/03075079.2015.1079702

Bøgelund, P. (2015). How supervisors perceive PhD supervision–And how they practice it. *International Journal of Doctoral Studies*, 10, 39–55, doi:10.28945/2096

Cooper, S. (2016). My first year as a research supervisor: Developing my own model of supervision. Available at: https://supervisorsfriend.wordpress.com/2016/10/ last accessed 30 March 2020.

Feldman, G. (2016). A reflection of my supervision process. Available at: https://supervisorsfriend.wordpress.com/2016/11/18/622/ last accessed 30 March 2020.

Francis, D. (1996). Moving from noninterventionist research to participatory action: Challenges for academe. *International Journal of Qualitative Studies in Education*, 9 (1), 75–86. doi:10.1080/0951839960090107

Grant, B.M. (2018). Assembling ourselves differently? Contesting the dominant imaginary of doctoral supervision. *parallax*, 24(3), 356–370. doi:10.1080/13534645.2018.1496584

Guccione, K. (ed.) (2017+). *SupervisingPhDs* blog. Available at: https://supervisingphds.wordpress.com last accessed 30 March 2020.

Hill, G. (2002). *Promoting congruence between the inquiry paradigm and the associated practices of higher degree research. Education faculty* (Doctoral Dissertation). Brisbane: Australia, Queensland University of Technology.

Hill, G. (ed.), (2011+). *The Research Supervisor's Friend* blog. Available at: https://wordpress.com/view/supervisorsfriend.wordpress.com last accessed 30 March 2020.

Hill, G. and Lloyd, C. (2018). Articulating practice through provenance. *Action Research*, first published 13 July 2018, doi:10.1177/1476750318786793

Hill, G. and Vaughan, S. (2018). 'Conversations about research supervision – enabling and accrediting a Community of Practice model for research degree supervisor development. *Innovations in Education and Teaching*, 55(2), 153–163. doi:10.1080/14703297.2017.1406388

Lovas, S. (1980). Higher degree examination procedures in Australian universities. *Vestes* (Australian Universities review), 23(1), 9–13.

Manathunga, C. (2005). The development of research supervision: Turning the light on a private space. *International Journal for Academic Development*, 10, 17–30. doi:10.1080/13601440500099977

Mewburn, I. (ed.) (2010+). *The Thesis Whisperer* blog. Available at: https://thethesiswhisperer.wordpress.com last accessed 30 March 2020.

Mewburn, I. (2011). Troubling talk: Assembling the PhD candidate. *Studies in Continuing Education*, 33(3), 321–332. doi:10.1080/0158037X.2011.585151.

Mewburn, I. and Miller, E. (eds) (2017+). *The Supervision Whisperers* blog. Available at: https://thesupervisionwhisperers.wordpress.com last accessed 30 March 2020.

Mewburn, I. and Thomson, P. (2013). Why do academics blog? An analysis of audiences, purposes and challenges. *Studies in Higher Education*, 38(8), 1105–1119. doi:10.1080/03075079.2013.835624

Phillips, E. and Pugh, D.S. (1987). *How to Get a PhD: A Handbook for Students and their Supervisors*. Buckingham: Open University Press.

Pilkington, R. (2013). Professional dialogues: Exploring an alternative means of assessing the professional learning of experienced HE academics. *International Journal for Academic Development*, 18, 251–263. doi:10.1080/1360144X.2012.717225

Salmon, P. (1992). *Achieving a PhD – Ten Students' Experience*. Staffordshire: Trentham Books.

Schön, D. (1983). *The Reflective Practitioner: How Professionals Think in Action*. USA: Basic Books.

Stenhouse, L. (1981). What counts as research? *British Journal of Educational Studies*, 29(2), 103–114.

Thomson, P. (ed.) (2011+). *Patter* blog. Available at: https://patthomson.net/ last accessed 30 March 2020.

UKCGE (2019) *Good Supervisory Practice Framework*. Available at: https://supervision.ukcge.ac.uk/good-supervisory-practice-framework/ last accessed 30 March 2020.

University of Sydney (2020). *Research Supervision*. Available at: https://sydney.edu.au/students/research-supervision.html last accessed 30 March 2020.

Veletsianos, G. and Kimmons, R. (2012). Assumptions and challenges of open scholarship. *The International Review of Research in Open and Distributed Learning*, 13(4), 166–189. doi:10.19173/irrodl.v13i4.1313

Wisker, G., Robinson, G., Trafford, V., Warnes, M. and Creighton, E. (2003). From supervisory dialogues to successful PhDs: Strategies supporting and enabling the learning conversations of staff and students at postgraduate level. *Teaching in Higher Education*, 8(3), 383–397. doi:10.1080/13562510309400

8 *The Supervision Whisperers*
Why a virtual community of practice for research supervisors did (not) work

Evonne Miller and Inger Mewburn

Supervising higher degree research (HDR) students is a rewarding, but often professionally challenging experience for academics. From teaching the research and writing process, advising on career dilemmas, and supporting students during life crises, the best supervisors are a mix of mentor, advocate and critical friend. Yet, who supports these supervisors? Where do they turn for advice, and to reflect on their supervisory practices, interpersonal skills and communication styles?

Despite a significant academic literature, and growing numbers of university-based training, online spaces for supervisors to seek support and share practice in virtual communities of practice (CoP) remain relatively underdeveloped compared to spaces for PhD students. With the exception of *The Supervisor's Friend* run by Geof Hill and *Supervising PhDs* run by Kay Guccione, there are very few blogs aimed specifically at a supervision audience and none that encourage supervisors to contribute their own stories of practice for the benefit of others. In recognition of this gap, in 2017, we launched *The Supervision Whisperers* (TSW)– a social media blog 'dedicated to the topic of supervising a thesis'. The blog consciously copied the community content model of one of our blogs *The Thesis Whisperer* (TW) in that it aimed to provide a space for supervisors to provide advice on everyday aspects of supervision to each other in the form of stories.

In this chapter, drawing primarily on the facilitators' perspective and data from the blog itself, we reflect on the processes, rewards and challenges of setting up and running a virtual CoP for supervisors. It argues that while TSW aimed to provide a 'safe space' for sharing, open discussion and reflection on how best to supervise students through their unpredictable research journey, overwhelmingly, research supervisors seemed reluctant to take up the offer to share. We still believe online spaces provide opportunity to foster practical global conversations and learnings about best practice in higher degree research supervision, but wonder if making such spaces radically open may be a step too far for academia as a community. Openness requires willingness to be vulnerable, and our failure to get supervisors to participate in a transparent community of practice highlights some problematic aspects of supervision practice in the academy, in particular the intimacy of supervision settings and the status of 'expertise'. The problematic practices of supervision

DOI: 10.4324/9780429274749-9

have been documented and analysed by many scholars before us, but rarely tested in practice. We hope our story of failure will provide valuable insights for others with aspirations to promote open communication about tricky areas of academic practice.

The origins of *The Supervision Whisperers* (TSW)

The idea for a blog specifically targeted to supervisors, and the experience of supervising HDR students, emerged late one summer night over dinner in a restaurant in Brisbane, Australia. As academics tend to do, we were reflecting on and sharing our own supervision stories, on the unique challenges our HDR students were facing and the degree to which we, with our different life histories, disciplinary expectations and unique career trajectories, were equipped to advise them. And while we all found the training offered by our respective universities helpful, it often was not timely or immediately accessible at times of crisis. What was needed, we realized, was an online resource like TW, but targeted to the uniquely different perspective and voice of the supervisor. And so, TSW was born.

How do academics learn to supervise research students?

Before we discuss the inception and evolution of TSW as a CoP, it is important to discuss research supervision. Learning how to supervise HDR students, and developing your own personal supervision style, is often a combination of responses to your own personal experiences of supervision and a process of trial and error as student problems arise. Traditionally, most supervisors draw on their own experiences (both negative and positive), informal conversations with colleagues, and some might even choose to read the literature on research education supervision (for example of only a few of the papers in this quite significant body of literature, see Kamler & Thomson, 2006; Wisker, 2012; Lee, 2018; Lee & Williams, 1999). HDR students frequently identify their relationship with their supervisor as the most critical element predicting the quality of their research journey. Becoming a good supervisor through trial and error is difficult, because the long timeframes of most candidatures mean that many supervisors do not get many opportunities to learn from their own practice.

Recognising the importance of research supervision pedagogy to successful completions, universities now offer formal supervisor development activities (workshops, courses, mentoring and awards) and accreditation schemes specifically designed to support and develop supervisors, endeavouring to standardise and enhance research supervision (Hill & Vaughan, 2018; Kiley, 2011; Lee, 2018). Face-to-face workshops and online training for supervisors within the university environment are often popular, with academics valuing the opportunity to reflect on and improve their supervisory practice (Hill & Vaughan, 2018). While these formally organised activities provide supervisors with valuable opportunities to learn from peers and experts in research education, they cannot capture all the contingencies of practice.

PhD supervision is acknowledged as one of the most challenging forms of teaching and learning; while it can be personally and professionally rewarding, it is not necessarily easy or straightforward. A supervisor must be a project manager, quality assurer, and counsellor, motivating, mentoring and pushing their research student to a timely completion (van Der Wath, Coetzee & Maree, 2016).

As well as providing guidance on key literature, methods and methodology, guiding analysis, and the all-important write up, a research supervisor is also frequently a source of important personal and emotional support to their student. And while formal university training sessions on research supervision are extremely helpful, the skills learnt there are often less immediately helpful in the moment when your PhD student breaks down in your office over challenges with fieldwork, negative reviewers' comments, battles with administration, or the impact of personal life events. While the supervisor is not usually the student's sole source of guidance, many academics develop close friendship-like mentoring relationships with their HDR students and provide critical support during times of professional and personal crises. The research education literature documents this delicate balancing act, noting how supervisors need to be 'guided in how to empathise with their charges' intellectual and emotional problems, whilst simultaneously achieving enough social and emotional distance so as to be able to effect the intellectual tasks of guide and critic' (Hockey, 1995, p. 208).

Stories are one of the best ways to learn how to achieve this kind of 'balancing act' in practice. See, as just one example, Cree (2012), which describes a relationship that resulted in one international PhD student asking if he could call her 'mother'. This personal story reflects on the learning process Cree has engaged in as a supervisor and her belief that supervision involves caring work. Stories like this enable us to learn from others' experience and give us tools to apply this knowledge in our own practice by helping us to enlarge our own repertoire for dealing with the problems of practice, and allow us to recognise similar scenarios, personalities and situations. Stories of failure and struggle have particular resonance, acting as both warning and lesson. Teachers have long used tearooms and office spaces to share 'war stories' about being academics, including research supervision. This social learning practice has extended to online spaces which can serve as 'virtual common rooms' enabling global conversations of practice to extend across time and space (Mewburn & Thomson, 2013). These online spaces can be understood as virtual CoP that enable peers to connect and learn from each other, and this sense of belonging can be comforting for those dealing with the intensely demanding profession that academia has become.

How academics use social media

Social media platforms can provide the space for a virtual CoP for supervisors to develop, with the potential to provide much needed real-time support and guidance. Academics increasingly use a variety of social media for professional networking and communication, social interaction, and real-time collaboration, connecting on Facebook, Twitter, YouTube, and blogs (Al-Daihani, Al-Qallaf, & AlSaheeb, 2018; Carrigan, 2016; Gasman, 2016). Stewart (2018), for example, outlined how using Twitter benefited academics by fostering 'extensive cross-disciplinary, public ties and rewarding connection, collaboration, and curation between individuals rather than roles or institutions' (p. 318). Numerous social media sites and blogs cover a range of issues related to academic work, from tips for academic writing and securing a tenure track job to strategies for work-life balance. Social media, therefore, could also be a rich resource for research supervisors; after all, as the other chapters in this book have adeptly demonstrated, doctoral students are avid users of social media for support, sharing, discussing and reflecting on problems, challenges and opportunities of the postgraduate research experience in real-time online.

The degree to which academics professionally use social media varies; some are active users, and strong advocates for the power of social media for learning, teaching, and connecting. Others are much less engaged. Research with academics in the United Kingdom revealed most used social media for self-development and the broadening of their social networks; a third did not use social media, citing negative opinions of social media and a lack of time, skill or interest (Donelan, 2016). Indeed, despite a growing number of books outlining why and how academics should engage in public scholarship via social media (see, for example, Mark Carrigan's *Social Media for Academics* and *Academics Going Public: How to Write and Speak beyond Academe* edited by Marybeth Gasman), many academics hesitate when it comes to social media – for good reasons. Lupton (2014) surveyed 711 academics across the globe about their use of social media in their work. While respondents reported many benefits, including linking with other academics and sharing their research, they also described many risks, including: concerns about privacy, time pressures, users' excessive self-promotion, being negatively targeted and the 'risk of jeopardizing their career through injudicious use of social media' (p. 3). As one respondent noted, they worried about

> making any flippant remarks that could be misinterpreted (or picked up by journalists with an agenda) ... I find some of the online academic disagreements I have come across quite scary and scathing and I hope I never end up in one of them.
>
> (p. 10)

The impact of a controversial blog post or an ill thought out, hastily composed tweet can in fact be catastrophic, as outlined in Jon Ronson's (2015) compelling book *So You've Been Publicly Shamed*. While beyond the scope of this chapter, the ongoing impact of online bullying, of internet trolls and entrenched misogyny means actively engaging online is more challenging for women, and those researching or posting about more controversial topics. This short tour of the state of academic practice on social media makes it clear that online spaces are contested, difficult terrain, another space where academics must negotiate the professional identity and manage their energies. We now turn to the difficulties of building sustainable, flourishing communities of research supervision practice online.

Building communities of practice online

Wenger (1998) famously defined CoP (whether online or face-to-face) as 'groups of people who share a concern, a set of problems, or a passion about a topic, and who deepen their knowledge and expertise in this area by interacting on an ongoing basis' (p. 4). The framework of a CoP requires three main elements: (a) domain, (b) community, and (c) practice. The domain (in the case of TW, PhD students) establishes the common ground and focus of interactions, with interest in the domain bringing the community together (in this case, PhD study). The practice (in this case, the blog posts) moves the group to action, with these three inter-connecting elements flowing in a cyclic manner as members share, reflect and refine current practices. CoP are learning partnerships that help foster critical reflective practice, defined by Schön (1983) as reflection-in-action and reflection-on-action.

Fook and Gardner (2007) define reflection is thinking about and understanding our experiences, with the intention of improving our practice in the future – and this definition guides our thinking. Much research has documented the value of virtual or online CoP in overcoming the challenges of location, time and distance. The asynchronous nature of online forums allows interested participants to engage and be involved at the time of their choosing, while creating a valuable archive of ideas, expertise, discourse and resources able to be accessed by anyone, anywhere, at any time; disadvantages include needing technology for participation and that it is easy to not participate (Byington, 2011).

Academics blog for a variety of reasons. In an analysis of 100 academic blogs, Mewburn and Thomson (2013) identified nine broad types of content with the largest being critiques of academic practice or their institutions. They argued that most participants were writing for other academics and this had the effect of creating a 'loose academic blogging community of practice' that they compared to a global common room (p. 1114). PhD students are also active bloggers. In a follow up survey of PhD students with active blogs, Mewburn and Thomson (2017) identified four different blogging practices, which they described as a repertoire, including creating a scholarly persona, 'slow thinking practices', pleasure seeking and knowledge sharing – but very little evidence that students were using blogs as part of a formal research process.

Mewburn and Thomson argue, following Foucault, that writing is a technology of self-formation. Building on Kamler and Thomson's (2006) concept of text work being a form of identity work, Mewburn and Thomson argue that blogging appears to offer a 'being and becoming' platform' for PhD students to construct their identity as an academic in public, reflexively and reflectively. By 'writing themselves into being', PhD students who blog are using online spaces to build community as well as build themselves an academic persona. PhD student willingness to engage in this kind of public, quite vulnerable process can be contrasted with 'grown up' academic's reluctance to do so, as we shall see.

Building *The Supervision Whisperers* (TSW)

TSW was founded on a content model pioneered by TW, which was established in 2010 by one of us (Mewburn). The TW is conceptualised as a 'local newspaper' for PhD students, including advice articles written by the editor (a professional research educator) and 'student journalists'. Articles from the editor share tips based on research and her experience in helping PhD students. Articles from PhD students take the form of stories about individual circumstances that share techniques, tips and ideas for solving problems encountered while studying. The blog is very popular: at time of writing there has been more than 9 million hits on the site and a social media reach of nearly 100,000. As Figure 8.1 illustrates, the TW has been read by people located in every country in the world. In contrast, TSW is in CoP in development.

The TW explicitly operationalises a community of practice model. Since the TW has been operating for nearly ten years, we assumed there would be a ready audience of readers who had 'grown up' in their PhD study with the TW and would be receptive to a similar site in the supervision space. We assumed that people would value a place to discuss and share their practices of supervision, similarly to their practices as PhD students. Our guiding vision for TSW was to create a safe space for honest, reflective and supportive truth-telling about the challenges, highlights and lowlights associated with being a research supervisor. As Figure 8.2 illustrates, the introduction to our blog reads: 'Research supervision is the most challenging form of teaching you will ever do. Luckily, the supervision whisperers are here to help PhD supervisors everywhere'. The commonality that links readers and writers of TSW is an interest and commitment in improving their practice as a supervisor, with the blog posts and subsequent comments and tweet exchanges an

Figure 8.1 Heat map of *The Thesis Whisperer* readership, by location from 2011 to 2019

Figure 8.2 *The Supervision Whisperers* homepage

opportunity for connections and learning across disciplinary, faculty, university, and geographic boundaries.

Deng and Yuen (2011) have argued that the networks created by a blog may be viewed as three distinct communities: a community of blog writers, blog readers, and blog commenters. In the following section, broadly drawing on Deng and Yuen's (2011) three key domains of blogging behaviour as a conceptual framework, we reflect on the development of the TSW blog and the opportunities and challenges of academic blogging about research supervision – as well as its limits.

Reflective writing on a public blog

Deng and Yuen's (2011) first domain of blogging behaviour is the process of actually writing blog posts. In terms of providing a space to discuss research supervision, the blog easily enables self-expression and reflection on practice. The literature tells us that the process of reflective writing has significant therapeutic and professional development value (Bolton, 2005; 2008), with educators often blogging as part of a professional learning process (Sackstein, 2015). Similarly, we have found the process of writing about issues we experience as HDR supervisors similarly cathartic; there is a surprising amount of things that supervisors often simply cannot say – issues that are difficult to verbalize about the student-supervisor relationship, which the literature in this space has explored.

Writing blog posts on supervision has, as is the aim of reflective practice writing (see Schön, 1983 and Bolton, 2005), forced a beneficial and powerful reflective process of learning and development, of rethinking past experiences and expectations – both of our students, our co-supervisors and of colleagues and professional staff. Learning, as Pereira, Pereira, and Cardozo remind us, 'happens when new meanings are made from experience' (2016, p. 8), and reflective writing blog posts about the ups and downs of research supervision has enabled us to better process the complexities and the impact of our own practice. Where the blog functioned less well was as a space for *other researchers* to share their supervision practice. Similar to the TW, the 'About' page on TSW contains a call to action to readers to participate with a set of editorial guidelines, reproduced below:

- *We want to be concise.* Academics have to do a lot of reading, so no posts will be longer than 1000 words.
- *We want to learn from people's stories* about supervising a research degree, but we don't need to hear all the details about the research itself. There's enough journals out there for that.
- *We don't want to just talk about writing* – successfully supervising a dissertation is about more than that. Please share your learnings, your dilemmas, practical tips and techniques.

- *We want to stimulate conversations*, so our posts will always be opinionated (hopefully, without being obnoxious). But we don't want to be sued, so we'll always keep it nice.
- *Respect for students, first, last and always.* This blog is a place to discuss issues of research supervision practice, honestly and frankly. This is *not* a space to whinge about, denigrate or demoralise research students.
- *We want to be good role models.* We hope students will be reading and learning in preparation for their future career. We want to dissect poor practice, without too much judgment, and learn together how to make things better.
- *We want to hear your voice.* Doing all the paperwork involved with thesis supervision can take the fun out of anyone's day. This is a place you can relax and connect with other supervisors who 'get it' – and might have some helpful suggestions!

An almost identical call to action on TW has resulted in a large volume of reader submissions. Since we launched the blog, we have asked friends and colleagues to contribute, and shared the blog link to multiple academic Facebook groups we belong to, requesting contributors. The comment from one female academic in response in early 2017 is telling: 'God. This is just what I need! Would like to contribute but may have to be anonymous!' (7/2/17, comment on Facebook group for academic mothers). This request for anonymity highlights the reality that engaging with social media has professional consequences; indeed, in her study of social work bloggers, Hickson (2012) noted some had been instructed not to name them their organization in social media posts. We can see this reaction to risk in a comparison of data stored on both TW and TSW. At time of writing, TW readers had contributed almost half of the 530 published posts, with at least one year's lead-time for new posts to appear. In the two years that we have been running TSW, we have only received ten offers of guest posts. Although the site functions as a place for both of us to share reflections on supervision practice and offer advice, so far TSW falls short in terms of providing a 'virtual common room' for others to do the same.

Additionally, while the TW receives some 80,000 hits per month, on average, TSW has had much slower growth: after 2.5 years, we have published 30 blog posts (~ a third guest posts), with ~1,400 subscribers and a total of nearly 30,000 international visitors (most from Australia (8,000 views), the United Kingdom (6,500), the United States (3,600), Canada (1,100), New Zealand (1000) and across Europe and Asia. Growth of readership on the site is much slower than we might expect with its close association with TW, which has over 35,000 email subscribers, 40,000+ followers on Twitter and more than 30,000 people signed up to the Facebook community page. This chapter, therefore, reflects on these differences and endeavours to account for the disparity in the two sites.

Success factors for a virtual CoP around research supervision

Building and sustaining a vibrant virtual CoP is no easy undertaking, as Hickson (2012) research with ten social work bloggers illustrates. These social work bloggers wrote 'for reflection, for debriefing, and for raising awareness', using their blog to share, reflect on, and learn from distressing and complex experiences. Only half reported receiving blog comments. While some felt disappointed and frustrated their blog was not generating connections or a rich discussion amongst other social workers, others were simply satisfied to be sharing their perspectives. As well as privacy concerns, limited time is also an impediment to academic blogging. One study of academic bloggers estimated that it took two hours to write a blog post, with one explaining how he quickly 'bangs out a tweet, but a blog takes a little bit longer' (Kirkup, 2010). Academics Smidt, Wheeler, Peralta and Bell (2018) described their own recent experiment setting up a private blog to discuss their experiences of tertiary teaching, using prompts and reflective tasks. Yet, the project ended after nine months, with the schedule of monthly blogging too onerous. In reflective statements, the group shared feelings of guilt for not sustaining 'the momentum of the project' and feeling 'disappointed with colleagues who were not able to meet the [deadlines for reflective tasks] or were not able to commit fully to the project' (2018, p. 482).

Hank (2012) outlined the motivations of academic bloggers, noting that while the bloggers she interviewed greatly enjoyed their blog (and benefited in terms of developing writing skills and academic connections), none felt it was a beneficial activity in terms of promotion. In terms of a very pragmatic cost-benefit time analysis, academics may very well place writing a blog post low on the priority list. Indeed, a global survey of how 3,500+ academics used social networking sites, and what they found to be beneficial and problematic, revealed that the most common concern (reported by a third) was time, with academics wary of the time commitment of social media networking (Jordan & Weller, 2018).

Lack of time accounts partly for academics' reluctance to participate in TSW, but the public nature of blogging as a space and an unwillingness to reveal 'private' stories of supervision practice needs to be acknowledged. All too often, it is the inter-personal aspects of supervision that prove the most challenging to navigate; and reflecting on and then publicly sharing these, often telling personal details, may be too difficult an undertaking. In their seminal paper *Forged in Fire: Narratives of Trauma in Research Supervision* Lee and Williams draw our attention to the intimate settings of research supervision, where teaching is often conducted in a one to one or 'dyadic' relationship that has echoes of a medieval 'master/apprentice' relationship where exercise of 'extreme disciplinary power' can be easily enacted. Kamler and Thomson (2006) further remind us that text work is identity work: in writing texts we write the self. There is an inherent tension between the PhD supervisor as 'authorised knower' and the open, transparent space of the internet. While PhD students seem willing to publish stories full of hesitations, vulnerability and unknowing (as can be seen on TW and in Mewburn & Thomson's 2017 survey), once these people become research supervisors the very identity of the supervisor seems to work against full disclosure of the discomfort and 'unknowingness' of practice.

The value of reading – the silent blog reader

Perhaps we should not view TSW failure – so far – to operationalise a virtual CoP as being a reason to stop blogging. Deng and Yuen (2011) identify 'silent reading' as the second key domain of blogging behaviour. They found that simply reading the blogs – not writing or commenting – was beneficial, with reflective learning was triggered by the process of silent reading. Others have also found that inactive online learners are also engaged in active learning, with Ellison and Wu (2008) noting that students found reading the blogs of fellow students *more* valuable than writing their own blog. Silent reading, Deng and Yuen (2011) concluded, is an important, yet often overlooked, dimension in understanding the impact and value of a blog-supported community. The literature on academic blogging and the motivations and experiences of academics using social media to form virtual communities of practice is much smaller. We suggest, therefore, that TSW, may still encourage discussion and reflection on the supervisors' experience, despite the lack of a diverse stories in blog posts themselves.

Commenting – reflective dialogue and developing connections

The third domain of blogging behaviour Deng and Yuen (2011) identify is commenting. Where TSW particularly shines is in how it lends legitimacy to those brief and snatched conversations with colleagues or at training course about supervisory challenges, and it encourages pedagogical experimentation. It has triggered a number of fruitful connections and conversations, providing critical time and space to reflect on supervisory practice. At times, the presence of a specific blog topic has saved workload; for instance, a link to the blog posts on how to manage research students while on maternity leave and experimentation with cohort supervision has been emailed around several times after discussions with colleagues about the challenges they were facing regarding managing their HDR workload or planning for supervision during periods of long leave.

Comments on blog posts are a critical indicator that the reflections shared on TSW have reached and resonated with a real audience, who at least occasionally, offer engaged and empathic feedback. An anonymous blog post in September 2018 about being 'the rescue supervisor' (that is, supervising students who you did not originally agree to supervise who now need a new supervisor due to staff retirement, relocation and, all too often, a breakdown in the relationship with the original supervisor) generated much discussion in the comments. Natasja commented 'I read this and it resonates with me on so many levels. It is as if I wrote it', while Al reminded the blog author and others who find themselves in the unenviable position of being asked to be a 'rescue supervisor' to simply say no: 'in the modern university NO is the most important and kindest word for all the people who matter i.e., postgrads and supervisors'. Naomi agreed with Al, explaining how she has learnt how to say no from Brene Brown, to 'chose discomfort over resentment'.

Miller wrote a blog piece about her experiences as a beginning supervisor (*Supervising your first research thesis student – learning from the 'IKEA feeling'?* August 2018), which she compared to that panicking feeling you get when trying to assemble kit-set furniture. Outlining the three key steps – starting by reading the instructions, accepting it is journey, and remembering there is a team (meaning that you are not the only resource for the student). This resonated with one reader, Stephen, who commented: 'Excellent piece, Evonne! There are a number of things here I've said, but not as well as this, to colleagues beginning to supervise for the first time'. TSW has also connected academics with shared interests, leading to research projects. For example, after connecting on Twitter via a discussion about the use of metaphors in research supervision, Miller has collaborated with a British colleague on a research projects asking Australian and British supervisory dyads to photograph metaphors used in research supervision (Vaughan & Miller, 2017). We are committed to continuing to try and build this community of practice, but how to move the blog forward without an emphasis on community story telling is a huge challenge.

Conclusion

The sustainability and strength of this CoP requires both active leadership and engagement with a tremendous amount of effort, thinking and rigorous planning going into the design, implementation and ongoing maintenance of blogs. In sharing our motivations, reflections and experiences of setting up TSW, we hope to raise awareness about the value and pitfalls of online communities of practice, and issues to consider when designing online communities for academics. TSW is in its infancy as a research blog and is best understand as an emerging CoP. Some of the topics we have blogged about, such as supervising while on maternity leave and being the 'rescue supervisor', are painfully honest reflections about the challenging aspects of supervision, and highlight the value of early, frank conversations between student and supervisor about expectations. Like some of the social work bloggers in Hickson's study, we also are working to engage a broader audience in conversation about best practice and innovation in research supervision.

We are, in Wenger's (1998) terminology, working to draw a greater number of people from the periphery into the core. However, given the fact that Smidt et al. (2018) could not sustain a private blog of four academics beyond nine months, there is no denying that the pressure of academic workloads is a key factor restricting wider participation. TSW remains, however, a valuable source of academic professional development, fostering reflection, connection and a deeper public dialogue about the all too often hidden practice of research supervision. Since we first wrote this chapter, the impact of COVID-19 across the globe (and on academia) has further limited our ability to drive SW forward – meaning it is currently on extended hiatus.

References

Al-Daihani, S.M., Al-Qallaf, J.S. & AlSaheeb, S. A. (2018). Use of social media by social science academics for scholarly communication. *Library Review*, 67(6/7), 412–424. doi:10.1108/GKMC-11-2017-0091

Bolton, G. (2005). *Reflective Practice: Writing and Professional Development*, 2nd edn. London: Sage.

Bolton, G. (2008). 'Writing is a way of saying things I can't say' – therapeutic creative writing: A qualitative study of its value to people with cancer cared for in cancer and palliative healthcare. *Medical Humanities*, 34(1), 40.

Byington, T. (2011). Communities of Practice: Using blogs to increase collaboration. *Intervention in School and Clinic*, 46(5), 280–291.

Carrigan, M. (2016). *Social Media for Academics*. London: Sage.

Cree, V. E. (2012). 'I'd like to call you my mother': Reflections on supervising international PhD students in social work. *Social Work Education*, 31(4), 451–464.

Deng, L. & Yuen, A. (2011). Towards a framework for educational affordances of blogs. *Computers & Education*, 56(2), 441–451.

Donelan, H. (2016). Social media for professional development and networking opportunities in academia. *Journal of Further and Higher Education*, 40(5), 706–729.

Ellison, N.B. & Wu, Y. (2008). Blogging in the classroom: a preliminary exploration of student attitudes and impact on comprehension. *Journal of Educational Multimedia and Hypermedia*, 17(1), 99–122.

Fook, J. & Gardner, F. (2007). *Practicing Critical Reflection: A Resource Handbook*. London: Open University Press.

Gasman, M. (2016). Introduction. In M. Gasman (Ed.), *Academics Going Public: How to Write and Speak Beyond Academe* (p. CXX). New York: Routledge.

Hank, C. (2012). Blogging your academic self: The what, the why and the how long? In D. Neal (ed.), *Social Media for Academics* (pp. 3–19). Oxford: Chandos Publishing.

Hickson, H. (2012). Reflective practice online – Exploring the ways social workers used an online blog for reflection. *Journal of Technology in Human Services*, 30(1), 32–48.

Hill, G. & Vaughan, S. (2018). Conversations about research supervision – Enabling and accrediting a community of practice model for research degree supervisor development, *Innovations in Education and Teaching International*, 55(2), 153–163.

Hockey, J. (1995). Getting too close: A problem and a possible solution in social science PhD supervision. *British Journal of Guidance and Counselling*, 23(2), 199–210.

Jordan, K. & Weller, M. (2018). Academics and social networking sites: Benefits, problems and tensions in professional engagement with online networking. *Journal of Interactive Media in Education*, 1, 1–9.

Kamler, B. & Thomson, P. (2006). *Helping Doctoral Students Write: Pedagogies for Supervision*. London: Routledge.

Kiley, M. (2011). Developments in research supervisor training: Causes and responses. *Studies in Higher Education*, 36(5), 585–599.

Kirkup, G. (2010). Academic blogging: Academic practice and academic identity. *London Review of Education*, 8(1), 75–84.

Lee, A. (2018). How can we develop supervisors for the modern doctorate? *Studies in Higher Education*, 43(5), 878–890.

Lee, A. & Williams, C. (1999). Forged in fire: Narratives of trauma in PhD supervision pedagogy. *Southern Review*, 32(1), 6–26.

Lupton, D. (2014). *Feeling Better Connected: Academics' Use of Social Media*. Canberra: News and Media Research Centre, University of Canberra.

Mewburn, I. & Thomson, P. (2013). Why do academics blog? An analysis of audiences, purposes and challenges. *Studies in Higher Education*, 38(8), 1105–1119.

Mewburn, I. & Thomson, P. (2017). Towards an academic self? Blogging during the doctorate. In D. Lupton, P. Thomson and I. Mewburn (eds), *The Digital Academic: Critical Perspectives on Digital Technologies in Higher Education*. London: Routledge.

Pereira, L., Pereira, I. & Cardozo, I. (2016). Writing to learn from experience: Unguided reflection as meaning making practices for teachers. In G. Ortoleva, M. Betrancourt & S. Billett, (eds), *Writing for Professional Development* (pp. 88–106). Leiden/Boston: Brill.

Ronson, J. (2015). *So You've Been Publicly Shamed*. USA: Riverhead Books.

Sackstein, S. (2015). *Blogging for Educators: Writing for Professional Learning*. USA: Corwin, Sage.

Schön, D. (1983). *The Reflective Practitioner: How Professionals Think in Action*. USA: Basic Books.

Smidt, A., Wheeler, P., Peralta, L. & Bell, A. (2018). Transformative and troublesome: reflective blogging for professional learning about university teaching. *Reflective Practice*, 19(4), 474–489.

Stewart, D. (2018). Crafting an online scholarly identity: Invention and representation. In M. Gasman (ed.), *Academics Going Public: How to Write and Speak beyond Academe* (pp. 71–84). New York: Routledge.

Veletsianos, G. (2013). Open practices and identity: Evidence from researchers and educators' social media participation. *British Journal of Educational Technology*, 44(4), 639–651.

Veletsianos, G. & Kimmons, R. (2012) Networked participatory scholarship: Emergent techno- cultural pressures toward open and digital scholarship in online networks. *Computers & Education*, 58(2), 766–774.

Veletsianos, G. & Kimmons, R. (2013) Scholars and faculty members' lived experiences in online social networks. *The Internet and Higher Education*, 16, 43–50.

van Der Wath, A., Coetzee, I. & Maree, C. (2016). A toolkit to support postgraduate research supervisors in supervisory processes: an integrative literature review. *Gender & Behaviour*, 14(3), 7993–8029.

Vaughan, S. & Miller, E. (2017). Metaphors and images as tools in doctoral supervision. Oral presentation at the UK Society for Research into Higher Education Conference, 6–8 December 2017: Celtic Manor, Newport, South Wales, UK.

Wenger, E. (1998). *Communities of Practice: Learning, Meaning, and Identity*. Cambridge, MA: Cambridge University Press.

Williams, A. & Woodacre, M. (2016). The possibilities and perils of academic social networking sites. *Online Information Review*, 40(2), 282–294.

Wisker, G. (2012). *The Good Supervisor: Supervising Postgraduate and Undergraduate for Doctoral Theses and Dissertations.* (2nd ed). UK: Red Globe Press.

Young, S. & Delves, L. (2009). Expanding to fit the (blog)space: Enhancing social work education through online technologies. Paper presented at the ASCILITE conference: Same places, different spaces. Auckland, New Zealand.

9 Academic identity, the supervisor and online communities of practice

Janet De Wilde and Gabriel Cavalli

In this chapter we explore academic identity and how it may be affected by online communities of practice (OCoP). We discuss the importance of sociocultural interactions in the academic identity development of both supervisors and their doctoral students. We consider this in the pedagogical context of communities of practice (CoP) (Lave & Wenger, 1991; Wenger 2002). We reflect on the influence of moving supervision online, and the implications for creating and joining online communities of practice (OCoPs) (Johnson, 2001; Sharratt & Usoro, 2003). We explore online interactions in OCoPs and how this may influence the identity development and self-efficacy for both the supervisor and doctoral student. We examine the interconnection between the doctoral student's identity development and that of the supervisor. Although online supervision has been growing over time, during the COVID-19 pandemic the use of online advising and supervising became the main way of sociocultural interactions between doctoral students and their supervisors.

Although there have been welcome developments in our shared understanding of supervisory practice (Taylor, 2019), these developments are not necessarily reflected in enhancement of practice on the ground within individual institutions. We note that within universities, due to pressures of research productivity, teaching commitments, and administrative duties and more, there is frequently a lack of creating time and space to reflect on and explore the practice of supervising and, importantly, the impact of supervisory practice being online. We suggest that the move online, as observed during the COVID-19 pandemic, has significant consequence for supervisory relationships, practice, and academic identity growth. We need to invest the time and create the space to discuss the consequences and impact of this move. Kumar, Kumar and Taylor (2020) offer practical advice on how to interact and manage online supervisory relationships. However, here we explore the impact of online communities of practice on the formation of academic identity for both supervisor and student.

Developing supervisory practice is an under-explored and under-discussed area of academic practice. Conversely, the practice of undergraduate (UG) teaching and learning and blended approaches have received an unprecedented amount of attention over the past two decades. Research supervisors

DOI: 10.4324/9780429274749-10

play a critical role in influencing a doctoral student's chances of completing on time, in determining the quality of their final outputs and, most crucially of all, in shaping their experience both as a student and as early career researcher. The importance of good research supervision is, therefore, hard to overstate. Moreover, doctoral students are in frequent contact with undergraduates and post-graduate taught students by taking small group seminars, laboratory demonstrations or input into degree research projects. Hence if the support for supervisors and doctoral students is given due attention the payoff is twofold as it helps develop not only the research culture but also the learning community and the taught student experience more widely.

To better understand supervisory practice, it is important to consider the doctoral phase as this is where a supervisor gains their first impression of what it is to be a supervisor. It is during the doctoral phase where a researcher starts to become independent and it is where academic identity is initially formed. Theories of doctoral student's academic identity development follow sociocultural shaping of identity rather than individual agency (Inouye & McAlpine, 2019). The sociocultural nature of identity development is supported by the fact that doctoral students are introduced as a newcomer into their academic practice through interactions with their supervisors, post-doctoral researchers, and peers (fellow doctoral students). Baker and Lattuca (2010, p. 813) state that 'the social nature of learning is manifested in the sociocultural conceptualization of learning as increasingly skilled participation in the practices of a social group'. This research environment can be considered a community of practice (CoP). Doctoral students grow through relational interactions in this community and they develop their academic identity and a feeling of belonging.

Supervisors create their community of practice, some unconsciously, based on their experiences. A supervisor's identity is strongly linked to the community they have created. The extent to which their community is open to external input may depend on the supervisor's keen sense of academic identity. McAlpine et al. (2014) describe academic identity development as a trajectory through time where academics learn from experience. It is often observed that when a supervisor's identity is threatened by external support for their own doctoral students, they may close off external input as a result. As Knights and Clarke (2014, p. 336) state

> Insecurity is tied intimately to the notion of identity in the sense that the latter is always precarious and uncertain because it is dependent on others' judgements, evaluations and validations of the self and these can never be fully anticipated, let alone controlled.

Further challenges for supervisor's professional identity are also highlighted by Wisker and Robinson (2016, p. 123) 'the balances between responsibility and autonomy; uncomfortable conflicts arising from personality clashes; and the nature of the research work, burnout and lack of time for their own work, all cause supervisor stress'.

During the COVID-19 pandemic most of these communities became online communities of practice (OCoPs). It has been reported that regular contact with others online has helped to keep these OCoP alive (AdvanceHE, 2020). However doctoral students who have not successfully been established into a community of practice, online or in person, may face significant challenges. Insecurity, lack of confidence, or curiosity may result in doctoral students turning to multiple other sources for supervision guidance such as the wealth of social media advice and information shared through a range of platforms. Being online has advantages and disadvantages. The availability of other advice has the potential to create a defence reaction in supervisors. Illeris (2014) presents two defence reactions, one is a defence against the complexity of impulses and influences that we are exposed to, which can become overwhelming, and the other is the identity defence. An identity defence reaction in the supervisor may occur as their academic identity can feel threatened by the wealth of external supervisory input, over which the supervisor has no control. This may be a more common reaction for those supervisors who have not strengthened their own sense of academic identity, whether they are early career supervisors, or not. Additionally, in OCoPs there are many more potential interactions which also come with additional levels of judgement.

The evidence is telling us that the sociocultural aspect of supervisory practice is crucial, and we can extrapolate that this is complexified by online practice. Kumar, Kumar and Taylor (2020) recognise the challenges of communication and the development of research skills with peers. Online, the nature of the sociocultural context has changed, supervisors no longer have the somatic experience of seeing students in the lab or office, there is no 'water fountain' nor 'coffee machine' small talk. There is no physical sensory input into the practice, this affects both the supervisor and doctoral candidate, and their CoP alike. Their mutual practice and identity development is purely through online communication. A supervisor typically works within their defined community of practice which provides shape and meaning to their practice; however, some supervisors allow more porous boundaries to these communities than others. Online supervision and online communities of practice create new challenges where the boundaries have been changed and may not be visible to the supervisor or members of the community. The social world of the internet is different from and more complex than the social world of the physical department. Furthermore, as the supervisor may no longer be setting the boundaries or seeing where the boundaries are, students can grow their own personal OCoP which was not so feasible previously.

The online environment offers many opportunities, one of which is to play with one's identity. Crossouard (2008, p. 63) points out that 'an online environment 'gives people the chance to express multiple and often unexplored aspects of the self, to play with their identity and to try out new ones'. Increasingly, social network users adopt different identities and ways of being on different platforms. For an early career researcher this may be a way to explore academia and its reactions, this can be observed on platforms such as

Twitter, Instagram and Facebook. A downside though may be the early career researcher may lack the expertise to read the stories that are shared online. How do we validate online when the normal frame of reference has been removed or blurred? Furthermore, as Kimmons (2014, p. 97) identifies, 'we need to carefully consider what we are transforming education into by placing it within social networks and question how we are transforming ourselves in the process'.

Additionally, Petrovsky (2015) examined the role of social media in the PhD journey and shared that social media platforms may engage PhD students in promoting and building their identity as a junior researcher. She highlighted that they use it for socialization as 'much of the PhD journey is rather lonely, the most natural use for social media among PhD students is to connect with others'. However, the impact can be that they lose their connectedness with their supervisor, peers and host institution. Gray and Crosta (2019) describe belongingness to be 'the sense of connectedness of an individual experience with their supervisor and peers' and crucially when supervising online there is the potential for this connectedness to be underdeveloped. What is not addressed is the potential impact on the growth of the supervisor's CoP or OCoP, nor do they identify the impact on their supervisor's identity development given that the two, student and supervisor identity growth, are mutually dependent.

Crucially, Bengtsen and Jensen (2015) argue that online supervision 'is a pedagogical phenomenon in its own right'. They discuss how the supervisory context is challenged by the diversity of digital tools and platforms. These environments have significant impact on the supervisory dialogue. To the extent that they termed online supervision as a form of 'torn pedagogy' stating that 'that online tools and platforms destabilise and 'tear' traditional understandings of supervision pedagogy 'apart'. We find that a consequence of disconnection between doctoral students' and supervisors' CoP/OCoPs and of the 'torn pedagogy' is the potential for loss of trust at multiple levels. Sindlinger (2012) states that online supervision can encounter aspects of the online disinhibition effect described by Suler (2004). Suler shows that online disinhibition can manifest as 'Anonymity (you don't know me), Invisibility (you can't see me), Delayed reactions (see you later), Solipsistic Introjection (it's all in my head), and Neutralizing of Status (we're equals)'. In addition to the potential for disinhibition on the part of the student, supervising online means that supervisors often lose first-hand ('first sight') access to students' work. Interaction online is often limited to students reporting on their work, where they can be extensively selective about what is reported and how it is reported. These experiences can undermine the relational nature of supervisory practice and result in lack of mutual trust.

This lack of 'first sight' interaction can be equivalent to supervisors exerting their supervisory practice blindly. In contrast, face-to-face interaction and supervision provides plenty of opportunities for supervisors to exert their research competencies in judging students' work and abilities, often in an informal manner outside of scheduled reporting sessions, such as incidental observation of student work when a supervisor walks through a laboratory or works together with students in a field trip. These instances, while informal, are vital to inform supervisors of the quality of work and abilities of doctoral students in the practices of their research field. In turn, these will strengthen supervisor confidence and trust, not just of students' work, but of themselves in assessing progress and ability from students' reports, verbal and written. In the absence of these validating informal instances, supervisors, especially early career, may struggle to find the balance between adequate support, encouragement, or the need to be critical, and to what degree, of student progress. If a supervisor does not strike a balance in their judgement this may result in loss of student trust in their supervisor, for example, if they are perceived as unfair or harsh, but also overtly lenient.

The Postgraduate Research Experience Survey (Advance HE, 2020) showed that PGR student satisfaction is lowest in aspects of the research culture. For example, some students are quoted stating 'more opportunities to share my knowledge with undergraduate students would be nice, particularly in terms of teaching opportunities' and 'the community of researchers not sufficiently considered for the benefit they can offer each other' while others are calling for 'more of a coherent PhD student community and more interaction with other postgraduate students/courses'. This clearly shows an appetite for belonging in a CoP as part of the doctoral student development. Interestingly, PGR students who live in university accommodation with other students have much higher satisfaction with the research culture in their degrees than students living isolated from other students. Equally, the survey shows that part-time PGR students, who are much more dependent on OCoP for their socialisation and support are much less satisfied than full-time PGR students, who have a more direct access to their supervisor's CoP.

We do not argue here for an avoidance of online supervision, where needed. However, we do strongly argue for avoiding reducing online supervision to merely reporting meetings. Instead, online supervision should be as rich as face-to-face with students and supervisors finding online spaces to work together. Given current technologies, there is no excuse why a supervisor, for example in STEM subjects, cannot follow their students to the laboratory, field trip or similar, albeit remotely and asynchronously if needed. For non-lab-based subjects, supervisors and students can co-create online and other interactive practices that are suitable for their discipline. Working together on result interpretation, decoding, and analysis, is a powerful way of providing rich supervisory instances that will avoid the emergence of 'dissociative anonymity, invisibility, asynchronicity, solipsistic introjection, dissociative imagination, and minimization of authority' (Suler, 2004, p. 321). In other words, supervision should be a lot more about being and doing together (learning by doing), and less about updating on progress, whether online or not.

We propose that a solution to the 'torn pedagogy' of online and distance supervision is that supervisors and students invest in connected pedagogy. By connected pedagogy we mean that they invest in the space to work together. This is space in the diary, space in time, and mental space. Learning is a social experience and investing in creating and maintaining the OCoP is vital by the supervisor(s) and their research team(s). Roumell and Bolinger's (2017) research showed that within the context of distance doctoral advising, faculty felt, although they could meet their managerial duties for supervision, they were unable to build relations for socialisation into the profession. Hence it is necessary to recognise the need for socialisation when creating an OCoP. A community which has a clear identity and that nurtures the doctoral students lessens the need for the doctoral students to seek other communities and to depend on them. We are not advocating that doctoral students should not create their own CoPs, or seek others, but their main source of doctoral supervision should come naturally from their supervisors' OCoP as this is who they have chosen to study with and as such should be their main OCoP.

We need to emphasise 'the practice' element of the OCoP, 'learning by doing' is key. In Refocusing learning on pedagogy in a connected world, Chee (2002, p. 10) reminds us that 'outer-to-inner translation highlights the importance of experiential and socio-cultural dimensions of human learning that have their basis in human activity and behaviour'. Supervisors need to practice with their doctoral students, this should not be forgotten or overlooked in the online environment. Earlier, we advocated observing practice for building trust but sharing practice is also vital for the learning. If the OCoP is supportive, creates the learning experience and builds trust, it creates the environment whereby the students or early career researchers can seek other OCoP with a better understanding and hence ability to judge what other communities are saying.

There is a need to develop supervisors' understanding of the important role of socialisation and communities in the development of good supervisory practice. The importance of socialisation is supported by Billot and King (2017) who found that induction programmes for academics that encourage and educate individuals to take responsibility for their socialisation can enhance positive outcomes. The need for considering socialisation is further supported by the recent concept of the 'Hidden Curriculum' of supervisory practice (Elliot et al., 2020). They identify the key needs for supervisor development as academic, personal, social and psychological. This is supported by Wisker and Robinson (2017), who reported 'Supervisors identified stress and concerns of well-being deriving from interactions with students, related to emotional, professional and intellectual issues, which affected their own sense of identity and well-being in emotional, professional and intellectual terms'. Building communities is central to socialisation. However, the situation is more complex for online supervision and hence there is a case for staff development for supervisors concerning online supervision. This is emphasised by Roumell and Bolliger (2017) who from their research on distance supervision identified that 'faculty felt they had not had sufficient training in supervision and did not have enough institutional support to adequately provide a healthy context for distance doctoral research supervision'.

For this to succeed, supervisors must undergo a paradigm shift on their perceived role as a supervisor, and hence, their identity as supervisors. This implies a recognition of the developing identity of the doctoral student as interconnected but separate from the supervisors, and a point of focus of the supervision. This should not be in detriment to the relevance of the shared research. On the contrary, we would like to argue that when supervisors focus on developing the academic identity of doctoral students, research outcomes are richer and more impactful, than if the supervisor focus is the research itself. This may call for a rethink of supervision evaluation and research student assessment. Emphasis should be placed on recognising doctoral student potential, beyond replicating the supervisor's identity. For this to happen, supervisors should disentangle disciplinary (and interdisciplinary) 'ways of being' and their own expression of this as part of their unique identity. In other words, supervisors must start by recognising that their own ways of expressing what it means to be a competent practitioner in their discipline is not the 'only way' of being in their discipline, to support and enable doctoral students to find their own ways of being competent practitioners.

A struggle emerges for academics to develop strong student-supervisory identity due to conflation between the role of research leader and the role of supervisor. This is especially the case in Science and Engineering, where, more often than in the Humanities and Social Sciences, doctoral students become integral to advancing their supervisors' own fields of research. The vital relevance for academics in becoming successful research leaders for their careers puts pressure on academics to be more invested in the outcome of their doctoral students' research and less so in their doctoral student's development as an independent researcher. This may be particularly pertinent in the case of early career supervisors. It is interesting to note that co-supervision with second supervisors who play a distinctive role in student development is not common. As academia increasingly supports the emergence of academics specialised in education rather than in disciplinary research, there may be a space for these academics to play a student development-focused role in the supervisory teams. There are also researcher development teams based in universities which also contribute to the wider academic development of researchers.

Academic identity is a multifaceted concept, including but not limited to, a sense of belonging, roles and responsibilities, power dynamics, engagement in a community of practice and importantly academic literacy discourse. The influential role of the academic discourse has been shown by Jacobs (2007) that in developing lecturers' understanding of the embeddedness of academic literacies within disciplines, is at the core of expanding the narrow disciplinary identity of lecturers, to incorporate a broader academic identity and associated broader practices. For newcomers into the community of practice, it is not to learn from talk but to learn to talk (Lave & Wenger, 1991, p. 109) in the disciplinary discourse. Hence for online supervision, creating the communities understanding of, and opportunities for, academic discourse and its social practice is crucially important for both the student's and the supervisor's identity development.

Conclusion

Academic researchers develop in communities through shared practice and discourse. Both the student's and the supervisor's identity are challenged and developed through this relational process. The significance of the socio-cultural identity development and its role student-supervisor co-development needs to be recognised and promoted at an institutional level. We suggest that by reconsidering institutional research culture as a social practice will underpin the need for socialisation.

To ensure a connected pedagogy, we strongly advise that supervisors and students practice together and move beyond update, check-in meetings. We also advise that institutions create time and space for the discussion of supervisory practice, in order to develop academics' understanding of the social nature of researcher development as well as the disciplinary nature. Developing awareness of the complex nature of supervision-student relationship and the recognition of communities of practice and the role of the lived trajectory in that community and how a sense of belonging is crucial.

To ensure that supervisors are, at least, aware of these issues playing a role in their supervisory practice, by design or default, we strongly advise institutions to embed a discussion of supervisor-student identity co-development as part of supervisor training. We recommend that this discussion could be framed from an academic literacies and communities of practice perspective, as a starting point to enable supervisors to evolve from a self-centred research leader role into a student-centred supervisor role.

In addition, such training should bring into the open issues of trust during supervision and propose this is discussed openly with students. Finally, institutions should be aware that if supervision is left to individuals as a 'lonely' practice, this will impact negatively on doctoral student experience. We strongly advise institutions and disciplinary societies to foster and promote supervisory OCoPs.

References

Advance HE (2020) Postgraduate research experience survey. Available from www.advance-he.ac.uk/reports-publications-and-resources/postgraduate-research-experience-survey-pres

Baker, V.L., & Lattuca, L.R. (2010). Developmental networks and learning: Toward an interdisciplinary perspective on identity development during doctoral study. *Studies in Higher Education*, 35(7), 807–827.

Bengtsen, S.S., & Jensen, G.S. (2015). Online supervision at the university. Available from https://pure.au.dk/ws/files/90974878/Bengtsen_Jensen_2015_.pdf

Billot, J., & King, V. (2017). The missing measure? Academic identity and the induction process. *Higher Education Research & Development*, 36(3), 612–624.

Chee, Y.S. (2002). Refocusing learning on pedagogy in a connected world. *On the Horizon – The Strategic Planning Resource for Education Professionals*, 10(4), 7–13.

Crossouard, B. (2008). Developing alternative models of doctoral supervision with online formative assessment. *Studies in Continuing Education*, 30(1), 51–67.

Elliot, D.L., Bengtsen, S.S.E., Guccione, K., & Kobayashi, S. (2020). *The Hidden Curriculum in Doctoral Education*. Palgrave Macmillan.

Gray, M.A., & Crosta, L. (2019). New perspectives in online doctoral supervision: A systematic literature review. *Studies in Continuing Education*, 41(2), 173–190.

Illeris, K. (2014). Transformative learning and identity. *Journal of Transformative Education*, 12(2), 148–163.

Inouye, K., & McAlpine, L. (2019). Developing academic identity: A review of the literature on doctoral writing and feedback. *International Journal of Doctoral Studies*, 14, 1–31.

Jacobs, C. (2007). Towards a critical understanding of the teaching of discipline-specific academic literacies: Making the tacit explicit. *Journal of Education*, 41(1), 59–81.

Johnson, C.M. (2001). A survey of current research on online communities of practice. *The Internet and Higher Education*, 4(1), 45–60.

Kimmons, R. (2014). Social networking sites, literacy, and the authentic identity problem. *Tech Trends*, 58, 93–98. Available from https://doi.org/10.1007/s11528-014-0740-y

Knights, D., and Clarke, C.A. (2014). It's a bittersweet symphony, this life: Fragile academic selves and insecure identities at work. *Organization Studies*, 35(3), 335–357.

Kumar, S., Kumar, V., & Taylor, S. (2020). A guide to online supervision. UK Council for Graduate Education. Available from https://supervision.ukcge.ac.uk/cms/wp--content/uploads/A--Guide-- to--Online--Supervision--Kumar--Kumar--Taylor--UK--Council-for--Graduate--Education.pdf

Lave, J., & Wenger, E. (1991). *Situated Learning: Legitimate Peripheral Participation*. Cambridge University Press.

McAlpine, L., Amundsen, C., & Turner, G. (2014). Identity-trajectory: Reframing early career academic experience. *British Educational Research Journal*, 40(6), 952–969.

Petrovsky, D. (2015). The role of social media in the lives of PhD students. *Advances in Nursing Doctoral Education & Research*, 3(1), 5–9.

Roumell, E.A., & Bolliger, D.U. (2017). Experiences of faculty with doctoral student supervision in programs delivered via distance. *The Journal of Continuing Higher Education*, 65(2), 82–93.

Sharratt, M., & Usoro, A. (2003). Understanding knowledge-sharing in online communities of practice. *Electronic Journal on Knowledge Management*, 1(2), 187–196.

Sindlinger, J. (2012). *Doctoral Students' Experience with Using the Reflecting Team Model of Supervision Online*. ProQuest, UMI Dissertation Publishing.

Suler, J. (2004). The psychology of text relationships. In Kraus, R., Zack, J., & Stricker, G. (eds), *Online Counseling. A Handbook for Mental Health Professionals*. London: Elsevier Academic Press.

Taylor, S. (2019). *Good Supervisory Practice Framework*. Available from https://supervision.ukcge.ac.uk/about-rsrp/ (accessed 15/10/2020).

Wenger, E. (2002). *Communities of Practice: Learning, Meanings and Identity*. Cambridge: Cambridge University Press.

Wisker, G., & Robinson, G. (2016). Supervisor wellbeing and identity: Challenges and strategies. *International Journal for Researcher Development*, 7(2), 123–140.

10 Interview with Mel Haines

Julie Sheldon and Victoria Sheppard interviewing Mel Haines

Mel runs *Write That PhD*, on Facebook and Twitter, for research students across the world.

Could you describe Write That PhD, *its offer and the needs it responds to amongst its followers?*

A few years ago I was working at a university and they wanted to start using Facebook and Twitter for research training and development, and so I trialled a few concepts under the university brand to see what benefits social media could provide. I was trying a 'Live' quick Q & A portal for students. The content that I found that stuck the best was in the 'How To' space. I replicated that concept in a personal account which I call *Write That PhD*.

One of the things that I've tried to do with *Write That PhD* is to share resources that in academia we would treat as credible. Most of the time they're peer reviewed articles but sometimes not. I share a lot of book chapters as well. On the odd occasion I do get people saying: 'We don't believe in that'. That happens in academia too, right? We agree to disagree sometimes, and yes, it's an interesting space.

My background is quantitative science but I've been working in the space across disciplines and across faculties for a number of years now. I did my PhD in 2004, and I thought quantitative research and the way that I did my very experimental science was the only way to do research. Then in the jobs I've had since then, qualitative research has been part of my journey – sort of learning along with the students I guess. I share things from both sides of the fence. I think, too, because I have that mixture it does open people up to seeing that there's more than just a tunnel vision sort of approach. Sometimes, yes, a lot of the time, if I share something for science people will, for hard science, people will write back and say: 'We want the equivalent for the soft science. Can you provide something?' So, people do make that differentiation themselves. I think it's important for them to start reading some stuff that's sort of not necessarily meant for them either. You can learn from the different genres, can't you?

DOI: 10.4324/9780429274749-11

How do you see your role in relation to supervisors?

My default position is: 'Check with your supervisor'. That's I think really important for a whole lot of reasons. If the supervisor starts feeling undermined, it's a problem. I think it's really important for the student too, to seek out help from their supervisor in the first instance. I always say to people that contact me: 'Check with your supervisor on this. Check if they like this approach'. Everyone has different ways and different styles and different expectations but at the end of the day, in a supervisor-student relationship, the supervisor has to be the decision maker, along with the student obviously. I don't know whether that helps with that. I'm always very mindful of the supervisor having the final say.

Do supervisors ever appeal to you for any advice?

Yes, on the odd occasion, I do post resources for supervisors. I'm also of the impression that students can benefit from seeing resources that are for supervisors because they get to peek over the fence. I think having insights into what the supervisor's role is and how the supervisor might be seeing it actually helps them to be more understanding as a student because I think there's mystery there in that relationship because of the complexities of it. I think it's always helpful and I always tell supervisors too, to reflect on the other side of the fence. I think if you can have those synergies and you can understand the different view-points, that it actually helps with the relationship.

How much demand is there for writing advice?

Writing is probably the number one issue that people want resources on. A lot of people don't seem to understand until quite late in the PhD exactly what it is they're doing, and what an original contribution to knowledge is, and things like that. In my experience, a lot of fundamentals seem to escape people. Supervisors often say: 'Go off and do a literature review' and the student has no clue what that even means. So, a lot of the stuff that I share is really basic stuff about the literature review is, what its purpose is, how to go about it, the different strategies and that sort of thing.

I think some people come to my site when they're too scared to actually ask their supervisor to define these things because they don't want to look like an idiot.

Are conversations on Facebook different to the conversations that your followers have on Twitter?

Twitter has about 70,000 followers. On Facebook it's about 185,000 followers – but it's a totally different demographic. There are a lot more international followers on Facebook compared to Twitter.

The audiences, and the way they behave, and the comments they leave are quite different. On Twitter there's less commentary and they are least engaged from a comment perspective. On Facebook a lot more sharing happens. The Facebook audience seems to be from countries which are not as affluent or are least fortunate, where resources and books and knowledge is harder to source. Often times I'll share a book chapter and the reason I share it is to give people a taster for the book and, in those regions, you see followers writing to each other: 'Can you get me this for free? Can you share the full text with me? Can you email this?' I don't have that happening on Twitter.

Have you seen any changes in doctoral writing whilst you've been working on the forum?

I guess the big change I've seen is the move away from the big book thesis to PhD by publication. The change in the PhD that's really evident to me out here is it becoming more of an industry-led, solving a problem type of thing, which is more like what the Prof-Doc is. Here in Australia a lot of the PhDs are solving industry driven problems and, yes, you're making a contribution to academia but often also to practice or society or policy all at the same time. The pressure to publish during the PhD so you can get a job as an academic at the end, if that's what you aspire to, is something that's gathering traction.

Once the PhD was just the pathway to academia wasn't it? Now it's the pathway to a lot of different places and careers.

What do you think PhD researchers get out of social media?

We always train our students to try and maximise everything they do – like if you publish a journal article, you want to tweet and Facebook about it for exposure. Convert it into a short piece for the media or a platform like *The Conversation*. We try to teach it as a way to basically slice and dice one single output into many, with the least effort. So, it's all about profile building too. Social media for me has opened up opportunities like this, I guess, and it can be the same for students. If they've got a profile and they publish a paper, it can get seen by people that maybe they would never have a chance to meet or connect with otherwise. So, there's some great benefits about getting reach for low cost. I've had people that have contacted me from all over the world and I've asked presenters, I've seen ... I just recently met a lady called Niamh Brennan from University College in Dublin. You might know her; she's just published two papers open access. One's 100 rules for researchers and one's 100 rules for PhD students. She posted that under the PhD Chat hashtag. I saw it. I wrote to her and said: 'This is really good. Would you like to do a webinar for me?' Then she wrote back and said: 'I'd love to. I'm actually visiting Sydney at the moment. I'm in Australia', and so she's done two webinars for me. We've had over 500 people at both. The papers are open access. She's got heaps of downloads off the back of that. So, it's kind of like sharing the love, and I think the same can happen for students. They can just by chance put something out and something marvellous can happen off the back of it. For the amount of effort, it takes you to just tweet a link – if nothing happens, it's not a big deal but you're giving yourself a chance for something to happen and for someone to pick it up.

What's been the impact of online communities, such as yours, on the development of the doctorate?

I think largely I provide a just-in-time service and people feel like they can dip into the resources that I share at any time. The doctoral journey is an isolating one if you let it be. Some people are doing it from a distance and that sort of thing, so I think the role that I play is sort of a bit of gap filler. Content's there when people want it. I think some people just feel like it's a constant stream of support. If they haven't got anything else, they can just tune into my feeds, either Facebook or Twitter and feel like someone's there and someone's listening. Even though technically maybe they're not. It's just sort of a bit of a lifeline. They can go there and have a bit of a read. This is what some of the students tell me. Even if they're not looking for a particular thing, they can read something, and it makes them feel better. So, I think it's just something that's really publicly available, really visible. It is sort of ... a signal of support and I think that feeling of support is something that a lot of students don't feel. It feeds into this whole mental health, wellness, imposter syndrome, sort of thing. You know none of those resources are mine. I just really act as the aggregator. I search around and find stuff that meets my criteria and I think will be helpful and I post it up. So, really, I'm just the conduit. Some universities support students better than others. Students at universities that are least supported, find that they can get from my social media, what they can't get from their own universities. I think really, it's just support.

How do you know when your service has been successful for your followers?

From the comments, I get quite a few emails and people comment you know on Facebook and Twitter. They leave me comments saying: 'Thanks very much. You're a lifesaver'. A lot of people have sent me the acknowledgement sections out of their thesis, where they have credited me and others often. A lot of people when they submit, they'll write a tweet where they say: 'Thanks to all the '@ handles' that have helped along the way' and things like that. So those are the indicators to me. I've got hundreds of emails where people have PDF'd the acknowledgements page and things like that which is just so cute. Those are sort of the main ways. I look at the metrics too about the reach and engagement and that sort of thing, but it's more the comments and the sending of the acknowledgement sections that are meaningful. For the amount of time it takes me to do a social media post, just one or two of those comments, makes it all worth it for me. If I've helped one person that's a success to me because I know over the years, I've seen people in the depths of despair over certain things. If I've managed to lift someone up that feels like that, that's success to me.

Do you think there's anything that institutions should be doing more to encourage researchers to engage and raise their profiles on social media?

Yes, it's really interesting because there's just so many inconsistencies in the doctoral experience and doctoral journey. And depending on where you are and where you enrol – and you don't know those things when you're naïve and new to the system. I mean even between countries, there are huge variations in the resources provided and in the actual experience. I think there's quite a bit of research happening in this space, isn't there? A lot of universities have things behind a password protected area so you can't see the resources so in some cases you just don't know how much support is there. I'd like to think we could do things better and more efficiently and have an approach where there's a lot more sharing and caring. In a lot of instances universities are all replicating similar resources, they're all spending budgets on doing similar things. If there was a more open access collaborative approach where everyone contributed to something bigger, then it might be more efficient, more consistent for everyone. With universities at the end of the day, it's a competition and money game too, isn't it? There are all of these other factors that sort of come into the equation. I found social media a very good and easy way to get engagement, but I started in the middle of 2015 and I don't know whether the game's changed. I think perhaps a lot people have come into this space and maybe my timing was sort of before the rush. I'm not sure how easy it is to establish communities now so much. I haven't tried to establish any others, so I don't have a comparison. In some ways it does worry me about how people find you because there's so much information in some ways now because of social media. How do you cut down and find the good stuff or the stuff that's relevant to you or stuff that's helpful? So, I think that's sort of a concern on the other side as well.

Are there different demographics between Facebook and Twitter?

I've got a whole mixture. It's a bit different between the two platforms. My following on Twitter is more Australia, UK, America. On Facebook it's the whole world. The age demographic is very variable on Facebook. On Twitter it tends to be sort of the more 24–45 type of age group and predominately females there. It's more 50/50 on Facebook with gender. On Twitter it's more like what I see in real life. In real life I see more women engaging or asking for help per se and engaging in professional development and they seem to be less afraid to say: 'Can you help me, I need help. I want to learn'. That is more like what I see in my day-to-day context, with men being less likely to turn up to things, to come to professional development and engage in materials and I think that's a more cultural thing and something that is a bit of a phenomena across the board too. Other colleagues in higher education have sort of expressed the same sort of trends.

Have you got a sense of how long your audience stays with you?

There are new people coming all the time. Then at the other end of the spectrum, there are people who have finished, who are still following but they're not engaging any more. It's a funny thing with social media. People sort of tend to open accounts and either leave the account dead, but they don't seem to unfollow very much. I think you maybe come for a reason or a season. There are platforms where you can look and see how much, what percentage of your followers are still engaged. There seems to be a percentage of mine that would have graduated and moved on although in saying that, some of the people then become a supervisor themselves and so they're still connected with me and still engaging but their role has flipped. They are now looking at the resources to give to their students. It sort of becomes a bit of a pipeline. The student becomes the supervisor and shares the good resources that they have used, or they stay connected so they can help students and point them towards certain things. In a lot of cases, I've found that universities advertise *Write That PhD* on their link pages and say: 'Follow this Twitter handle'.

Do you have an online persona?

I try to be the resource that I would have liked to have accompanying me on my PhD journey. I think something like *Write That PhD* would have helped me so that's sort of the rationale really.

I think we're all looking for our purpose in some ways. This is really important to me. It's sort of become part of who I am this *Write That PhD* persona and my way of giving back. Even though it's not my name or anything, it's actually become a critical part of who I am, and I post every single day and its really part of my routine. I am doing webinars and things now in my role and people are quite funny because I haven't got any photos of myself on social media. It's just an unbranded thing, and people now say on the webinars: 'Oh Dr Mel from *Write That PhD*'. People say: 'You've been there for me', and you don't even realise that you have been there for them but that's the way that they see it. People do feel like they know me quite personally but it's really *Write That PhD* they know.

Is there an insight that you'd like to share that we haven't covered?

There's so much to say about this whole social media thing. I wonder where it will actually all end up. The one thing I would say about this space is that I do think we can build more of a community around PhDs and I think social media can certainly be a part of that. I mean the big thing with PhDs that possibly doesn't need to be … is this well-being and mental health angle that's really gathering momentum now. I'm hoping we can improve that. A PhD is hard, but it doesn't need to be *that* hard.

11 Interview with Katy Peplin

Julie Sheldon and Victoria Sheppard interviewing Katy Peplin

Katy is a coach who specialises in working with graduate students. She has been running *Thrive PhD* since 2017.

Could you tell us about how the programme works?

Thrive PhD was born out of an understanding that a lot of doctoral students need advice but also needed a community beyond their departments. *Thrive PhD* is the best of both worlds.

The twelve–week programme runs once a quarter, and the students are sorted into groups, sort of, like cabins at summer camp with usually eight or nine people. Every week there is a curriculum and there are discussions that are open for everybody, and a couple of open thread questions on the topic of the week. For example [*at time of interview*] this is week four and it's all about reading, organising your notes but the topics range anywhere from career prep to how to get hold of your schedule to how to use project management skills. It really is the twelve things that I think most PhDs will find the most value in. Alongside of that there is also a daily rhythm set by an accountability post. It is, sort of, modelled after a stand up meeting and Agile project management. Basically it is the same three questions every day which helps habit and routine. The questions are 'What is on your done list?' so, what are the things you have accomplished since you last checked in? 'What things are going well and what things could use support?' And then, 'What is your plan for what's coming next?' The repetition helps students normalise the idea that some days things are going and some things don't so nobody is ever storing up to report on them at the end of the week. It is, sort of, really normalising the ups and downs, that not every day is going to be a day when you turn in a chapter so to speak. I comment on those most days but also the group comment on one another's so they remember when important dates are and they cheer for each other. I see them sending messages all the time to each other like, 'Hey! I know you had this meeting today. How did it go?' or, 'I haven't seen you in a couple of days. How are you doing?' The real magic I think happens when they can see that they aren't the only ones that might be struggling with a particular issue, that they aren't the only ones that have questions about how the PhD works and they aren't the only ones who have

DOI: 10.4324/9780429274749-12

good and bad days. I know that a lot of people, even after they have graduated, have kept in touch.

What has the uptake been like?

Every quarter we get bigger and we, sort of, get bigger at both ends because I allow people to stay in the programme for as long as they need after those twelve weeks so the first twelve weeks is a fixed price and then after that they can remain in the network for a reduced price. We get new people coming in every twelve weeks but we have had better and better retention after every cohort. I think we had like 70 % retention which is amazing and way beyond what I thought it might have done so that is exciting.

What does the Thrive model offer?

I think that I initially draw a lot of people who are reticent to explain what they are struggling with publicly for whatever reason so there are a lot of people who get support at Twitter and that's how I find that majority of my people. They find my Twitter presence and then go from there but because the network is not just closed but, like, extraordinarily closed, so it runs through a separate site and you don't need a Twitter handle to log in and you don't need a Facebook page. You can set your own profile name and can also vary the amount of information so I have a rough idea of where people are but I often don't know their specific degrees and I really also don't know their supervisor's names.

I have one client who uses a pseudonym who has obscured their location and I only know generally that they are in humanities. That person has become more and more open as they have stayed in the network and have dropped more hints but for whatever reason that's the level of privacy they feel they need to have and because of the way it is set up as long as I have a billing email address, which is just a Gmail so address so it doesn't even have an institutional identifier, it works for me.

A lot of the academic Twitter support, for example, starts as disciplinary and then it, kind of, goes out from there but if these are people you met at a conference more than likely they are people you will go up against in the job market and you'll compete for other jobs and so because this is so dispersed I think it really gives people a chance to be more authentic within a network. There is no need to worry about being scooped by somebody or sharing your research normally and some people are more cagey than others about what they are doing but it's all client led.

What motivates your clients to join, do you see that your programme is fixing things that have gone wrong within the grad school or is it more about building on support that they are already getting?

I would say that about a third of the people in the group are people who for whatever reason have great support, great supervisory support but who have had some sort of life or research event that has taken them off track. We have quite a few people who have had significant breaks, who have been on leave and are coming back and looking for, sort of, the support that they don't even necessarily expect their university to have in terms of their life issues.

I would say one third of the people are truly under supervised. They don't have the support. There are one or two extreme cases that come to mind where I had to step in from my professional stand point and say, 'What you are experiencing goes beyond a hapless advisor and into something that I think your university should be involved in and hear. If you would like to talk offline one on one here's your university ombudsman and here are people you can talk to confidentially because I think this goes above and beyond what I would expect even in terms of a negative supervisory relationship'.

Then, a third, I would say, are students that for whatever reason are socially disconnected from their PhD programmes. They are people who are working on field research away from all of their communal support, they are parents or people who are care givers. Sometimes they don't have the flexibility to stay on campus and build that community in place or they are people who for whatever reason are working part time so we have quite a few people who have full time jobs and need this to, sort of, structure their work because they only report to their supervisor once a semester. I would say it is less than I expected in terms of people that I feel like I am actually providing support that a supervisor should.

How do your groups behave and are there any points where you need to modify or police behaviour in the group?

Right. I do. I was a facilitator in a teaching and learning centre for a long time and a lot of that experience came to bear here and so when I set up the community, I do a lot of work in the first couple of weeks to get users on board. So there are extensive terms and the, sort of, spirit of the network and things, and then I do things like the first week I comment my own responses to that first week of 'How's it going?' questions and the accountability groups so that people can see a model. The only time I have ever had to step in and modify behaviour, and I was present in the network, was when there was a person who came in ... how do I put this? They had a strong dose of self-flagellation which isn't uncommon and, sort of, wanes over the weeks. It's always inspiring for me to see people that start in the beginning and say, 'I have accomplished nothing' and by week three they are able to identify five good things they did that day but this person for whatever reason was unable to progress out of the, 'I don't do anything. I don't do anything. I don't do anything' and when one of his group members, sort of, gently refrained and said, 'Instead of focusing on what didn't happen, what are the things you did accomplish this week?' which is almost verbatim of a question I will use to redirect the client. He got really aggressive and said, 'What I do or don't do is a matter for me and not for this network' which isn't true. If he didn't want someone checking in on his accountability then you could not post and so it did require an offline conversation about the role of the group and the role of unpaid supportive group members. I would say that the biggest behaviour I see is that students will drop out. They will have a couple of really good weeks, they will post, feel excited and then something will happen and there will be this pressure to report something worthwhile so they will wait to check in until something has actually happened and then before they know it two or three days have gone by or a week has gone by. So I have an escalating scale, I will tag them in a post in the network if I haven't seen them in a couple of days. You could spend a week or so and I will send them a message offline and say, 'Okay, do you need to check in? Do you need a 30-minute call, just complimentary to talk about what might be happening?' and then I honestly leave them alone because they are adults and they have paid for this service and it's not my job to hunt them down in the way that I might a private client. So what's nice about that is that I do often see people after ten days or two weeks resurface. And there are things all over the network which say you don't have recap what's happened and it can be a fresh start if you need it and so we do have some people who take advantage of that fresh start once or twice a month.

Is the national context ever relevant?

It is relevant all the time. There is a post at the beginning to explain the difference between what a thesis is and what a dissertation is because many people in the U.S. will call a Masters project a thesis and then be confused. Funding requirements in the UK and Australia for example are much stricter. There isn't the possibility of an extra year but in the U.S. it can be much more common. As a coach I often ask very open-ended questions like, 'What would the possibilities be for extending?' especially if I don't know the disciplinary or even country nationality context. What I would say is that for 80% of the skill work, the only time that the curriculum really needs to be national specific is when we talk about job searching but, for example, we have several people who are students working abroad at UK universities for whom Brexit has added an immense amount of stress over the last couple of months. So as a coach it is something I am aware of. I often have to coach people around healthy consumption of news. For some people that means managing their intake of Brexit coverage and for people in the U.S. it also means being aware of what's happening in a way that is conscientious but it's something I am constantly aware of and it is made more difficult by the privacy settings in the network.

What are the most shared issues and problems?

The financial stresses are often shared, the lack of supervisory oversight is often shared and building a schedule and accountability structure that works for you is absolutely shared. I would say that 80% of the skills that we are coaching around are relevant across the board.

Do you think that there is anything that either institutions or supervisors should be doing to provide more support in terms of accountability or peer networking or the kinds of things that people have turned to this programme for?

I am very conscious that what I am providing isn't realistic for a supervisor to provide. It is often not realistic to ask a supervisor to check in every day or even weekly and so it is something that I try to be very clear in my messaging on Facebook, 'You can be empowered to build the support structures that you need'. Supervisors should understand that a student seeking extra support isn't necessarily an indictment of their supervision.

But I do think that supervisors should have an awareness of what level of support are they willing to provide. If they are willing to facilitate let's say a lab meeting once a week to help students be aware of each other's structure and if they aren't willing to do that in person, are they encouraging and offering space for students to self-organise and so offer that for example. But I think that it's incumbent on the supervisor to have a sense of their boundaries and say, 'This is what I am willing to provide. This is what I am not'. Let me put it this way, a lot of supervisors will not respond to a student email seeking feedback on work until they are ready to actually read it, but a student will take those two weeks as, 'I have done something wrong!' Anxiety really starts to spike. The supervisor should email back saying, 'Thank you for this. I expect to have it back to you by "x" date'. It's simple behaviours like that which can really help students adjust to the supervisor's boundaries.

Do you ever get institutions referring researchers?

I get a lot of peer-to-peer referrals and then I actually get a lot of referrals from mental health clinics on campus so I have two or three students say to me, 'I was sent here because I heard about you through a workshop on reducing stress and anxiety' which is completely ... I don't even often know my client's first names much less their institutions and much less if they are seeking mental health support so it's, kind of, always interesting to me that it happens.

What might the relationship between graduate schools and online courses be in the future?

Some services are available for institutional subscription. What I do is a little bit harder to institutionalise but I have started to make webinars and online courses that could be available for institutional subscriptions. I am still growing into that but more often than not I have been taking more and more meetings with career counsellors, with people who are interested in graduate student professional development more broadly and looking to say, 'Okay, as somebody who is in institutional support and is very limited by what I can do in terms of hours a day working, what can I learn from your asynchronous model and what things can we work together to provide in an institutional way?'

How do you measure success for your clients?

I have a variety of different outcomes that look like success. In the past month we have had two people defend, and defend well, which is a textbook example of what success looks like. But I have also had a student this week check in every single week day and they have never done that before and they have been in the network for a year and they checked in every single day so that was a real moment of excitement for me.

In terms of the most natural place to measure success it's when people exit the network and so we have had some people exit the network because they have built local support that is much more specialised and that's what they need after taking the general skills building that I offer. That looks like success to me because it was a person that had a pretty intense financial constraint and now they can remove what even I think is a small fee and build on that in their own lives in a way that causes them less stress so that feels good to me.

12 Interview with Amy Bonsall
Julie Sheldon and Victoria Sheppard interviewing Amy Bonsall

Amy founded the *Women in Academia Support Network* #WIASN on Facebook, which at the time of this interview, had around 11,500 members worldwide.

Can you tell us about the formation of the Network?

There is a dearth of research about women's experiences of becoming an academic and we felt that the *Network* would be a significant and important means of support network. We were quickly aware that a *Network* could offer a supportive space, where what's said in the room stays in the room.

Many of our members tell us, 'I've got this great project, can I include data about the group?' We are clear that the *Network* isn't a data source, although members are welcome to poll the *Network* as long as they're very clear about what they're polling for and which institution they're from, whether it's gone through ethics.

There's no fee to join, and out of 11,000 members, we've got six or seven thousand people who are actively responding to what's going in the group. We do from time to time have members who say, 'I've been a member for two years. This is my first post. I passed my viva. I said thank you in my acknowledgment page to you and you don't know that, I've never posted before, but I wouldn't be here if it wasn't for this network'. Yes, we get quite a lot of those.

You set it up when you were a PhD student in 2017. What drove you to do this?

I was a member for a long time of a PhD Facebook group, which was a wonderfully supportive group. I made brilliant friends there and I don't think I would've got my PhD without it. I made contact with a number of female academics who had young children and who felt quite isolated – not able to go to conferences because they were juggling so many different things. The group was open to men and women but, following an unpleasant altercation with a male member of the group, we found the dynamics were damaged. Whilst I appreciate that a group should be able to debate issues, surely there has to be a lexicon of how we do this. So I set up my own small group of like-

DOI: 10.4324/9780429274749-13

minded members, six people who I'd got on with very well, and now we're the six administrators. We've been joined by 11,000 others. So, I think I was right in thinking that there was a real and desperate need for a space where women could speak.

It is not overtly a feminist space. I hope a by-product of the work we do is equality for women but we're not an advocacy group, we're a network.

How do you moderate conversations in the Network?

By the time we had six or seven thousand members, we started to put together guidelines. Whenever we take an editorial view of a particular issue, we make it clear on the guidelines. The guidelines are now about seven pages long and it's developed a bit like a community of practice, reflecting the agency of the individuals in the group. So, it's a strength and it's a challenge but that's okay – we didn't set it up to be easy.

Have you got a sense of what people are getting from the Network or their common interests?

It's incredibly varied. Sometimes we simply put people in touch with each other for specific interests, say, writing CVs or advice for job interviews or advice for career progression, setting up informal mentorships. We also have writing groups, we offer practical support if somebody, say, needed a computer, another member might volunteer help. For example, there was one occasion when we managed the transportation of a computer from somewhere in Cornwall all the way to Birmingham through members going, 'I'm going down there for a conference, I'll pick it up from you and I'll take it'. And that's been wonderful.

And then we have members who provide support and expertise within their areas. For example, qualified lawyers, employment advice and other things as well.

Do you think there are any lessons for academia to take away from your experience of the Network?

If you have people who are coming from a minority group or a protected group who are telling you there are problems, then you know what, there are problems. You need to listen to that and you need to listen to it openly and try and work to put things in place that actually accept that that is true rather than trying to find justifications for why it might not be.

And that's really hard and I'm not pretending that we get it right all the time because we don't. But we've got resources now that we've collated that hopefully are there to help all of us better understand the challenges faced by BAME sisters in the academy so that they're not expected to do the leg work of giving you information as to why these structural issues exist and what the history behind them is. They're there, you need to go and read them, it's not incumbent upon them to do that work for you. So, that's been really important and to really look hard at your own privileges, where you stand, where you should be supporting, and where you actually are not supporting and you can rile against that as much as you like but you're not supporting.

What, in your view, does the online community give you that the physical one doesn't?

It's the immediacy of suggestions and advice. So, if you've just come out of a supervision meeting that didn't go too well you have a community of people, not directly involved in your experience, but who understand your journey. If you can get support quickly, then it can act as a safety net, I think.

I think it's also the levels of expertise you're able to access. If you need the advice of the vice dean, and somebody's there, you can tag them, and if they're available, they can give you that advice. I don't know where else that would be possible.

Typically how many pieces of advice might you be negotiating if you're posing a question?

I haven't seen many instances where people have had no responses. We have posts that have three, four hundred comments.

Do members have offline interactions?

Very early on we were asked by members if there could be smaller interest groups (mental health, BAME) and we debated having subsets, with arguments for and against. But it's an iterative process and we wanted to respond to our members. There's approaching 100 groups now. The writing group organises monthly writing retreats. Members' meetups take place in Pakistan, in South Africa, for example.

There's the grey space between physical meeting and being in the network as well whereby we have groups that have come together to collaborate on things beyond the forum – book editing for example, and peer reviewing publications.

What has your background in performing arts has brought to this?

As a performing arts professional you have to a) make your own work largely, and b) you've got to be able to network. You get very used to being told 'no', and being told that things aren't possible. Practice-led research can be messy because it's dealing with people and it's dealing with more variables than you could ever conceive of. So, you have to have a strong purpose.

There have been members who took issue with some of the things that we do and I feel able to deal with this. Because we also do so much good. We know it's not perfect and we are not pretending that it's perfect but it's a lot better than what was there before which was essentially nothing.

I've also done a lot of work in Malawi and South Africa and the differences are stark. It was incredibly important that we created a space for women that can get Facebook on their phone.

We ask people to debate robustly because that's very important, but we really try and discourage people being personally unkind to anybody. We really do. And we're not always successful in that, of course.

And there are cultural differences as well in the way people sort of speak to each other. we have members of course working in second languages, third languages. So, we try, often unsuccessfully, I'll be honest, but we do really try to be aware of those issues and to accommodate them and to be kind where we can, but firm.

What does community mean to a postgraduate researcher?

It's important to be aware that it isn't just your research community that has to serve as your community, that there are other communities that can latch onto your identity as a parent scholar or as a scholar who is dealing with disabilities, for example, or whatever parts of your identity are important but are strongly resonating with them at that time. I think the facility to be able to have a community who can understand the very particular challenges of being a postgraduate researcher, especially the older you get too, as life gets, becomes very, very complicated.

And trying to find a place that can facilitate giving you the support that you need and actually it's important to recognise that your needs change from being a scholar at the beginning of your PhD journey, even offering support, we do allow, for the network, sorry, we do allow MA students who are applying for PhD to come into the network because actually for various reasons, it's very hard to get help to do that, even to fill out the application form and to know, well how do I get a supervisor, how do I get funding for this? Lots of people, particularly women, are shut out of being able to find out even how you go about that process. And so, it's finding what community can meet your needs at that time that I think is really important.

A lot of PhD students are particularly active on Twitter but that's a very different kind of interaction.

Well our Twitter account is public and is very different in terms of the traffic and everything else in terms of what, as to what goes in, in the actual forum. And I think, yes, it's, I don't know, this is an unscientific statement so don't quote me on this necessarily but one thing that we have found is that overwhelmingly members are totally disillusioned and frustrated with the great glass ceilings, all that sort of stuff. Not to say there's not some work, good work going on, I don't know, but there is an awful lot of deep frustration at the problematisation of women because you do not need to tell me what I need to do better, it's the system that needs to do things better, not me. And why are you telling me how to be successful at an interview when you're not doing the same for that interviewer. There's absolutely no point.

2020 Postscript

The *Network* has proved to be really important to many members during the pandemic. Membership has continued to grow and we have now set up a committee, made up of volunteer members, who will be in charge of selecting moderators for the group. We have come to realise that for a network to be successful, it needs to retain its agility and its ability to change and develop. Being able to do this, while at the same time offering tangible support to members, is where we see the future of WIASN.

13 Interview with Pat Thomson and Anuja Cabraal

Victoria Sheppard interviewing Pat Thomson and Anuja Cabraal

Pat and Anuja run the @PhD-VirtualNotViral Twitter account, host weekly tweet chats and created a website of resources for doctoral researchers working during the pandemic.

Shortly before this interview, Anuja and Pat explained the story behind VirtualNotViral in their tweet chat, which is extracted from here:

AC: When the pandemic came, I knew there was going to be research disruption, especially for those in labs and those doing in-person data collection. I was thinking of how I could help people based on my skill set when Pat Thomson posted on Pandemics and PhDs.

I decided to write a post about what researchers could do instead of in-person data collection. I DMed Pat and asked if she'd take a look at it. She agreed. Within a day I posted this. This was the first time we'd ever directly communicated. I still wanted to do more. Pat and I decided to host a tweet chat. The rest all happened very quickly. We agreed on an account name, a hashtag and within four days VirtualNotViral was born and had over 1000 followers in 24 hours.

Interestingly, Pat and I had still never spoken! This is how the account came about. We made the website because we wanted to capture the resources that people would find useful, and this seemed the easiest way.

PT: I think we are an interesting example of how Twitter can act as academic speed dating – find people you like and can work with and get the work going. I've made lots of really helpful connections via social media but Twitter in particular. There's an old response to something I once said on Twitter which keeps coming back to haunt me – it's about Twitter not being a place for anything positive. I think there are lots of people who are doing constructive things on social media, including #VirtualNotViral. There's probably something to be learnt about collaboration from this.

From 'Taking Stock' #VirtualnotViral tweet chat, 15 June 2020, archived at: https://twitter.com/i/events/1272763777398616065
Also see Patter blog post https://patthomson.net/2020/08/17/running-a-tweetchat/

DOI: 10.4324/9780429274749-14

Interview

Could you tell us about your followers on the #VirtualNotViral tweet chats? Have you brought followers over from your own blogs and personal Twitter accounts or is this a different audience?

AC: I don't see a lot of my regular followers on the tweet chat. So for me it's a different audience on *VirtualNotViral*. I actually had a lot of UK followers for some reason, not as many Australian followers although I do have a lot in my immediate network that are Australian but I haven't seen a lot of that crossover onto *VirtualNotViral*.

PT: Yeah, I think the time zone's a problem [*tweet chats run every Monday at 9am BST and 6pm* AEST] and certainly when we had Raul Pachego-Vega from Mexico [as a guest] we had to try and find a time that he could do which was in between both our times, but that ended up being really early morning for him. So I think time is tricky for us, there's nine hours difference between the two places. I think both 9am and 6pm can be problematic in their locations and actually we were just discussing it this morning, any time is going to be problematic.

In relation to the followers I guess I had quite a lot of followers on Twitter anyway, and they've obviously not all followed me across because you know, we've got 4000 on *VirtualNotViral*, as of a few moments ago and I've got about 19,000 on Twitter myself, but I can certainly recognise some of the people who are involved. But I think we have also picked up some new followers too. I know that we have followers in Canada, South Africa, India and yesterday we saw somebody in Ghana retweeting.

Twitter followers are always a kind of a mystery really, in terms of how it happens. Some of our friends have been extremely helpful. So the ANU and La Trobe researcher development people – *The Thesis Whisperer* and *The Research Whisperer* – have been supportive. We had Deborah Lupton on for our first tweet chat and she did some promotion. She still retweets things. Raul Pachego-Vega's obviously got a very big following and I think some of his people may have come across it as well. With these things, it's always the mysteries of networking, how you tap into different people's networks and I think we probably have done that. *VirtualNotViral* is kind of at an intersection and my guess is we've mainly got PhD-ers, some graduate school and researcher development people, (some of those are quite supportive as well, in both Australia and the UK). There's some pretty solid retweeting going on from grad schools. And there will be a few other people around the place who are interested in our area, I guess they might research in that space.

How active are your followers in shaping the content?

PT: We started out with a general chat which asked, where is everybody at? And how are people feeling? and from that we got some clues about what people might be interested in [*early tweet chat topics included: online vivas, well-being, working from home, ethical issues of research during the pandemic, finding a job post-pandemic*].

Then last week we did another 'taking stock' tweet chat where we got a set of topics that people are interested in which we are now in the process of finding people to be guests for. So I think we try to be responsive. We get the occasional DM from people or the occasional how about this, but mostly we have to curate. I'll let Anuja talk about the resources because she actually deals with those, she spends hours doing Twitter moments.

AC: Yeah, it's interesting that the way we run *VirtualNotViral* has shifted in the months since it started. So initially, in the first couple of weeks, Pat and I were both tweeting and retweeting a lot, especially the resources that we felt would be useful. Things like working from home now, the stress about being in a pandemic, research has changed, what does it look like?

So at the start we were sourcing all those resources and retweeting a lot. But over the months and over the weeks, the focus has mainly been around the tweet chats and sharing resources that way.

Just a note on how we find people: the people that we get to run a tweet chat are really people who know what they're talking about, who either research the area or have a lot of experience in the area. So it's not just anyone, and this is something that I learned from Pat. We are providing something for students to really support them. It's great to have guests who knows what they're talking about to help with those chats.

But to go back to the resources. We collate all tweet chats every week in what's called a Twitter Moment. We like it because it then stays on Twitter. The Twitter Moments can take up to two to three hours sometimes to curate. So we've got every single tweet chat in our Twitter Moments on Twitter and on the website as well. Then we will try and share and retweet resources over the week as well. We've also got the website that Pat really deals with, and that has a bunch of resources in there too.

Is all of the VirtualNotViral work done by yourselves in your free time? Do you have any support e.g., from your institutions?

AC: I'm mainly independent, and don't belong to an institution as such so this is all done in my free time. This is all volunteer.

PT: I don't get any time for this from my institution at all, none of this is ever counted in my workload. But you know, interestingly for me as the institution went online, lots of people within the institution started referring to it. So you know, our school and our grad school are continually referring people to the tweet chats. I think a lot of people who spend a lot of time doing this kind of social media work do it on top of their usual work. Unless you've actually got it written in your job description, and you know you're specifically employed to manage social media, then it does just tend to be a bit of an add-on, really.

There's always a kind of dilemma for me about should I be spending this time on just working with the doctoral researchers within my school, within my faculty, within the University that I belong to? Or should I do it more generally? I guess I took a decision a long time ago that I was going to work more generally and not within the institution per se. And it's not that I don't do some things within the closed environment because I do. But with the blog and with *VirtualNotViral*, I think at least in part, I'm concerned for people whose universities don't provide that much.

So where do you think these resources sit in relation to supervisor support and/ or institutional support? Do you think do you think they are offering something that institutions haven't been able or quick enough to provide?

AC: I think Pat and I will have a different opinion on this one. Only because I don't sit within an institution, and I also think that people within institutions were probably going through their own challenges.

I think institutions have provided a lot of these things face-to-face stuff with writing workshops and support staff. But students don't always attend that kind of thing either. So I think being in the middle of a pandemic people were just drawn online. And *VirtualNotViral* came out so organically, so I don't know how much students turned to the institution at the time, even if the institutions had provided, I don't know whether students would have gone there.

PT: I think institutions are really variable about what they do, and you can certainly see that in the UK context. I think some of the Australian universities are actually miles better than most of the grad schools in the UK, which seem to be quite slow and cumbersome, and have a lot of institutional rules. Even the institutional blogs tend to be a bit corporate. When I started blogging (and actually I started about nine years ago) at the time our registrar had his own blog, 'Registrarism', and he's moved over to Wonkhe now, but he still maintains his own blog. So it's always been very helpful for me when people say why don't you blog on the University platform, to say, well, you know the registrar doesn't, so you know this is clearly a precedent here that I'm following. And our University does have a couple of very successful social media, it runs a couple of very big YouTube channels particularly coming out of chemistry, so the Periodic Videos. And I mean absolutely enormous in social media with millions of followers. But it's been much less successful in the rest of social media, like a lot of universities, and I think it's because they actually don't understand speed. They don't understand that the importance of social media is actually its quickness, and the capacity to develop a hashtag and if it doesn't work, you leave it, you dump it, if it gets appropriated, you go on and do something else. It's a kind of fleet footed media, I think that's not really what a lot of institutions do unless they've got a bunch of very savvy staff who know how to do it and stay sufficiently within corporate guidelines that they don't get themselves into trouble. I think a lot of people in University Marketing still see social media much in the same way that they see print media.

AC: The other thing to note is that there are two universities here that I think have used social media well, and we've shared some of their resources: La Trobe Uni and ANU where *The Thesis Whisperer* and (one half) of *The Research Whisperer* sit. They've been really great at running virtual write sessions, promoting them online and sharing them on social media. The La Trobe University researcher blog has been posting weekly, if not more frequently, and getting students and researchers to write about their experience and share that online. So it's been very organic, not very corporate at all, but they've been really agile in the social media space too, developing hashtags like La Trobe working from home (#LTUWFH), even Deakin University developed a hashtag so that researchers could start connecting. So there's been some interesting things, but apart from ANU and La Trobe, I don't know if it came from the University itself, I think it was just researchers launching it.

PT: It's their researcher development team, if they've got savvy people. So you can see that here in the UK too. You can see Glasgow's been quite quick off the mark for instance, and doing lots of interesting things. LSE's just kept doing what LSE does, which is considerable and important, and ground breaking, but they're not fleet footed. The structure they set up is slower than that. I'm interested in this topic. I'm actually interested theoretically in how you think about this sort of flexibility and quickness. I guess it's partly the capacity of the researcher developers to be able to read a mood. So it's being, I suppose Bourdieu would call it something like a fish in water; it's people who are in the social media environment who can very quickly see how to actually move with it and get things to happen.

I think that it is that kind of immersion factor, which I suppose a long time ago somebody tried to sum up hopelessly as digital natives and immigrants, but I think that kind of notion of immersion and that intuitive embodied understanding that you get about 'this is how the medium works'. Without necessarily even being able to consciously articulate everything that's going on, but understanding how you move in it, in the same way you know how to move on the tennis court or cricket pitch or whatever, if you've really been doing social media for a long time, then I think that's partly what's involved in being able to set things up quickly.

So do you think it's easier to do that in a small group, with a couple of people, or even individually, rather than in a large organisation?

PT: Absolutely, and I think we've seen a lot of examples of that, such as Zoe Ayres who's doing stuff around mental health, producing downloadable posters that people are using. There are people doing online writing retreats. So you can see there are people who've got something to offer which is a fit for what people are interested in and they also know how to set it up and make it work.

AC: I think that's one of the reasons *VirtualNotViral* came about is that Pat is very agile and she knows social media and, you know, she's a doer. So when we had that little email exchange, we were messaging back some ideas for hashtags that we could use, we settled on *VirtualNotViral* and Pat said great, I'll set up a *VirtualNotViral* account and so we had the idea, we both liked the idea and Pat just took it and ran with it and did it. Whereas if you sit there and you've got to answer a whole bunch of questions back and forth: is it a good idea? Are you sure it's a good idea? When are we going to do it? When are we going to launch it? Should we do it today? Should we do it tomorrow? No. So within three or four days of the first time I had ever contacted Pat Thomson, we had a Twitter account and I think that one of the reasons it came about is because of that agility that Pat's talking about.

Has your experience of running VirtualNotViral changed or confirmed your understanding of social media and its affordances?

PT: I still think it's pretty feral, isn't it? I still think that. But I think it is possible to create kind of expanding bubbles, and I guess that's what we've tried to do. I mean, we've scrupulously avoided getting into spats with people. We somehow managed to set some unwritten norms that this is about support that people can get. When we had Narelle [*Lemon*] doing well-being, we encouraged people to go offline if they didn't want to be identified and to DM with us. And so we're pretty conscious of not having topics where people are going to be vulnerable or exposed. So for example, we haven't really done a lot about Black Lives Matter. We save that for our personal accounts. And I have to say I manage my personal account pretty well, just as carefully because I'm just not interested in getting into – I just don't think Twitter is a medium to have those kind of debates. I would find it too stressful and I think, you know, if it's feral, there are also a lot of people out there that actually don't know how to behave, and they obviously do things on social media they'd never actually do face to face or in real life. And that's obviously one of the problems. And, I guess if that started to happen, I think we would move, change, shut down, do something. I think we were both pretty aware of that potential, and so we would shut down any gas lighting, let alone the kind of rudeness, the nasty stuff that goes on – I don't think it's (VNV) changed my view about that.

I guess I've been a little bit surprised at how quickly it did actually manage to establish itself, and as Anuja said, the Twitter chats now seem to be the backbone of it. Initially I think it was the resources and the website that people were looking at and I think people are still doing that a bit, but I think VNV is this kind of place where there's quite a focused discussion. I used to be involved in #AcWri which was an academic writing chat and I know that Helen Kara, for example, still does a creative methods chat once a month, but Twitter chats seem to have died down a bit and I think resurrecting it has actually been a kind of a bonus. In a sense, we were lucky in that it had died down and we were able to come up with an old form we knew that we could use.

And also the weekly format is quite unusual in the sector. Often tweet chats seem to be monthly or every couple of months, so maybe some of its dynamism comes from how often the chats run?

PT: Yeah, I think that is partly it. My hunch is there's a kind of energy about it. You know we're kind of on to stuff, and it's moving....

AC: And it's high engagement. A few people have tweeted to say they look forward to it every Monday morning. It's a great way to start the week, but I think it also links back to a previous point about what social media or Twitter is and yeah it can be quite feral. But Pat and I are both quite conscious of maintaining positive Twitter feeds and tweeting positively. It's a space where people come and for an hour, you're on social media, you're engaging with other people. But it's a focused conversation, it's on a topic that relates to work or research and it's positive and its engaging. There is an energy to it. And it's actually fun. It's very live and it's very dynamic. So kind of fun in that way too.

PT: And. I think the other thing that I found interesting is that we've evolved this process. Anuja and I get onto WhatsApp about 15–20 minutes before the tweet chat goes on. We've now got to the point where we know there are roles that either of us have in terms of curating and we swap those about. So there's an introduction, there's a set of questions that we start with, which we've communicated to the person or people who are on beforehand, so they've done some pre-prepared answers so we can get that first bit of it actually happening with some kind of momentum. We ask people, one person will manage the intro and the other person will manage a kind of Hello, who's out there and then be checking on the kind of acknowledging people. And if there's a lot, Anuja and I will be online saying, oh, there's this person or what about that? I'll do this one, you do that one. I think the volume of it would actually be quite hard for one person to manage – it actually takes both of us an hour of quite concentrated attention to keep track of everybody, because I guess we're wanting everybody who comes on and makes a contribution to feel acknowledged and to be acknowledged and responded to, even if it's just a kind of hello I'm so and so. We want to take the heat off the person who's the guest and allow them just to focus on their topic, and so sometimes we actually number the questions for people because they find that more help. Sometimes it's just a kind of open chat, depending how people feel, but I think the guests are variously used to this kind of medium. But for us, it does take quite a bit of management during that hour and we are constantly to-ing and fro-ing about you know who is going to do what. And sometimes we have to DM the guest person with a kind of – can we tweet this back to them to see if they notice it this time, if something's been left dangling for a while? There's a kind of very active, fast production value in this, and I said a while ago to Anuja that I think it's like Talkback radio. I mean, I've got a background in radio. It does feel to me a lot like radio, the way that it's working at the moment is that kind of active, very active sort of studio engagement where there's a lot of ad libbing and a lot of improvisation that goes on in that hour to keep it on track, keep it moving, you know. It's not at all uncommon for Anuja to say to me, you know oh there's nothing happening right now…. If we've prepared something we'll put a few things in now to kind of keep things happening, so we're kind of reading the rhythm of those tweet chats all the time.

AC: And we get hundreds of tweets in that hour, we get hundreds, so four to five tweets every minute are going out for our tweet chats.

PT: So I think it's kind of an evolved tweet chat. I don't think it's like the old tweet chats used to be. I think it's just much more intense actually and busy. I think that also gives that kind of impression of energy as well.

Do you have a sense of where it is going to go next? Are you going to carry on doing weekly tweet chats?

AC: We revisit this conversation every now and then and I think we are going to let it be a bit organic. We don't have anything set in stone. We've toyed with different ideas, but we are still going with the weekly for now.

PT: I mean, I guess being in the UK for this, we are obviously behind Australia in terms of lockdown. And you can see that a lot of doctoral support is still going to be online, probably until Christmas. I'm conscious that Anuja's working in a different lockdown environment (but then this changed). Although, it's really hard to predict and I guess it'll be a bit of a hole, probably for both of us, when we stop it and I'm not quite sure how we would go about that, but obviously we will have to at some point.

Is there an insight you would like to share that we've not yet covered?

PT: Just maybe to stress that you often hear people say that you have to do face to face in order to have a working relationship with people, and I think VNV demonstrates that's absolutely not true. But I think like any kind of collaboration, it does rely on trust, give and take, respect for each other's knowledge and capacity, and preparedness to say what's on your mind, and all those things actually make a collaboration work. There is something about a commitment to working in a particular kind of way that makes this and other similar kinds of things work, whether they're face to face or online. There are people that you can work with and others that you can't.

AC: It strikes me that we started this collaboration with someone new, in the middle of a pandemic, I don't know how, but there is a lot of trust, flexibility, understanding in this and there's just something about the energy and dynamic between Pat and I that does make it work and Pat's absolutely right – I don't think it could work for everyone, but it just has worked and all through Twitter.

The other point that I would like to make is that if you have an idea, you can jump on it. I mean this *VirtualNotViral* came out because of an idea and then we just jumped on it so you know things are possible. That's one thing about social media, it can make positive things possible too. But it's been interesting. Great, actually.

Afterword

Julie Sheldon

When I first started supervising in the mid-1990s, research students used to ask, 'Is there a book I can read on how to do a PhD'? Even though my answer was invariably 'no' they would pitch up with the 'how to' books they were compelled to buy and I would have to stay on my toes as they tested my view on any divergent advice. *Plus ça change* – doctoral researchers continue to solicit extra-supervisory advice about the mechanics of crafting a PhD. Whilst I used to be familiar with the clutch of the 'how to write a thesis' books and could adjudicate accordingly, I cannot possibly know the individual merits of the legions of online bloggers, vloggers and curators of content that provide advice and information to doctoral researchers.

I came to this topic as a bit of a sceptic. Googling offers of PhD support yields millions of results and I was concerned that this cacophony of online voices might overwhelm research students. And, if I am truthful, I was threatened by the presence of what I considered an unstable proxy for authorised supervision and support.

My view has shifted.

In the intervening years the principles of Open Access have naturalised the dissemination of research online. The maintenance of research networks through Facebook, LinkedIn and other groups is commonplace. The formation of a research persona in and through Twitter and Facebook is perfectly acceptable, as is talking about what you do across platforms and audiences. Indeed, research has been reinvigorated by blogs and micro-blogs that allow researchers to post items, develop ideas and then issue neat capsule summaries of research.

This appetite for digital platforms is indivisible from the changing contours of researcher development in the last two decades. As a supervisor hailing from the pre-Roberts era (this refers to an influential report in the UK in 2002 that heralded a sea change in the provision of skills and career support for research students) I inherited an unreconstructed view of 'support'. Support was restricted in my thinking as something tangible (equivalent to the manuals on how to craft a thesis) and it took the appointment of dedicated researcher development personnel, and the wisdom embodied by my co-editor Victoria Sheppard, for me to accommodate concepts such as 'resilience', 'personal effectiveness' or 'engaging research'.

DOI: 10.4324/9780429274749-15

These days I have strategic and operational responsibility for the doctoral researcher experience at my institution. One of my responsibilities is to harmonise services to ensure that the academic and social interests of postgraduate research students are appropriately provided for. Those services have been overwhelmingly virtual since the pandemic, and will continue to be so for the short to medium-term.

The articulation of research in and through social media is predicated on a level of access and technical proficiency that, as we see in this volume, might not be universal. Doctoral researchers' knowledge of the technology of online interaction generally outstrips their supervisors', yet many are insecure about inhabiting social media platforms as researchers. So, how might supervisors help them? And what role does the institution play?

First, doctoral researchers need time to hone their academic online persona. At the most basic they might be guided in their use social media for academic networking, for example, advice on how to create a professional online presence and how to build external connections. Some supervisors are role models with a thriving online presence, but many of us are not exemplars and, if that is the case, we may at least be able to point to examples of good practice within our fields. Most institutions have a social media policy, and guidance on social media etiquette should be shared early in a candidate's registration – better still made a part of induction events.

Within subject areas we might curate (filter and group) a small set of reliable sites related to the doctoral process in general (writing advice, stress management, connecting common situations such as for part-time researchers).

Finally, and as resoundingly acknowledged in this volume, participation in online networks is driven by researchers' desire to be part of a peer community rather than a sign of deficient supervision. Many of us have attempted to compensate for the lack of impromptu interactions during the pandemic with departmental or institutional virtual mixer events. However well intentioned, virtual networking events often feel artificial and fail to kindle a shared sense of purpose. What seems to have worked better has been research-focused activities that also, and without over-planning, double up as mixer events. We have seen an uptake of interest in writing groups, with doctoral researchers electing to stay on after the allotted time to chat with others in the group. There is a balance to be struck between engineering communities from the top and subcontracting activity to students and hoping for the best. Virtual community-building, if it is to be successful, should be researcher-led and organic. But it might also require a little behind-the-scenes management. Ultimately, community-building has to be enabled synergistically.

To sum up, researchers gain most confidence and take ownership of their research when they are informed about their peers and discover connections within their environment and situation. The contributions to this volume converge in this simple message: online support and advice has the capacity to foster a sense of belonging, build rapport and prepare doctoral researchers to demonstrate their expertise in a variety of contexts.

Index

Note: locators in *italics* and **bold** refers to figures and tables respectively.

abundance 13–14; knowledge 9–13; scarcity and 13–14; of social media 17
academia 9, 110; contribution to 135; hierarchical nature of 20; and reactions 126–127; status hierarchies 9; to supervise research students 111 *see also* academics
academic blogging 118; about research supervision 116; gift economy of 106
academics 10, 16, 111–113; blog/bloggers, motivations of 15, 114, 118; community 51, 55, 57–58, 83; conferences 14; cyberdistrict 53; degree to 113; discourse 130; emerges for 130; future generation of 58; identity 124–130; institutes, intimidation in 57; marginality, intersections of 10; online communities for 83; practitioners 4; professional networking for 101; Queen Mary University of London (QMUL) 84; reputational economy 17; sense of 85; with shared interests 120; staff 87; structures 17–18; supervision in 4; tribe 28; in United Kingdom 113; working practices 1
academic writing 102; books on 102; online discussions of 102; practices 102
accountability 54, 75, 140, 142–144; for networks 75
accreditation 98, 111
affiliation 3, 10, 38, 49
Agile project management 140
Altmetrics, use of 2
authorised knower 4, 118
autoethnography 11–13
autonomy 125
Aznar, S. 54

balancing act in practice 112
BCU *see* Birmingham City University (BCU)
behaviour 24, 28–31, 43, 46, 57, 74; and relationships 105; on social media platforms 57
Bengtsen, S.S. 127
Bennett, E. 24
Bennett, L. 3, 46
bewilderment 23
Birmingham City University (BCU) 97–98
Black Lives Matter 156
Blackmore, C. 3
blended learning 1, 83–84
blog/blogging 1–3, 8, 12–13, 23, 39, 96, 103, 114–115; behaviour, domain of 116; controversial post 113; online spaces of 95; posts, comments on 119–120; posts on supervision 116; relational impact of 16; use of 25 *see also* Twitter
blogsites 96–97, 106
Boas, tradition of 12
Bolliger, D.U. 129
Bonsall, A. 146–150
Borzillo, S. 54–55
Brennan, N. 135
Brexit coverage 143
Brooks, C.F. 86
Brown, J.S. 86
bullying 57–59, 113

Cabraal, A. 5, 151–159
Canada Research Chair 16
career scholars 10–11, 15
Carter, S. 28

Index 163

casual contracts, variety of 12
choice 57
choral commentary 2–3, 17
Clarke, C.A. 125
collective knowledge 51
collective virtual space 60
commenting 77–78, 91, 102, 119–120
communication: personal mode of 105; processes 56; styles 110; system 2
communities of interest 70
communities of practice (CoP) 54–56, 110, 120; definition of 89–90, 114; framework of 114; pedagogical context of 124; of research degree supervisors 99; sustainability and strength of 120; virtual/online 114, 118
community structures, language of 52
computer-based self-help programmes 69
confusion 23, 76
connectedness, cyber-embodiment of 59–61
connection–cultivation–integration (CCI) 58–59
consumer markets 69
CoP *see* communities of practice (CoP)
Cornwall, J. 147
counter-spaces 58
Creative Commons CC-BY license 18
Cree, V. E. 112
cross-disciplinary peer group approach 76
Crossouard, B. 126
Crosta, L. 127
curriculum design 90
cyber communication network 52
cyber community 52, 60
cyberstreet 3, 52–54, 57
cyber-terrorism 57

data surveillance 8
democracy disruption 8
Deng, L. 116, 119
Denicolo, P. 50–51
developing connections 119–120
Devine, K. 57–58
digital academia 6, 38
digital communications 14
digital education 13
digital engagement 15
digital identity: within discipline community 31–33; managing 34
digital knowledge, artifacts 9
digital learning 83–84
digital literacies scholarship 9
digital microcelebrity 10
digital photography, accessibility of 76

digital platforms 6, 160
digital practice 9, 14, 16, 35, 44
digital savoir faire (savvy), 38
digital scholarship 1, 5, 10, 16
digital technology 69–70
Disabled and Ill Researchers' Network 72, 74
discipline community 28–29, 31–33
discourse: aspects of 100; registers of 100
discrimination 56
dissertation 8–9; autoethnography 11–13; networked participatory scholarship 14–17; process 11–12; proposals 14, 17; scarcity and abundance 13–14; scholarship for knowledge abundance 9–11; social media scaling 17–20; tradition 17–18
distance learning module 90
doctoral community 25, 55, 62, 104
doctoral experience 38, 54–55, 76, 137
doctoral learning process 54, 68–69, 75
doctoral research/researchers 8, 23–25, 27, 29–30, 38, 45, 66–68, 70, 75, 79, 95, 97, 98, 135, 140, 146–147; academic identity of 130; anxiety in 102; Chat hashtag 135; choosing not to engage 26–27; choosing whether to blog 27–28; conservative attitude of 27; engaging with 25–26; identity of 105; investigations of 2; learning 28; mimicry 28–29; oscillation 30–34; practice, online communities for 84; pressure on 103; programmes 142; program, structures 8–9; supervision, source of , 112, 129; supervisors of 4; stuckness 29–30; voices 24–25; website of resources for 151; well-being of 3
doctoral self-reflection 78–79
doctoral writing 135
dual identities 23, 32
Duguid, P. 86
dyadic relationship 5, 118

Eckert, P. 85
education/educational 38; development programme 87; discourse 99; technology 13
emotional labour 101, 105
Emotionally Demanding Research Network 71, 73–74
emotional reassurance 102
energy, impression of 158–159
engagement, modes of 45
English language 53

ethnography 10, 12, 18
explorations of doctoral researchers 38
extreme disciplinary power 118
Eye, G. G. 9

Facebook 1, 8, 10, 47, 97, 126–127, 133, 136–138, 144, 149; audience 135; community page 117; conversations on 134–135; first decade of 8; groups and apps 101 *see also* social media
face-to-face workshops 76, 79, 111
financial constraint 145
financial stress 143–144
'flipped classroom' model 1–2
'fly-in faculty' nature 87
Folley, S. 3, 24, 46
Fontainha, E. 86
Fook, J. 114
Friedman, T. 11

Gannon-Leary, P. 86
Gardner, F. 114
gift economy 6, 106
Gogia, L. 19
good partnership 72
Good Supervisory Practice Framework 97
Google+ community 71–72
Gouseti, A. 44
graduate schools 144–145, 152
Gray, M.A. 127
Gruzd, A. 52
Guccione, K. 3

Haines, M. 4, 133–139
Hank, C. 118
hashtags 18, 24, 44, 46, 95, 97, 100–101, 154–155; #AcWri 156; #Immodest-Women hashtag 45–46; #phdchat community 27; #PhDlife 104–105; #PhDsupervisor 104; #phdweekend 56–57; #stateofmyphddesk 59; #WIASN Facebook group 5; popularisation of 97
Hayano, D. 12
HDR *see* doctoral research/researchers; higher degree research (HDR)
HE *see* higher education (HE)
Hernández, E. 58
Hickson, H. 117–118, 120
higher degree research (HDR) 110–112, 116
higher education (HE) 24, 56, 87; economies of 9; reconfiguration of 50
Higher Education Academy (HEA) 50

Higher Education Institutions 83–84
Hill, G. 4
hopelessness, sense of 29
humour 100–101, 105
Hunter, K. 57–58
hybrid learning 83–84

identity 87; development 86, 124; and engagement 53; formation, aspects of 28; sense of 87
IDERN *see* International Doctoral Education Research Network (IDERN)
imposter syndrome 30, 45, 59, 68
in between, theme of 77
independence 4, 67
individual agency 125
individual practitioner 1 06, 98–99, 104
individual reflection 97–99, 104
individual supervisory relationship 18
informal learning, for researcher well-being 68–69
innovation, freedom of 88
insecurity 125
Instagram 10, 97, 126–127
institutional/institutions: committee 15; funding 13; identity 12, 14; interactions 10; leadership 88; program, belonging to 17; referring researchers 144; research, formal structures of 11–12; social locations 17; subscription 144–145; support 154
intellectual capability 67
interaction: first sight 127; online 127
interactive content 5
International Doctoral Education Research Network (IDERN) 96
interpersonal relationships 52
interpersonal skills 110
isolation 33, 35, 58, 61, 72, 105

Jensen, G.S. 127
Johnson, C.M. 30
John, T. 50–51
Jones, Q. 52; reflections on cyber communities 52

Kamler, B. 114–115, 118
Kiley, M. 29
Kimmons, R. 15–16, 127
Knights, D. 125
knowledge abundance 8–9, 11, 13

language 55–57
Lave, J. 83, 87

learning 83, 116, 128–129; agenda 84; apprenticeship model of 84; assessment for 85; environment 54, 67; experience 2; online platforms in 70; and social environment 58; theory 84
Le Cornu. A. 53, 58, 85
life commitments, balance in 50
line management 68–69
LinkedIn 40, 97, 160
Lupton, D. 113

Marwick, A.E. 55
Massive Open Online Courses (MOOCs) 1, 13, 70
Masters project 143
McAlpine, L. 125
McKiernan, E. 19–20
media visibility 11
mental health 50, 57; beneficial for 76; well-being and 139
mental space 128–129
Mewburn, I. 4, 30, 114–115
micro-blogging platform *see* Twitter
mid-career educator 8
Miller, E. 4, 120
mimicry 28–29
MOOCs *see* Massive Open Online Courses (MOOCs)
mutual engagement 85

Network 146; experience of 147–148
networked/digital identity 12
networked participatory scholarship 8, 14–17
networked scholarship 2, 10

O'Connor, K. 85
OCoPs *see* online communities of practice (OCoPs)
offline power inequities 11
online affiliations 38
online behaviour 74
online coaching programme 4
online communication 85
online communities 29, 44, 148; accessibility of 47; active engagement with 42; behaviours 53; benefit of 85; creation and maintenance of 6; emerging landscape of 1; engagement in 1, 85; facilitators of 4; impact of 136; landscape of 2; participation in 33; platforms 103; potential value of 66 *see also* social media

online communities of practice (OCoPs) 83–84, 124–130; case studies 87–91; creating and maintaining 129; identity and sense of belonging 86; learning by doing 129; of practice 3–4; theory of 84–86
online content, motivations for engaging 40, **41**
online courses 5, 144–145
online education 1
online forums 44, 90–91, 114
online media 1, 31, 35
online NHS Apps Libraries 69
online platforms 4, 43, 70, 107
online resources 38, 40, 43, 95–97, 106–107, 111
online sharing of information 86
online social networks 15–16
online space development 72
online supervision 130; avoidance of 128
online training for supervisors 111
open access articles 5
open courses 1–2
open dissertation 17–20
'Open Dissertation, The ' concept 2
openness 110–111
organisational services 79
oscillation 30–31

Padlet board 76–78
Pandemic Pedagogy 83
Parent-PGR Network 72; limitations and considerations for practice 74–75
participatory blogging 13
participatory networked spaces 19
Peach, D. 3
peer 69; learning 89; networking 144; reviewed articles 10; reviewed research 96; reviewing publications 148; review processes 9; supportive community of 99
Peplin, K. 4–5, 140–145
persistence 9
personal identity 12
Petrovsky, D. 127
PGRs *see* doctoral research/researchers
@PhDForum 50–52, 60; activities on 59; communication 60; community 52, 57, 60; curation of 55; cyber-embodiment of connectedness 59–61; as cyberstreet 52–55; dimensions of 57; equality within online community 55–57; evolution of 51; growing function of 53; identity and engagement with 53; inclusive academe 57–59; tweets 61

Index

photography: for reflection 79; in STEP project 79
photo-sharing 78
photo-themes 79
podcasts 5, 86, 100, 102
police behaviour 142–143
postgraduate researcher 38, 149 *see also* doctoral research/researchers
Postgraduate Research Experience Survey (PRES) 38–39, 128; motivations 40–41; online communities' questions 39, **40**
practice-led inquiry 96
practice-led research 148
precarity, exploration of 105
procrastination 27, 105
professional dialogue models 98
Professional Doctorate programmes 98
professional identity 114
professional learning process 116
project management skills 140
provenance 100
psychological well-being 70
psychology 39
public audiences 19
public blog, reflective writing on 116–118
public health 39
public scholarship 113
public scrutiny 28
purposive sampling 38–39

QMUL *see* Queen Mary University of London (QMUL)
Quality Post graduate Research (QPR) 96
Queen Mary Engineering School (QMES) 87; mission 88; specific staff in 89
Queen Mary University of London (QMUL) 87; academic practice 84; educational development at 89–91; educational development programmes at 90; leadership 88; in London transition 89

racial inequality 56
reader submissions 117
reflective/reflection 76; change, areas of 78; definition of 114; dialogue 119–120; effective photo-taking 78; on practice 116; pragmatic forms of 78; writing on public blog 116–118
relationships, network of 16
replicability 9

reputational economies 11–13
reputational economy 10, 13
rescue supervisor 119–120
research degree supervisor development 95–96, 99; community of practice 97–99; context 96–97; feeding back into online communities 106; online offline to raise awareness 100–104; online PhD resources and spaces 104–105; pandemic postscript 106–107; supervisors 99
researcher-supervisor relationship 66–67
ResearchGate 40
research/researchers: blogs 5; in coaching/mentoring settings 67; community 78; degree supervisors 95–97, 100, 106; development, activities 42–43; self-evaluation of 75; students 38; supervision pedagogy 111; supervisors 124–125; support, modes of 1; training and development 133; use of social media 44; well-being, informal learning for 68–69 *see also* doctoral research/researchers; research supervision
research supervision 118–119, 125; community of practice 97–99; context 96–97; conversations about 96; feeding back into online communities 106; international conferences 96; nature of 97; online offline to raise awareness 100–104; online PhD resources and spaces 104–105; pandemic postscript 106–107; supervisors 99; *see also* doctoral research/researchers; PGRs
resilience 4, 28, 160
Robinson. G. 125
Ronson, J. 113
Roumell, E.A. 129

'safe space' for sharing 110
satire 100
satisfaction with research culture 42
scaffold engagement with resources: 98
scalability 9
scarcity 13–14; practices of 9
Schmitt, A. 54
scholarship 11; extensions of 10; for knowledge abundance 9–11
Scholarship of Teaching & Learning (SoTL) 88
searchability 9
SEDA *see* Staff and Educational Development Association (SEDA)
self-agency 4

self-efficacy, development 124
self-expression 78, 116
'self' in social media platforms 59
self-reflection 76, 79
self-selection 38–39
semi-structured interviews 38–39
sensemaking 76
sense of being 12
sense of belonging 14, 76, 83, 86–87
sense of community 105
sense of identity 89–90
shared learning agenda 84
shared practice 88
shared repertoire 3–4, 86
share productivity apps 61
sharing, segmentation of 85
Sheldon, J. 3
Sheppard, V. 3
Sindlinger, J. 127
Skype 1, 10, 107
Smith, R. 51
social community 89
social content, motivations for engaging 40, **41**
social distancing 1, 60
social environment, learning and 58
socialisation 4, 28, 54, 129
social learning of hierarchy 59
social media 2, 8–9, 13, 41, 47, 88, 112–115, 135, 137–139; abundance of 17; academic practice on 113–114; apps and websites 51; awareness of 27; behaviour 30; channels 88–89; communities 9; contemporary practice 15; doctoral researchers use of 2; engagement 25–26, 39–40; hashtags 95; identities 153; institution-specific questions on 38; mentoring 48; networks 11, 13, 118; platforms 43–44, 97, 112–113; potential of 26; profiles on 137; relational impact of 16; role for 2; role models 48; scaling 17–20; use of 23, 30; variety of 112–113; working 153–154
social media savvy: interview results 42–48; motivations 40, **41**; research design 38–39; survey patterns 41–42; survey results 39; types of online engagement 39–40
social networks 12–13, 113, 127
social relationships 89
social work bloggers 117
Society for Research into Higher Education (SRHE) 96
Solipsistic Introjection 127

SoTL *see* Scholarship of Teaching & Learning (SoTL)
special interest networks for researchers: activities and impact from networks, examples of 73; disabled and ill researcher's network 74; Emotionally Demanding Research Network 73–74; Parent-PGR Network 74–75; rationale for 71; underpinning principles of 72–73
SRHE *see* Society for Research into Higher Education (SRHE)
Staff and Educational Development Association (SEDA) 98
Stewart, B. 2–3
stigma 57
stress 78–79, 158–159
structured questionnaires 38
stuckness 23, 29–31
student–supervisor interactions 4–5
Student Transitions through Engaging with Photography (STEP) project 76, 78; doctoral self-reflection 78–79; learning design 76–77; limitations and considerations for practice 79; outcomes of pilot project 77–78; rationale for initiative 75–76
studio engagement 158
study strategies 67–68
supervision/supervisors/supervisory 101–102, 111–112, 124–130, 134; community 99; defence reaction in 126; development 95, 97; development of 124, 129; of doctoral research 4; Hidden Curriculum of 129; impact of 124; inter-personal aspects of 118; pastoral role of 104–105; practices 110, 117; professional identity 125; relationships 103; resources for 134; role in relation to 134; and student relationship 134; virtual CoP for 112–113
supportive community 48, 58, 99, 101
survey participants 29

'taking stock' tweet 153
teachers/teaching 2, 9, 70, 83, 112
Teams meetings 1
technology in well-being 69–70
Thesis Mentoring programme 67
Thesis Whisperer (Mewburn) 4, 6, *115*
The Thesis Whisperer (TW) 96, 110; community of practice model 115
The Supervision Whisperers (TSW) 96–97, 110–111, *115*, 117–120;

building 115–116; inception and evolution of 111; origins of 111; readers and writers of 115; reflective dialogue and developing connections 119–120; reflective writing on public blog 116–118; social media 112–115; supervise research students 111–112; value of reading 119; virtual CoP around research supervision 118–119; vision for 115
Thomson, P. 5, 114–115, 118, 151–159
Thrive model offer 141
time management 51
torn pedagogy 127–129
traditional scholarship, reputational economy of 9
transitional/transitions 76–77, 83; to doctoral education 67; learning 68–69, 79; to postgraduate study 67; process of 67; themes 77
transnational education (TNE) 87
trolling 57
trust relationships 12–13
2020 Postscript 150
Twitter 1–3, 8, 10, 14, 17, 23, 30, 38, 46–47, 58, 97, 113, 117, 126–127, 133–138, 141, 149–150, 153; active engagement with 53; activity and hashtags 43–44; chats 5; formation of 53; communities 30; conversations 2; doctoral candidates' experiences of 24; feed sourcing 5; first decade of 8; hashtags 104, 106; interactions and profiles 46; intimacy of 24; knowledge abundance and 11–12; learning environment for doctoral students 52–53; networks 13; retweeting, resources and; use of 25, 153; voice 43–44 see also social media
Twitter site: content curation 3; cyberdistrict of 3; cyberstreet 3
Twittersphere 52

UK Council for Graduate Education (UKCGE) 1, 50, 97
undergraduate (UG), teaching and learning 124–125
University Counselling Service 72–73

University of Sheffield Emotionally Demanding Research Network 72
University Research Ethics and Integrity Team 72
University Research Ethics Committee 73
University Staff Parents' Network 72
unpaid labour 75

value of reading 119
value of sharing 27
Vaughan, Sian 4
Veletsianos, G. 15–16
vicarious trauma 71
video platforms 70
virtual cohort 14
virtual communities 100
virtual CoP 118–119
VirtualNotViral 5–6, 151–159
virtual settlement 52
viva survivors 102
vlogs 39

webinars 138
websites 39
WeChat 88
well-being 66–68; beneficial for 76; leveraging informal learning for researcher 68–69; and mental health 139; use of online platforms in learning 70; use of technology in 69–70
Wenger, E. 83–84, 86–88, 114, 120
WhatsApp 1, 101, 103, 157 see also social media
White, D. 53, 58, 85
Willinsky, J. 9, 19–20
Wisker, G., 125
Women in Academia Support Network 5, 146–150
work, balance in 50
work-based community of practice 85
working relationship 158–159
workspaces, shared photographs of 59
World is Flat, The (Friedman) 11
worthiness 57
Wright, F. 60

Yuen, A. 116, 119

Zoom 1

Printed in the United States
by Baker & Taylor Publisher Services